BEHAVIOR MODIFICATION:

AN EMPIRICAL APPROACH TO SELF-CONTROL

BEHAVIOR MODIFICATION:
AN EMPIRICAL APPROACH TO SELF-CONTROL

John A. Glover
Albert L. Gary

Nelson-Hall 𝑛ℎ Chicago

Library of Congress Cataloging in Publication Data

Glover. John A.,
 Behavior Modification.

  Bibliography: p.
  Includes index.
  1. Behavior modification. 2. Habit.
3. Emotions. 4. Psychology, Pathological.
I. Gary, A. L., 1935-   joint author. II. Title.
BF637.34G54   153.8′5 79-88
ISBN 0-88229-298-6

Manufactured in the United States of America

10   9   8   7   6   5   4   3   2   1

Acknowledgments

We must first acknowledge the many hours that Theresa Glover and Dot Gary spent in reading the manuscript and making many highly pertinent suggestions. Thanks are also due to Dr. Helen Barrett for providing guidance, knowledge and constructive criticism in the physiological aspects of this book.

This book is dedicated to our wives, Theresa Glover and Dot Gary, and our children, Sarah Glover, Elizabeth Glover, Scott Gary, Erika Gary, and Kandace Gary. Without their help and support and the sacrifice of many evenings, this book could not have been completed.

Contents

PART I
Problem Behaviors

1

Problem Behaviors

"When in trouble or in doubt, run in circles, scream and shout." We doubt that this is the approach that many people take to their problems. Most of us use some kind of roughly systematic method of dealing with various problems, and since we live through them, our techniques must be reasonably effective.

Most of the population of the United States face some similar problems. Overweight, which has been linked to heart disease, diabetes, early death, poor health, etc., is a very common problem in America today. Many people are not obese in the clinical sense, but are, rather, overweight enough to cause discomfort either physically or mentally (the cosmetics of overweight are quite complex). Many other people smoke and are convinced that they should stop smoking for any number of reasons. Smoking is a personal and social problem. The advantages of not smoking are manifold while the advantages of smoking are limited; you get to smoke.

Other problems include speech habits. Many of us are desirous of editing our language for one reason or another. Most of us have a difficult time adequately making these kinds of changes in our behavior. Budgets, alas, are the bane of us all. We never seem to be paid enough to do what we want. (Like buying this book!) Is there a good way of developing a proper management program to adequately maintain a proper budget, to control our weight, to quit smoking, or change our speech habits?

These problems, and others of a similar nature all pertain to what we might call self-control, self-discipline, or self-management. Any book that announces that it will aid you in developing these forms of control is automatically in trouble. We hope that we will not be associated with body-building courses, figure development or psychic-prowess enhancement programs.

There are several different and often conflicting views of human behavior that properly interpreted and applied (so say their proponents, so say we too) can help people develop appropriate self-management. Of the several possible views of behavior, psychoanalytic, phenomenological, cognitive, and behaviorist, we will be presenting a variant of the behaviorist approach, behavior modification. Most of these methods have been applied to the management of personal behavior.

Ah, ha! You've been trapped and are now in the clutches of some writers who are behavior modifiers. Aren't behavior modifiers some sort of blight on the land? Aren't they unethical and unscrupulous—evil people with devious and sly techniques who warp minds, make strong men weak, and generally louse up the good quality of American life? Haven't these kinds of people been banned in Boston, prisons and mental institutions for doing bad things?

Well, if you share the sentiments behind any or all of these questions, it's time for us to define our brand of behavior modification. Behavior modification is the systematic application of learning theory to behavior in an attempt to change that behavior. Notice that this definition leaves out several things. It leaves out any change in behavior brought about by anything other than the application of learning theory (in the next chapter we will outline operant theory, a learning theory, specifically as it relates to human behavior). Behavior modification, as a discrete field, does not include chemotherapy, shock therapy, physiotherapy, or brain surgery. Behavior modification is external to the individual. Those individuals who perform various forms of therapy that amount to surgery, chemical treatment or the like are not behavior modifiers. No doubt these people modify behavior, but they do not do so in a manner that is acceptable by the field of behavior modification. By representing themselves as behavior modifiers, they are performing a disservice to those of us who are behavior modifiers. Their techniques and results should be judged solely on their own merits and not through association with those who practice behavior modification based on learning theory (often referred to as contingency management). No doubt, this is a position that some behavior modifiers would disagree with. Oh, well, it's a free country.

Well, enough preaching and side-stepping around the process of behavior modification. We'll get to that in the next chapter soon enough. We still haven't said what we are. Behavior modifiers are people who believe in cause and effect. We tend to be systematic and meticulous in our approach to the study of behavior. We really believe that the consequences of behavior govern the appearance, strength, and frequency of behaviors. We also believe (as we will soon point out) that not everything is as it seems. We love our families, vote for the candidate of our "choice," write in the plural even when there is only one writer, go to ball games, buy cars and houses, and we do all the things that your average Joe or Jane on the street does. There is a difference, however, in how we deal with certain of our own behaviors, outside of our dealings with the behavior of others in clinical, counseling or teaching situations. We deal with our own behavior in a systematic fashion and manage it according to a system of principles generated from research in learning.

So, Who Needs It?

Chances are that if you don't smoke, aren't overweight, sleep well, have no speech trouble, manage your budget beautifully and live a happy, successful and fulfilling life, you don't really need this book or the techniques contained herein. If you never have any problem with the management of your own behaviors, you may read the book for its literary quality alone (choke!). Most of us, though, fight a constant running battle with cream pies, Phillies Cheroots, a little unnecessary purchase here and there or other similar kinds of personal behavior problems. Most of us need a little help, too, or we wouldn't have started smoking or overeating in the first place. Other habits can be equally hard to break. Establishing new habits to replace old ones is a job—a real job. It is very easy, for instance, to reach into the refrigerator for a banana and then into your pocket for a cigarette. The behaviors become so nearly automatic that they go almost unnoticed by many of us.

Extraneous influences don't make the prospect of changing behavior any easier. We are constantly confronted with model after model on television urging us to try the new cereal Crudwheats. We see happy, healthy people eat generous portions of what is obviously a very wonderful food. Why, if we eat this food, we will become successful, happy, healthy, our luck will change, and we'll become one of the beautiful people.

And what about the new Gutbomb burger? Quick, filling, easy, inexpensive, sexy waiters and waitresses, low-caloric, great-tasting burgers that are eaten in front of your very eyes by handsome, well-built people. Have you ever noticed that you seldom see fat people in food advertisements?

Drinking doesn't really give you a break either. See all those happy, frollicking folks quaffing huge quantities of whatever beverage it is that's being advertised? Notice how thin, chic, and obviously successful they are?

Ah, yes, the smokers. They're not on television any more, but they're in magazines and on billboards. Rugged, individualistic, sexy, and successful people smoke. Are they rugged, individualistic, sexy and successful because they smoke? Certain folks would have us think so. Advertisers have a job to do just like anyone else. Problems arise, though, when advertising "over-kills" and sells things in the extreme. For example, one banana split eaten with a concomitant decrease in intake of other foods that same day will cause little, if any weight gain. Advertisers seldom take weight problems into account because their job is to sell as many of the banana splits as possible. What results is the constant harangue for the banana split, implicitly telling the consumer that he or she should eat them three or four times a day, every day.

We don't want to pick unnecessarily at banana splits. They are only an example of the nature of a large and influential business structure in America. It is not our purpose to develop a philosophical analysis of overt American consumerism, but we feel that it is necessary to point out (not because it isn't obvious, it is, but because we take it so for granted) the unbelievable emphasis on consumption in America. We are urged to trade reasonably good cars away yearly. We are urged to buy more and different clothes yearly. Our refrigerators are not adequate if they do not possess external ice and water dispensers. In fact, almost any product you can name is pushed in this way. It is hard to resist repeated and repeated and repeated demonstrations of how we should be consuming things. It seems almost un-American not to buy and buy and buy and consume and consume. The tremendous pressure to consume, of course, has got to lead to problems. Smoking is probably the one habit in the world that could be dispensed with completely and have no one but the growers of tobacco and the tobacco companies suffer for its loss. Cigarette consumption, however, goes up yearly.

Food and drink companies, naturally, also take similar positions in selling their products. It is expected that the consumer is more likely to emulate the bean-eating behavior of actors and actresses drenched in sex-appeal than they would be to make wise decisions based on nutritional and cost factors. Hence, the pitch that you are more likely to have an enjoyable sex-life if you eat Blasto beans than if you were to eat (horrors) brand X. Naturally, brand X counters this and so round and round we go.

All advertising isn't bad. Some advertising serves a very useful purpose and many enterprising advertisers are actually trying to sell products on their merits these days.

Well, the problem goes on and on. There seem to be many more cues in the environment for us to perform activities that may be harmful than there are for us not to perform them. To master these kinds of situations, we need: will power! (Whatever that is.) Our definition of will power may be considerably different than others you've heard of or seen. Will power, for us, refers to a set of conditioned responses. A lack of will power is similarly defined as a set of conditioned responses that result in undesirable outcomes.

What About Me?

How can any systematic program be adopted by the reader and be successful if other efforts haven't worked in the past? Here are seven reasons why behavior modification may work for you.

(1) Managing behavior is hard work. We feel that there are no in-

stant, easy, or automatic ways of changing behaviors. If there were, then no one would have problems controlling their behavior; we'd be out of work; there would be no overweight people, no alcoholics, no smokers, no tobacco farmers, no mental hospitals, etc., etc., ad infinitum. There have been, and are, many successful techniques for changing behavior among so-called "normal" people with some form of problem. All of them mean hard work. Ask any Weight-Watcher if the change in eating behavior came easily. Human behavior is an unbelievably complex topic. No behavior change is ever easy or simple. Compulsive smoking, eating, or spending is as difficult to understand and treat as any other form of compulsion. Such compulsions are not as frowned upon as, say, compulsions for neatness or compulsive stealing, but they are just as difficult to remove. Anyone claiming to have instant, easy or effortless "cures" should receive very close scrutiny, indeed, before their techniques are adopted.

(2) You have to want to make the changes in your behavior. Restating this somewhat, you have to want to change more than you want to stay the same. (We'll define this more appropriately in the next chapter.) Many of us give lip service to losing weight, quitting smoking, balancing our budget, or managing our time more beneficially, but few of us do anything about it. If you are not interested in really making a change, then this, or any other method, will not work. As we will keep pointing out, over and over, nothing comes easy in the behavior modification racket.

(3) You must be consistent and persevering. Consistency is often prescribed by coaches, politicians, accountants, psychologists, and other equally strange people. Consistency in itself is no answer for it is as easy to be consistently wrong as it is to be consistently good or right. Perseverence goes right along with consistency. Changing your behavior for one week will not do a whole lot for you. Changing your behavior permanently will.

(4) Organization is a necessary function of properly following any program. This will, no doubt, mean much more to you after reading chapter IV where we point out methods of organization.

(5) Satisfaction with results is necessary. If you are not satisfied with a change that you once felt was all-important, you are not likely to make that change permanent. Weight loss, for instance, does not bring about instant sexiness, droves of males or females pounding down your door demanding dates, social success, academic success, or job promotions. Your expectation of the consequences of change must be realistic.

(6) Set your goals realistically. Do not attempt to over or underachieve some change. One might be harmful, the other unsatisfying.

(7) Constant evaluation and re-evaluation of any program is a necessity for the success of that program.

Our approach is only one among many that may be very successful. If you meet the seven criteria above, you will probably do well with a behavior modification approach. Behavior modification is definitely not a cure-all or an end in itself. It is a very potent tool generated from several years of operant theory (learning theory) research. Used properly it can enhance your lifestyle and bring about significant and positive changes. Used sloppily, carelessly, or improperly, it will be just as unsatisfying, unworkable, and depressing as any myriad of techniques you could choose.

2

Behavior Modification/ Operant Theory in Action

Behavior modification is a systematic technique for analyzing and modifying behavior. The principles that spawned behavior modification are traceable to the roots of behaviorism, or other specific cause and effect theories. B. F. Skinner has probably made the greatest contributions to behavior modification. His theories certainly have had the greatest impact on the field. Other theorists, however, have made important contributions to the field. We will be mentioning some of these folks throughout our discussions.

In its simplest terms, behavior modification stems from one very simple premise: organisms (including people) tend to emit more frequently those behaviors they are rewarded for and tend to emit less frequently those behaviors they are punished for or receive no reward for. Now that sounds very simple. No fuss, no muss. It sounds very like hedonism taken to an extreme and applied as a theory to explain behavior. Organisms do those things that make them feel good and do not do those things that either don't make them feel good or make them feel bad.

THE SIMPLICITY OF IT ALL

Can human (or any organism, for that matter) behavior really be that simple? Yes, no, and certainly maybe. On first reflection, behavior modification makes some premises that seem to be very obviously true. All of us do things that are rewarding. We eat, sleep, read, watch television, and love. We go out to dinner, go to plays and movies, buy cars, and root for our favorite football team. If you think about it a while, however, certain discrepancies pop into the forefront. How many people do you know who do things they don't like? How about ourselves? We all pay income taxes, go to work every morning, change diapers, wait in long lines, get drenched in the rain running errands, become frozen running around in cold weather, and generally do things that are really noxious. The list of discrepancies gets even worse when you consider people in wartime conditions, or other forms of extreme stress.

Can we really make a case for the idea that behavior is reward oriented when we consider behaviors that are so obviously at variance with our stated premise? How about altruism, selflessness, or humanitarianism? We all, at times, avoid personal gain in many situations to comply with our beliefs or attitudes, or to work for some higher purpose, such as the Christian Ideal, American Patriotism, or belief in the goodness of man. During the remainder of this chapter, we hope to provide adequate explanations for our behaviors that will subsume these seeming discrepancies.

GETTING STARTED

The best place to start in a discussion of an operant (behavior modification) approach to behavior is with stimuli. A stimulus is anything that any of your sense modalities allows you to perceive. These stimuli can be auditory: bells, buzzers, symphonies, words, explosions, and any other form of vibration that can be processed by your auditory senses. These stimuli can be visual: pictures, people, pinpoints of light, etc. They can be olfactory; in fact, they can be of any form of thing that allows perception in any or all of the sense modalities. A train, for instance, can be heard, felt, smelled, seen, tasted, etc. Some stimuli, a spot of light in a dark room, can only be seen.

Stimuli can be very simple or complex. A leaf in a painting of a forest is a stimulus. The entire picture is a stimulus too, or it can be interpreted as being a whole set of stimuli. Generally such things have a time and place effect. You may see the leaf as a separate stimulus or you may see the entire painting as a stimulus. The same kind of complexity can, of course, be found in auditory, tactual, olfactory, and other kinds of stimuli.

Incidentally, if you do not perceive a stimulus, it's still there. If you don't perceive a car coming down the street, and walk out in front of it, it will still hit you. Some people can have cancerous growths and not be aware of them. If a person does not perceive a stimulus such as a tumor, the person cannot act on it. It's the old question about "does the tree make noise if it falls in the forest and there is no one to hear it?"

There are several kinds of stimuli that have different effects on behavior. These are:

(1) *Eliciting stimuli.* These stimuli elicit (bring out or cause) a reflex action. (The reflexes are generally referred to as respondents.) An example of this would be sitting on a tack (the eliciting stimulus) and jumping up (the reflex).

(2) *Reinforcing stimuli.* We'll discuss these in the text immediately following this list, so let us save these for now.

(3) *Punishing stimuli.* These are discussed a little further on in the text.

(4) *Discriminative stimuli.* Discriminative stimuli are stimuli that control behavior, and will be discussed later.

(5) *Neutral stimuli.* Those stimuli that are perceived but have no

effect on behavior are called neutral stimuli. An example might be the color of walls in a classroom. This is perceived but has little or no effect on behavior.

Our general feeling is that the organism's interaction with various stimuli govern the behavior of the organism. Stimuli alone, however, do not give an adequate explanation for behavior. However, when we examine some of these in depth, a few answers begin to emerge.

THE GOODIES

Reinforcing stimuli, reinforcers, and reinforcement are those stimuli that we often think of as rewards, good consequences, or good things. A reinforcer, by definition, is a stimulus that when applied to some behavior causes that behavior to be strengthened, to appear more frequently, or to increase its level of probability of occurrence under similar circumstances in the future. What we are saying is that this stimulus, the reinforcer (reward), causes whatever behavior it is directed toward to strengthen. Notice, that nowhere in the definition do we say anything about the form a reinforcer must take or when it appears, how much of it must appear and so on. Some of these things will be discussed later, but at this point it is necessary to further confound the issue by mentioning that there are two specific forms of reinforcement.

Positive reinforcement is a reinforcer (reward) that is a consequence of a response. It is a stimulus that occurs after a response and strengthens that response. Not to let things become too simple at this point, we need to mention that the form of this stimulus has little or nothing to do with whether or not it is reinforcing. It is reinforcing if the behavior (response) increases in frequency, strengthens, or is more likely to occur in the future. Very specifically, a reinforcer is defined by what it does to the behavior and not by what it looks like. Remember, for instance, that at times (perhaps when you were nine or ten years old and had done something that an aunt or uncle thought was really wonderful) somebody tried to reinforce (reward) you (the aunt or uncle hugged and kissed you in front of your friends) and your behavior definitely did not increase in strength. In fact, you may never have performed that behavior again. Or remember the time you worked very hard to complete a job and for a reward (reinforcer) you were given a pat on the back and that's all?

For the writers, chocolate cake, oozing with creamy, thick, deep, rich, dark brown frosting is a very powerful reinforcer. (As you might have noticed, the writers were almost drooling over the description of what started out as a rather simple piece of cake.) Many people, however, are allergic to chocolate and either become ill, break out, or for other reasons are made very uncomfortable by chocolate cakes. For these people, and for those who just don't like chocolate cake, the cake would not be a reinforcer.

One of the writers has a very strong aversion to melons of all types while the other enjoys melons very much. For one of us it is a reinforcer and for the other it is not.

Just because something is meant as a reinforcer or reward has nothing at all to do with whether or not, in fact, it is a reinforcer. Each one of us has separate and distinct sets of stimuli that are reinforcing to us. Reinforcement can only be defined by its effect. If the behavior a stimulus follows is strengthened, it (the stimulus) is a reinforcing stimulus. For instance, if you spank a child for talking in class and his talking behavior becomes more frequent (i.e., is stronger) you have reinforced the talking behavior. Just because spanking does not *seem* like a reinforcer has nothing to do with its effect.

Generally speaking, it is impossible to predict what will be reinforcing to all people, although we may well predict that some things will be reinforcing to a great many people. Going a little bit beyond this, there is no way to predict, *a priori*, the potency of a reinforcer for any group of individuals.

Potency, the new term that we sneaked in above, refers to the strength of a reinforcer as compared to other reinforcers. (Reynolds, 1969)

Negative reinforcement. A negative reinforcer is a stimulus that when *removed* from a situation causes the response that removed it (or seemed to have removed it) to increase in strength. Notice that the stimulus that is a negative reinforcer occurs (by the nature of the definition) *before* the response that terminates it. This stimulus is also perceived as a noxious stimulus by the organism. Again, superficial appearances can be quite deceiving. The stimulus may appear to be very rewarding or pleasurable to the observer, but it is defined only by the effect that it has on the response.

An example of a negative reinforcer would be the termination of discomfort to your foot by having a pebble in your shoe. It works like this: you're minding your own business walking down the street when all of a sudden—whammo! You feel pain on the surface of your foot. This pain is the noxious stimulus. You then remove your shoe, terminating the pain. This termination of the pain is the reinforcing stimulus, or rather, lack of stimulus. The response that is reinforced is removing the shoe.

The whole process is very much like wearing shoes that are too small because it feels so good when you take them off. Another example may clarify further the process of negative reinforcement. Do you remember instances where things like affection and attention were given to you in circumstances where they were not rewarding at all? Perhaps being hugged and kissed by a parent or other adult in the presence of your peers? This, for you, could have been a noxious stimulus. If it was, you would react to it in much the same way as you would to a rock in your shoe. The behavior that terminated the noxious stimulus (the hugging and kissing in this case was the noxious stimulus) would be the behavior that would be strengthened because of the termination of the noxious stimulus (making a horrible face, going "ugh," or shaking yourself free).

Note: It is possible to "accidentally" negatively reinforce behavior. If some behavior is going on as the noxious stimulus ceases, whether or not it causes the stimulus to cease, it will be reinforced. The same effect can be generated through positive reinforcement. Accidentally reinforced behavior, that is, learned vicariously, is called *superstitious behavior*. Examples of this effect will make the concept more lucid.

When you have a difficult problem to solve or when you are deeply immersed in thought, you may find that, like the authors, you scratch your head, rub the bridge of your nose, or stroke your beard. None of any of these mannerisms really help you think. How could scratching your head help you think? It doesn't stimulate the brain or anything like that. Well, this behavior has been learned because it has accidentally been reinforced. If you have ever solved a problem while scratching your head, the solution, a reinforcer, reinforced all the behaviors going on at that time, not just the problem-solving process. Hence, the head-scratching business is superstitious. It might be quite interesting if we could discover all of our superstitious behavior. We all, no doubt, possess many forms of superstitious behavior.

Escape and avoidance behavior. While on the general topic of negative reinforcers, the topic of escape and avoidance behavior needs to be discussed. Going back to our example of the unsuspecting reader picking up a rock in her shoe, we will attempt to point out how avoidance behavior is learned. Avoidance behavior is behavior (a series of responses, or, perhaps, just one response) that postpones or avoids completely the onset of a noxious stimulus. Suppose that the next three times you walk across a particular field, you get a rock in your shoe at about the same place in the field. It does not take long for you to learn that this part of the field (a discriminative stimulus) is the part of the field in which you experience pain. Eventually, after several trips through the field, you will start avoiding the spot where you pick up the rocks. You have then successfully learned an avoidance behavior.

Escape behavior is the behavior that we described earlier in which the organism escapes the presence of a noxious stimulus. In avoidance behavior, the reinforcer is the avoidance of pain, and in escape behavior, the reinforcer is the escape from or termination of the pain.

Most of us have rather well-developed systems of both escape and avoidance behaviors. If we foresee a noxious stimulus, a boring night at someone's party, we avoid the party to avoid the noxious stimulus. The avoidance and escape behavior may either be well-thought out, or may, in fact, be an unconscious response.

LEARNED OR INNATE

As you have probably inferred from the preceeding discussion, there is one other basic division, of reinforcing stimuli. Some are learned and some are innate. *Innate reinforcers*, also referred to as primary or unconditioned reinforcers, are those stimuli that are reinforcing to us by our basic biological nature. Fcod, water, air, sleep, rest, climatic comfort, and sex are some of the major forms of innate reinforcers. If a person is very hungry and he has, for instance, never before encountered chocolate cake (we'll assume that there are no allergies or other confounding conditions), that cake presented after some response would almost certainly reinforce the behavior that obtained it. Innate reinforcers need never before have been encountered for them to have properties to reinforce our behavior. Very obviously, our survival on a day-to-day basis depends on obtaining these reinforcers. Without them we would die either individually (lack of food leads to starvation; lack of water to dehydration; lack of air to suffocation, etc.) or as a race (no sex means no babies, hence, no future generation).

Have you ever, as an example, been swimming and inadvertently stayed underwater to the point where you had to fight to the surface and get air? If you have, you will remember the powerful feelings of relief and pleasure that something as simple as a breath of air could provide to someone deprived of it. Incidentally, those actions (responses) that brought you to the surface and obtained the air for you were reinforced by the attainment of air. If in the future you should, heaven forbid, ever be in the same situation, the probability is that those responses that were reinforced by providing air will have a much higher probability of appearing again.

To demonstrate the fact that you need never have experienced innate reinforcers in the past for it to be effective now, let's go through one more example. Let us pick a native Hawaiian for our subject. Our Hawaiian friend has lived on the islands for all of his life and has never experienced (not an unreasonable assumption) an uncomfortably cold temperature. In the middle of January, let us whisk away our unsuspecting subject and transport him to Northern Siberia (where the nights are cold and long indeed) in his usual attire and leave him a few hundred yards from a warm log cabin which is quite comfortable. Well, it doesn't take long for the −60°F to have its effect on our scantily dressed friend. Now he is cold and very uncomfortable (a noxious stimulus, a natural one at that). His goal will most certainly be to escape this arctic nightmare and become warm. If all goes right, he'll run for our warm cabin and become comfortable once again (successfully avoiding a noxious stimulus). He need never before have been freezing cold for it to affect him now. He need never have experienced the comfort of moving into warmth from cold for it to be a reinforcing event in his life. What has happened is that he has been negatively reinforced for his behavior of running to the cabin (escaping the cold, a noxious stimulus).

noxious stimulus -------- escape and reinforced

It can be argued that the process of becoming warm and comfortable is also a positive reinforcer. It matters little for our example, however, as the strength of his cabin-entering behavior has no doubt increased regardless of whether we view it as the termination of a noxious stimulus (which it was) or the onset of a pleasant stimulus (which it also was).

response + reinforcement = increased strength of response

Our example is somewhat silly, but it does bring up the point that there are unconditioned negative reinforcers and positive reinforcers. An unconditioned negative reinforcer is some unlearned noxious stimulus that, when removed from a situation, causes the behavior that brings about the cessation of the noxious stimulus (or at least, seems to from the point of view of the organism in question) to increase in strength or in future probability of occurrence in similar situations. These noxious stimuli can be in any form that causes physical discomfort to the organism.

As can be imagined, there are many more learned reinforcers than primary or innate reinforcers. These *learned reinforcers* are also called secondary reinforcers and conditioned reinforcers. There are many examples of secondary positive reinforcers. Some of the possible positive secondary reinforcers are records, clothes, money, cars, new shoes, poker chips, etc. etc. How do these stimuli, that are not reinforcing in and of themselves, gain reinforcing qualities? Generally, there are two ways which we will discuss momentarily.

Let us stop for a moment and examine the most common of all secondary reinforcers, money. Pull out a five-dollar bill. Hey! We are talking about you. Don't pretend you didn't read it. If you don't have a five-dollar bill, put out a one. A two-dollar bill or a thousand-dollar bill will do just as nicely. Take a good look at the bill. Not very esthetically pleasing, is it? Smell it. That's right, hold it up to your nose and inhale. The bill doesn't smell especially nice, does it? Rub the bill over your skin. It doesn't feel as nice as cotton or silk, does it? Now for the supreme test, taste the bill. Pretty repugnant, huh? Not to make a point to the extreme of bludgeoning it into the ground, money cannot be eaten or drunk, it doesn't feel good, look good, or provide any sort of reinforcing stimulus by itself. In fact, we can imagine very few stimuli as worthless, relatively, as money. How can such a neutral sort of stimulus gain the reinforcing value that it obviously has? After all, we all work for it, want certain amounts of it, and unfortunately have a large portion of our lives dedicated to accumulating or spending it.

There are generally two ways in which a neutral reinforcer can gain the properties of a primary, positive reinforcer: by pairing and by exchange. (1) *Associative pairing* is the process wherein a formerly neutral stimulus is paired with a primary, positive reinforcer until it gains the properties of the primary positive reinforcer by itself.

```
                     primary reinforcer
response ---               +              = increase strength
                     neutral stimulus      of response --
                     (after several trials)
                     formerly neutral now a secondary reinforcer
```

In such a process the neutral stimulus (let us choose 3 " x 6 " index cards) is paired with some primary positive reinforcer (we'll use food). What we mean by this is that we're going to pair an index card with food every time food is consumed by the person we are training. Those responses that lead to gaining food are reinforced by the food and by definition are more probable in the future when the person is hungry. After a while we start to reinforce the person with food less and less often, but always with the index card. Eventually, if we keep this up, the index cards by themselves will have some of the reinforcing properties of the food.

All this sounds pretty silly, doesn't it? After all, index cards are worthless by themselves. You can't eat them or drink them. In fact, they are very much like money. Can something as insane as what we have just described really happen? The literature in operant theory is full of examples of similar forms of associative pairing. But to bring it closer to home, let's go over an example that we are likely to be much more familiar with. Have you ever played poker, monopoly, yantzee, or other games in which tokens, chips, or playmoney were used? In poker, chips of various colors are used. These chips by themselves have no real reinforcing value. However, most poker players try very hard to gather as many chips as possible because they have a highly reinforcing effect. Why? Because they have so often been paired with money, another secondary reinforcer. One other reason, which brings up the second way in which secondary reinforcers are developed, is also important: *exchange* for other reinforcers.

When some relatively neutral object can be exchanged for other ·reinforcers, it will tend to gain some of the reinforcing value of those other reinforcers. Think of our eating behavior for a rather mundane example. If we are hungry and near a McDonalds, we go in and exchange money for food. The food is a primary reinforcer that strengthens the responses we made that led us into the restaurant in the first place. The money, by being exchanged for food, obtains some of the value of the food as a reinforcer. Every time we make such an exchange, the strength of the reinforcing qualities of money is increased.

Money is not only exchanged for food, it is exchanged for drink, clothes, comfort, lodging, protection from the elements, and transportation. Some individuals, we understand, also try to exchange money for esteem, affection, attention and prestige. Little wonder, then, that money is such a powerful secondary reinforcer. Other objects could just as easily obtain the value of money if they could be exchanged in the same way. Very few of us would continue to collect dollars if we changed to a wampum economy. They would have values very much like Confederate money does.

We all have so many secondary reinforcers that it would be impossible to list them all. In fact, each of us has an entirely different set of secondary reinforcers than each other. Remember, that we have all learned either by pairing or by exchange that many different stimuli are reinforcing. And since each of us has lived a life different from others, different kinds of things will necessarily be learned. This is not to say that many of them will not be in common, but it is to say that many will not be in common. An example of this might be some particular song. If one song was paired with a gay or happy experience by hearing it several times while the experience was happening (winning an important ball game, being on a pleasant vacation, etc.) the song itself will gain some of the reinforcing characteristics of the event that it was paired with. How many songs make you "feel better" or make you "happy"? Almost certainly you have learned this by associative pairing. Obviously, the same song that brings about good feelings in one person could have the opposite effect on another. The song could have been paired with sad experiences and have derived noxious characteristics.

Negative reinforcers can also be learned by this technique. Neutral stimuli can become noxious after repeated pairing with noxious stimuli. For example, if you walk through a field six times and step on a nail each time you go through the field, the field will derive some of the noxious properties of those nasty nails. If you don't believe it, think about how you (and we too, for that matter) would avoid such a field after so many repeated bad experiences.

Interestingly, many things that would seem to many of us to be reinforcing are perceived by some people as noxious stimuli. The opposite, perception of seemingly noxious stimuli as very reinforcing stimuli, also happens. It is a matter of past reinforcement history, the pairing of various neutral stimuli with other stimuli. Some stimuli that may not really be neutral, can also be conditioned in this manner. One of the writers, for instance, once became ill eating too many ripe olives. The olives had been a reinforcing stimulus, but after being paired with the illness, they are now seen as noxious stimuli. This example, of course, deals with a primary reinforcer, but the same thing is possible with other stimuli.

Blue books, the type used by college students to take exams, are generally rather neutral stimuli. They may have some value, either positive or negative to different students and, hence, are not truly neutral. The point is that if some students were to do poorly in consistent fashion on exams when using the blue books and others to do well in consistent fashion when using them they would attain the values of either positive reinforcers or noxious stimuli. After a time of either repeated success or repeated failure paired with the blue books, the books themselves will take on some of the qualities of success or failure as the case may be.

As we will see throughout the remainder of this book, the associative pairing process has a great influence on many of our behaviors and may be used in changing some of them.

PUNISHMENT

We all have rather specific ideas of what punishment is. Spanking, taking away candy, sitting in a corner, receiving a fifteen-yard penalty, being thrown out of some situation, and being rapped on the knuckles with a ruler are all seen from time to time as punishment. Punishment, for an operant psychologist, has a rather different meaning than for the average person. Punishment is a stimulus, that when applied to some behavior, causes that behavior to decrease in strength, frequency or probability of occurrence (Johnston, 1972). Again we are defining a stimulus by the effect it has on behavior, not the way it looks, feels, or smells. You might rightly ask about the guy you remember who used to get the daylight spanked out of him for talking in class. His talking behavior never decreased in frequency. Or what about the person who continually eats too much and as a consequence gains weight and gets stomachaches? Aren't these examples of people for whom punishment doesn't work? No. Regardless of how nasty a consequence may appear to be, it is not a punisher unless the level of the behavior it is directed toward decreases. A punishing stimulus can only be identified by its effect, not by its appearance or properties.

The authors have had several occasions to see children "punished" for improper behavior only to see the behavior continue at its previous rate or to increase in strength. Spanking, suspension, and verbal "punishment" are not necessarily a punisher for all people. In fact, these stimuli are generally paired with some highly reinforcing stimuli. It is impossible to spank a child, suspend the child, or direct comments at the child without paying attention to the child. Attention is such a powerful reinforcer for many children that it far outweighs the effect of noxious stimuli such as spanking. Attention is also probably not the only reinforcer connected with the misbehavior. Have you ever seen a young boy who has just been spanked strutting around and saying: "It didn't hurt a bit."? This kind of behavior garners more attention, prestige, and adulation. All of these things are also powerfully reinforcing.

Well, what about our friend, the overeater? Evidently for such a person to continue to eat in the face of some seemingly nasty consequences, the consequences must not really be punishers according to our definition. The other stimuli that surround the ingestion of food must be highly reinforcing for him for the noxious stimuli to have such little effect. These reinforcers could include taste, tactile and olfactory stimuli, social stimuli, anxiety attenuating stimuli, etc.

Punishment, as you have no doubt by now gathered, is applied after a response only. If a punishing stimulus occurs before a response, it will affect the response it followed and not the response it was aimed at.

Punishers can also be innate or learned. The learned punishers are developed in the same way as reinforcers, via associative pairing. This means, as was pointed out in the discussion of the acquisition of secondary reinforcers, that each of us has a completely different set of punishers. Each human being is totally unique in that certain stimuli will be punishing or reinforcing and they will not be identical to those of any other person.

We generally do not use punishers *per se* in any of our treatments, preferring to use a positive approach. Punishment, theoretically, should be just as effective in changing the level of behavior.

Implications of Operant Theory

At the outset of this chapter we brought up several behaviors that seemed not to fit the operant paradigm. Let us re-examine these in light of our definitions and discussions and see how such behaviors might be explained.

How do we explain away altruism, generosity, or selflessness? Our answer is that these behaviors have become very powerful reinforcers by themselves, far outweighing other things such as money, self-gain, or power. How can such a thing happen? To determine this we'll follow the history of Joe Altruism. Joe was a normal kid at birth. Kicking, crying, and fussing occupied the major portion of his time. Somewhere during his formative years something very like the following happened to Joe.

Joe is playing with some toys and his little brother comes up and grabs away one toy. Joe doesn't do anything about this because he is interested in the other things at the time. However, at this moment his mother sees the action, runs over to Joe and proceeds to hug and kiss him while saying: "Joe, you sure are a good boy, being so generous and unselfish." Ah, ha! Joe's mother has applied copious amounts of attention and affection to Joe's behavior. By definition, if these things are reinforcers for Joe (they are reinforcers for most of us) this behavior will increase. Now, the next time Joe is in a similar situation, the probability is higher that he will make a similar response.

The next day Joe is eating some candy and a neighborhood child asks for some. Joe, in a situation similar to the day before, gives him some and is thanked profusely by the child (more reinforcement). Further, his father sees him doing this. Immediately his father runs out the door and hugs Joe, telling him what a kind child he is and how proud he is of him (more reinforcement). Now Joe is even more likely to behave generously in such situations. If we extrapolate a bit, we find that the generous behavior eventually gains reinforcing qualities by itself by being paired so often with other reinforcers. In fact, in the absence of external reinforcers, Joe may reinforce himself. How many times have you ever done a good job at something without external reward, but "felt good" inside because you have done it? Eventually such altruistic behaviors developed by reinforcement over a long period of time became self-sustaining and self-reinforcing.

This one cursory look at behavior can be generalized to include all our behaviors. We believe that all behaviors are learned in this way and that we all internalize the majority of our behaviors. There still are several questions left that need to be looked at, e.g., how do we know when to behave certain ways, and how do we eliminate behaviors from our repertoire of behaviors?

DISCRIMINATIVE STIMULI

A discriminative stimulus is a stimulus that tells you when to do something. It is a stimulus in whose presence you have been reinforced for certain behaviors in the past and, hence, are likely to perform those behaviors again when you again perceive that stimulus. (Bandura, 1969) For example, classrooms are stimuli that are all roughly similar and will tend to evoke similar responses from people who have previously experienced them. When you walk into a classroom with some person up front lecturing about something, you are apt to sit down at a desk quietly and listen to the person. Different discriminative stimuli, such as recreation rooms, are likely to evoke entirely different behaviors.

Discriminative stimuli are those stimuli that govern our behavior based on past experience. How do we account for the fact that we all seem to "know" how to behave in new situations? This phenomenon, behaving appropriately in new situations, can be explained via a process known as stimulus generalization.

STIMULUS GENERALIZATION

Stimulus generalization is a term that describes the process of behaving similarly in the presence of different stimuli. You need never have been in a theater before for you to behave appropriately. Theaters are roughly similar to classrooms, auditoriums, and churches. This rough similarity is enough to cause you to respond in a manner similar to the response you have previously emitted in the similar situations. Roughly, the more similar two discriminative stimuli are, the more likely stimulus generalization is. As long as there are some points in common between two different situations, stimulus generalization is a possibility.

There is another phenomenon that seems important enough for inclusion at this point: shifting control of stimuli. Shifting stimulus control (changing the discriminative stimulus you are responding in the presence of to another stimulus) is accomplished by pairing the discriminative stimulus with the new stimulus, gradually fading out the old discriminative stimulus while maintaining the new discriminative stimulus after the pairing. This associative pairing process will shift stimulus control from one discriminative stimulus to a new one.

To digress at this point, it might be interesting to the reader to note the similarity between discriminative stimuli and eliciting stimuli, briefly discussed at the start of the chapter. Eliciting stimuli are those stimuli—a sharp pain, a surprising feeling, a sudden perception—that *cause* a reflex to be produced in the organism. If you step on a tack, you *will*, very likely, jump up and shout. If a puff of wind hits you right in the eye, you *will* blink. The stimulus, a puff of air, makes the blink occur. The blink is a reflex, often referred to as a respondent. An organism, of course, can be conditioned to respond to a formerly neutral stimulus instead of the eliciting stimulus through the process of associative pairing, wherein the eliciting stimulus is paired with the neutral stimulus until the formerly neutral stimulus will *elicit* the response by itself. This is an example of respondent conditioning, often refered to as Pavlovian or classical conditioning.

RESPONSE GENERALIZATION

A phenomenon that accounts for much anomalous behavior is known as response generalization. Response generalization is the generalizing of the same, or very similar, responses in the presence of more than one stimulus. In other words, you will behave the same way in the presence of two dissimilar conditions.

Well, how do we explain the unexplainable? Where do new, never-before appearing, behaviors come from? Do they just pop out of the sky into someone's behavioral repertoire? Do the id and ego conspire to implement new behavior? Does the Big Programmer in the sky add a punch card to your hopper? Happily, the answer is none of the above. New behaviors are added to an organism's repertoire by a process known as shaping and sometimes called successive approximations. (Note: There is considerable evidence [Bandura, 1969] that seems to show that most of the new behaviors we learn are acquired through a process known as modeling. We will devote one entire chapter to modeling later.)

SHAPING

Shaping is a process whereby new behaviors are added to the

behavioral repertoire of organisms by reinforcing closer and closer approximations of the final goal behavior until the goal behavior is attained. An example of the process will clear up any confusion, we hope. Suppose we want to train a pigeon to peck at a key inside an elongated cage. (There is no good reason for this as far as we can see, but stay with us for now because examples from animal research are less complicated than experiments with humans.) We cannot tell the pigeon what to do because the animal does not understand our speech. We cannot show him what to do because he would have extreme difficulty in interpreting our actions with his limited intelligence. The only way left to develop the response we want is to shape the pigeon's behavior.

What would be reinforcing to a pigeon? Food is the most commonly used reinforcer in animal experiments, so we shall use food (the process with people will obviously be more difficult because we have to find appropriate reinforcers for each individual). To insure that food will be reinforcing, we will keep food away from our pigeon until we are sure that he is hungry (generally animals in such experiments are deprived of food until they weigh 75 percent of their free-feeding weight). Now we put him in our elongated cage at the side opposite that of the key we want him to peck and place our food dispenser on the wall near the key. We wait. The pigeon will be emitting several sorts of behaviors. We wait until he moves in the direction of the key and presto, we give him a pellet of food. This pellet of food reinforces the act of moving in the direction of the key. We remove the bird after he has eaten and replace him at the end of the cage. We wait until he moves a little farther in the direction of the key than previously and then reinforce him. Again, we repeat the process. After several trials the bird will enter the cage and walk directly to the wall on which the key is placed. Now we wait until he pecks at the wall and then reinforce him (pecking is a common behavior among pigeons). As soon as he pecks on the wall, we again reinforce him. Now we repeat the process and wait for him to peck closer to the key than before and reinforce him at that point. Eventually, after several more trials, we may place the bird in the cage and he will walk to the wall and peck the key. We have now obtained the final goal behavior by reinforcing successive approximations of the final behavior.

Okay, you may believe this for animals, but what about people? Aren't the processes much more complex than with animals? You couldn't condition me that way if I didn't want to cooperate. Our answer is a humble, "Oh yes, we can." Have you ever played "hot or cold"? It is a game played by children and slightly eccentric psychologists. In the game, a person is brought into a room and expected to produce some behavior. The person is not told or shown what to do. The "guinea pig" is guided entirely by cries of "hot" or "cold" from his peers in the room. The word "hot" denotes getting closer to the goal behavior (a positive reinforcer) while the word "cold" indicates moving away from the desired goal (a noxious stimulus). At any rate, although it may take some time, any of us can learn new and rather complex behaviors in this way.

Games are artificialities but we do learn a lot of our behavior through the informal game of life when we are reinforced for approximations of goal behaviors and punished or ignored for poor or inappropriate behaviors. To make this discussion a little more cogent, let us briefly examine one human behavior and see how it might have been learned via shaping or successive approximations.

Eating everything on your plate, being a clean-plater, not wasting food, etc. are some of the cries and directions that we will remember from our childhood. Many of us as adults still eat everything set in front of us and have never learned when to stop eating, or have learned to stop only when the food has all been consumed. Let's go back in the life of Barbara Cleanplater and see how she has grown up to become a locally famous table cleaner (in the sense that she cleans everything off the table and into her rather large stomach).

Barbara is seated at the dinner table one evening with the rest of her family. On this evening the dinner is one that is especially delicious to her. While the other young'uns are playing with their food, Barbara consumes all of the food put on her plate by her generous mother. Her father notices this and compliments her on being such a good girl. He further points out Barbara's wonderful behavior to her recalcitrant siblings and states: "Why can't all of you do as well as Barbara? Barbara knows that food is expensive and she eats all her food just like a grownup." Notice: Barbara's father has just meted out several different kinds of verbalized reinforcers. Not only is Barbara a good girl because she eats everything on her plate, she is more grownup and is to serve as a model for the other siblings, gathering even more prestige and attention. Well, not to let things stop here, Barbara's mother makes several similar comments and then hugs Barbara and gives her a kiss for performing such wonderful behaviors.

By definition, Barbara, after being reinforced, is much more likely to perform similar behaviors in the future under similar circumstances. If this kind of reinforcement goes on night after night, as it is very likely to, it will not be very long before this behavior is a permanent part of Barbara's behavioral repertoire. The shaping, of course, occurs as greater and greater amounts of food are consumed more and more frequently for the same amount of reinforcement. Shaping certainly preceded the encounter we looked at. In days previous to the evening we examined, Barbara was almost certainly reinforced for making closer and closer approximations of eating all her food. Finally, of course, she did eat all the food on her plate.

There are still some unanswered questions concerning how such a behavior could go on after the reinforcement ceases, as it almost certainly would after Barbara's behavior became a regular occurrence, and especially after she started to become somewhat overweight. The next section of this chapter should help explain this.

REINFORCEMENT SCHEDULES

"I don't get reinforced every time I do certain things." "I do lots of things and only receive some reinforcers at very infrequent intervals." These statements and others like them bring up some very interesting phenomena. Reinforcement schedules are, as the name implies, schedules by which reinforcement occur for various responses. There are four basic schedules of reinforcement.

1. *Fixed interval schedules* of reinforcement are schedules that provide reinforcement for some responses after fixed intervals of time. This may be every five minutes, every minute or every several days. Fixed interval refers to fixed periods of time.

2. *Fixed ratio schedules* are schedules of reinforcement that provide reinforcement after a set number of responses, hence the term ratio. Reinforcement may occur after every response (continuous reinforcement), after every five or after every two thousand responses.

3. *Variable interval schedules* are schedules that provide reinforcement for responses after varying periods. Reinforcement may occur after one minute, after seven minutes, and then after three minutes. The time interval between reinforcements is varied and is not constant.

4. *Variable ratio schedules* provide reinforcement after variable numbers of responses. Reinforcement may occur after the first, third, twenty-seventh, and twenty-ninth responses. The number of responses between reinforcements is varied and is not constant.

Most behaviors are learned or originally maintained on a constant or close to constant schedule of reinforcement. Behaviors are eventually maintained under more and more variable schedules of reinforcement with the reinforcers occurring less and less often. Finally, some behaviors can be maintained on a one-for-every 10,000 responses schedule. This process is known as schedule "stretching."

Most human behaviors are maintained on some form of variable schedule. Most of our behaviors go unreinforced for long periods of time and yet they continue to appear in more or less regular fashion. How many of you are "vending machine coin slot checkers"? You may check the coin slots many times before you find the change someone else has inadvertently left behind and yet your behavior is maintained at a fairly constant level via this variable schedule. How about gamblers? More specifically, how about those folks who play slot machines hour after hour? The payoff for gamblers occurs only at irregular, variable ratios. Yet we have seen gamblers play for tens of hours at slot machines without winning, quitting only when they have exhausted their supply of money. It is an easy deduction from such a behavioral example that behavior can be maintained at a high and relatively constant rate with only miniscule reinforcement with very large numbers of responses (or periods of time) between reinforcers.

There are many variations of reinforcement schedules and each of them will have a different effect in the maintenance of behavior. We feel, however, that the four we listed above should be sufficient to describe most situations. Our friend Barbara, of course, fits in very well. After her behavior has been learned and maintained for a while, the reinforcers can occur less and less frequently to the point of occurring only at very, very infrequent intervals and still her behavior remains well established. We mentioned previously the internalization of reinforcement and of course this also takes effect as Barbara has had attention, affection, and prestige paired over and over with her eating behavior. It is relatively easy to learn such a behavior pattern but much, much harder to unlearn.

E<small>XTINCTION</small>

You may have been hoping that we would get around to the discussion of how to eliminate (extinguish) behaviors or how behaviors stop occurring (are made extinct). Extinction occurs when a response ceases to be reinforced. Is this a sort of contradiction in terms when we look at the maintenance of behavior on extremely variable and rarely occurring reinforcement? No. It is a process that will cause behaviors to cease fairly easily if the response was maintained on a rather frequent schedule of reinforcement, but it is also a process that can be rather long and difficult if the response has been maintained on an infrequent reinforcement schedule.

Imagine, for example, walking out to your car this evening and finding that your keys will not unlock the car. Your response (turning the key) will not be reinforced (the reinforcer is opening the door successfully). You may bang on the car a while, jiggle the keys, curse at the car and kick it once or twice. Eventually, however, if you are not reinforced, the response will become extinct and you will look for other ways to get into the car.

Other, seldom-reinforced behaviors will be much harder to extinguish because the conditions may not be too dissimilar. The extinction process can be hastened, generally, by not reinforcing one response and systematically reinforcing a competing response. Competing responses are two responses that cannot occur at the same time, e.g., you cannot stand up and sit down at the same time. By punishing one of the competing responses and reinforcing the other, the process can be speeded up even more.

Are responses ever really "lost" or "unlearned"? That's a good question and we have no real answer for it. The closest we can come to an answer is a discussion of *spontaneous recovery*, a phenomenon that amounts to a response being accidentally reinforced during or after (the response may continue for a lengthy time in very sporadic and sparse fashion) extinction and returning nearly to its original strength or frequency of occurrence. The fact that such a phenomenon exists, indicates to us that many responses are not truly "lost" or "unlearned."

SUMMARY AND COMMENTS

In this chapter we have summarized in brief terms the basic principles of behavior modification. A stimulus is any perceivable item. Stimuli have various effects on our behavior depending on the form of the stimuli and the past experiences we have had with these stimuli. *Reinforcing stimuli* are those stimuli that when applied to a behavior cause that behavior to be strengthened or to become more probable in the future. These reinforcing stimuli may either be *positive* (follow the response) or *negative* (a removal of a noxious stimulus prior to or simultaneous with the response). Reinforcing stimuli may either be *innate* or *learned*. The majority of our reinforcers are learned via *pairing* with or in *exchange* for innate reinforcers.

Punishing stimuli are those stimuli that when applied to a response, cause that response to be weakened or to be less probable in the future. These punishing stimuli may also be learned or innate.

Discriminative stimuli are those stimuli in whose presence we have been reinforced for certain responses in the past. In a way they "tell us what to do" in different situations.

Shaping is the procedure of developing a new response in an organism by reinforcing successive approximations of the final, goal behavior. Many behaviors are learned in this fashion. Certain behaviors evidently appear with very infrequent reinforcement. *Reinforcement schedules* are the schedules whereby reinforcement appears for various responses. The schedules can be "stretched" until reinforcement for some responses appear only very infrequently.

Extinction is the process of removing reinforcement for a response until it is removed from the repertoire of behaviors.

In this chapter we have skimmed over some of the important parts of operant theory and we have prepared you for the rest of our text. If you have successfully waded through this formidable chapter, take some time off and reinforce yourself with a cold drink, some relaxation, or a good movie. If you couldn't quite force yourself through all of it, go back and try again. We feel that the information in this chapter is essential to the rest of the book.

3

Modeling

In the last chapter we described the process of acquiring behavior from the standpoint of operant theory. While much of our behavior is undoubtedly learned in the process of conditioning, there is at least one other important form of learning that we need to discuss. Modeling amounts to an observer watching some model and then reproducing the responses he has seen the model perform. This is very much like a monkey-see, monkey-do paradigm. There are many possible explanations for modeling (Bandura, 1971). As yet, however, there seems to be no consistent and generally acceptable explanation for the phenomenon of modeling. (Mikulus, 1969).

Even though there is no generally acceptable explanation for modeling, the work of Bandura and his associates has provided us with some pretty good characteristics of modeling behavior. By way of explaining the effects on modeling, we should develop a functional understanding of modeling and the variables that affect modeling.

RESPONSE CONSEQUENCES AND MODELING

On reflection, you can note that any response has three possible outcomes in terms of response consequences. Responses may be reinforced (rewarded); they may be punished; or there may be no consequence, i.e., neither reinforcement nor punishment is the result of a response, it receives nothing. As you might imagine, a model experiencing each of these outcomes will be perceived differently by the observer and will have a different effect on the learning of the response by the observer. If the model is reinforced for his responses, it is more likely that the observer will produce this response (or one very similar to the observed response) in a similar situation than if the model is not reinforced or is punished. If the model is not reinforced and not punished, the observer is likely to imitate the model's behavior at nearly as high a rate as though the model were reinforced (Bandura, 1965). Models punished for their responses generally are not imitated at levels anywhere approaching the level of reinforced or no-consequence models (Bandura, 1969).

There is reason to believe that observers learn at nearly the same rate regardless of the consequences of the model, but that observers who have witnessed punished models inhibit their responses. Bandura, Ross & Ross's (1963) study of incentives and model consequences demonstrated very convincingly that given the right incentive, responses that observers had seen models punished for would appear at levels equal to those levels of reinforced or unpunished model responses.

There are several important implications of these findings. Although responses can be learned equally well regardless of the consequences the model receives, punishment of the model's responses is likely to inhibit these responses in the observer. What does this mean? Quite bluntly, it means that given the correct incentive (the proper situation, motivation, etc.) an observer will emit those responses that he or she has seen lead to punishment. Does this sound familiar? These findings tell us that using someone as an "example" of what not to do is not a technique that we would want to use. Even though the responses might be inhibited at present, the possibility exists that these responses could be emitted at any time the incentive becomes strong enough, or if the situation changes enough. So, pointing out how "bad" someone has been and then punishing them probably serves to teach the behavior rather than not.

OTHER MODELING VARIABLES

One very important variable in the modeling process has been pointed out by Bandura (1969) in a series of his research. The more similar an observer perceives the model to be to him or herself, the more likely modeling is to occur. This is not to say that modeling will not occur with dissimilarly perceived models. In fact, Bandura, Ross & Ross (1963b) reported modeling with films, cartoons and puppets! What this says is that the more like ourselves we perceive someone to be, the more likely we are to imitate that person. If we picture ourselves to be middle-class, intelligent, verbal, athletic, witty and well-educated, we would be more likely to imitate a person whom we saw as being like us than if the person was drastically different. This perception of self and others need not be accurate. An inaccurate perception of another or of self can lead to imitating the behavior of a person who is unlike what we are really like, but, perhaps, like what we want to be or wish to be.

Since imitation can and does occur from cartoons, films, puppets and, in fact, any animate object or device capable of mimicking human behaviors, we need to consider some interesting implications of modeling and the basic variables that seem in some way to govern it.

Let us give you a couple of things to think about. Picture yourself in the despicable and horrible position of having to kill someone. (We realize that this is noxious, but play along with us.) If you had to name where you gained the response that would enable you to perform such a ghastly deed, what source would you give? If you have not witnessed a real murder, been in combat, or trained in combat, the answer must be films, television, radio, or printed matter. The behavior, in one fashion or another, has been modeled for you and you could, given the proper incentive, imitate the behavior. Does this sound unbelievable? Let us refer you to the work of Bandura for as much evidence as you might care to consider concerning the modeling of aggressive behavior.

Most of the inappropriate modeling that goes on is far more subtle than the sensational modeling we often read about. How many of you remember reading about people who have either seen a crime committed on television or in a movie and then gone out and reproduced the crime? Few of us, luckily, are unstable enough to run into the streets and maim and murder people after seeing such responses on television or in movies. It's not that we haven't learned how, we have. It is because we inhibit the response for any number of reasons. First and foremost, we all spend most of our lives learning not to physically harm other people. After a lifetime of such learning the behavior itself is aversive. Second, we generally do not see ourselves as the kind of person the murderer is. We might more readily imitate Kojak, Mannix, Shaft, or some of the other "good guys." They may be violent, but always for good reasons. Third, we really haven't the incentive to perform such noxious behavior. Fourth, we fear punishment. The possible list of reasons for inhibiting responses is almost endless. Each of us has particular reasons for inhibiting various responses.

The more subtle modeling that goes on over the visual media is concerned with other rather repugnant forms of behaviors. Notice how you never see a fat person eat any of those goody-goos that are always being advertised? *Successful* wives serve their husbands Acido, the coffee for athletically developed males. Check out that sexily-thin couple eating double-ick banana split cheeseburger pies with a side order of fries. How about those beer-loving characters who are all ruggedly handsome or sleekly beautiful? Have you ever seen a beer belly on a *model* for one of those advertisements? Notice how the alcohol drinker is more masculine/feminine (the viewer chooses depending on his or her frame of reference) than the other poor schnooks in the picture? How come we never see them inebriated to the point of losing consciousness or throwing up freelunch on the plastic scenery (both of which are probable outcomes if too much of the beverage is consumed)?

Ah, and what of the now-extinct cigarette commercials? Nicatinos, as you'll no doubt remember, were for *real* men.

Commercials are not insidious "big brother" forays into mind control. They are, however, an attempt to show the product in the best possible light. Only the best possible models are chosen to make the response of buying the product as likely in the observers of the models as possible. We obviously wish to see ourselves as more like the ideal models who are presented than the possible fat, drunken, or cancerous models.

So What ? What Do We Do About It ?

The easiest answer is: quit watching television, listening to the radio, reading, and seeing other people. This is a patently ridiculous solution to a very complex problem. Part of the solution must be an awareness of what commercials are. As long as you are going to watch television, you are going to learn the behaviors appropriate to the various products modeled on television and in other media. The trick is to inhibit those that are inappropriate and emit only those that are appropriate. If you are having trouble with your weight, do not imitate eating behavior. If you are fat, compare yourself to the model. If he or she is fat, okay. But if the model is thin, remember, you do not resemble him and the consequences of your eating behavior will be far different than for the thin model.

Our best advice is to purposely inhibit responses that are modeled on television and in the other media. The consequences of the behavior for the observer must always be more important than the identification with the model. Your weight loss, health, or other consequences must be more important to you than being like the model you see.

Summary

Modeling is the process of learning via imitation of some model. Observers are more likely to imitate models when the models are reinforced for the behavior than if the behavior has no visible consequence or if it is punished. Evidence exists that even when a model is punished for some response, the response is probably learned but is inhibited because of the observed punishment.

One other important factor in determining the effect of modeling is the perceived similarity between the model and the observer. The more similar an observer perceives a model to be to himself or herself, the more likely modeling is to occur.

In using knowledge of modeling to help control one's own behavior, comparisons to models and reflection on the outcomes of the behavior should be seen as more important than identification with the model.

4

Charts, Graphs and Other Helpful Paraphenalia

Thus far we have described the background for explanation and analysis of behavior. For the reader to adapt these principles and techniques to modify his own behavior, or to help in the modification of another's behavior, some of the tools described in this chapter will be extremely helpful.

At What Level Is the Behavior Occurring ?

To change behavior it is necessary to know at what level the behavior is occurring now. This may seem like a very stupid statement. The reader would not be mulling over this book if he or she were not already aware that some behavior was occurring at an unacceptable rate. It is, however, very likely that we seldom know exactly what the levels of some of our behaviors are. After all, the difference between gaining weight, holding a stable weight, and losing weight is not particularly great. Unless accurate records are kept, it is highly difficult to ascertain what the optimal level of some behaviors are. For example, ask yourself the following questions: (1) How many cigarettes have I smoked today? (2) How many bites of food did I take today? (3) How many times did I say the term "you know" inappropriately today? We can all approximate answers to such questions, but unless we have kept accurate records, we cannot be sure of our answers.

A determination of current levels of inappropriate behaviors is very helpful in choosing what technique will be used in modifying the inappropriate behaviors. Further, to determine if the treatment has been successful, we need to know if the level of the behavior has changed from the period before the treatment to the periods during and after the treatment. Clinical terms such as treatment always seem to creep in. By treatment we mean anything done to change the behavior, not necessarily a treatment in the medical sense. Hard as it may be to believe, it is highly possible to bring about a successful change in behavior and to be unaware of the results of such a change in behavior. If a person initiates some change that brings about a consistent loss of one-eighth of a pound a day, the person can become highly frustrated because the results are not easily seen. He may discard the technique when only a minor addition to it could have made it a highly successful technique. Throwing out a technique without a sound basis in fact is not exactly the way to succeed in the behavior modification business. Keeping accurate records of the behavior you wish to change allows you to determine whether or not it has been successful, how successful it has been, what parts of it are most successful, and lastly, what addition to the technique may result in improving the technique. Merely trying a technique out "without bothering with all that record-keeping business" cannot possibly provide the basis for intelligent decisions concerning a person's behavior. After all, a treatment is of very little use if we cannot determine whether or not it has been successful and how successful it has been.

Why not use subjective impressions? After all, won't we know if we lose weight or stop smoking? Yes, chances are you will know, but keeping orderly track of your behavioral data should make decisions concerning your behavior far easier. For example, if the implementation of a technique results in greatly reducing the level of a person's smoking, but has not completely stopped it, a simple addition to your behavior change technique may result in complete cessation of smoking. One thing that many people overlook is that behaviors may occur at many different rates, i.e., inappropriate behavior is not an all-or-none proposition. Hence, if some technique reduces the level of inappropriate behavior it should not be discarded because it has not brought about the total extinction of the inappropriate behavior. In such situations, additions or changes should be made in the technique rather than discarding it out of hand.

Let us not mislead the reader. Certainly, some techniques are not going to be successful at all. If accurate records are kept, then such unsuccessful techniques can be discarded, based on the results of the technique, and new techniques can be tried. The problem of using an unsuccessful technique for too long is just as frustrating as the problem of discarding a partially successful technique. At any rate, decisions concerning behavioral change techniques must be based on their level of success or failure as inferred by the data the person has recorded. Changes in treatment become far more logical if based on sound data rather than on "feelings."

Since we now believe that a sound reason has been established for the use of accurate data gathering and recording, let us present some simple techniques adaptable for personal use. (For a more in-depth treatment of the topic, see Williams and Anadam, 1973.) No sophisticated statistical models will be presented as we doubt that they would be worth inclusion in a personal behavior management book, but they are available from several sources, notably Winer (1971) and Champion (1970) as our favorites.

The simplest technique available for recording the level of some behavior is the frequency count. As the name indicates, a frequency count is merely a record of how often some bit of behavior occurs. If you smoke ten cigarettes in one day, for example, a frequency count of that day's smoking behavior would be ten. If you place something in your mouth twelve times in a day, your eating behavior, defined as placing something in your mouth, regardless of size or consistency, would be twelve. If you talk ten times in a day, a frequency count of your talking behavior would be ten.

Ah, but here is the problem. What constitutes a smoking behavior? What constitutes an eating behavior? How much of something is one behavior? If only two puffs are taken from a cigarette, does it count the same as taking forty puffs? An even more difficult problem is eating behavior. How can eating (consumption) behaviors be measured in any accurate sense? Everybody knows that one taste of soup is not equivalent to one mouthful of chocolate cake, don't they? Well, maybe they do and maybe they don't, but this kind of discrepancy certainly makes for problems in keeping accurate records of behavior.

There are several techniques available for eliminating this problem (Williams and Anadam, 1973) but we will prescribe only the simplest. It is necessary for any behavior that one seeks to change, to be specified exactly in concrete, observable terms so that there will be no ambiguity in arriving at easily determined measures of a behavior. Eating behavior may be defined, for example, as *any* ingestion of any substance. Hence, a twenty-bite piece of cake would count for twenty times as much as one bite of meat. In this manner your frequency count will be consistent. A forty-puff cigarette would be forty times as much as a one-puff cigarette. We are aware that bites and puffs can be of different sizes, but such fine discriminations are difficult to make. At any rate, as we will point out in the chapters that deal specifically with problem behaviors such as overeating and smoking, the techniques for changing the behaviors have built into them techniques that allow for the proper specification of behaviors.

A frequency count would appear much as the one pictured in figure 4–1. For our example we chose days and puffs.

Well, that's very nice, but what does it do besides adding one more superfluous task to the day's routine of drudgery? That is a good question. A frequency count provides an objective measure of the rate of occurrence of some behavior or behaviors (more than one could easily be included). Did you smoke more today than

FIGURE 4-1

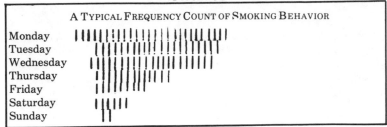

A TYPICAL FREQUENCY COUNT OF SMOKING BEHAVIOR

Monday
Tuesday
Wednesday
Thursday
Friday
Saturday
Sunday

Note: Each mark represents one puff. No attempt was made to regulate the size of individual puffs. Such a record may be kept directly on a card used for the purpose of recording data, or the data may be transferred to the chart from a note pad, or a counter.

yesterday? How do you know? One way for you to be absolutely certain is to organize your data in effective form. (By the way, keeping track of behaviors in this fashion alone tends to reduce the level of occurrence of some behavior, but more about this in the appropriate chapters.)

Well, aren't all those slash marks pretty hard to interpret too? Isn't there some better way to see if there has been progress or to determine if a change in the levels of behavior has occurred? Yes. A frequency count may easily be changed to a frequency graph which allows for greater ease of interpretation. A frequency graph, such as the one in figure 4-2, can easily be constructed directly from your frequency count and it doesn't take much time. As you can easily see, the individual in question gradually decreased his smoking behavior and then ceased altogether. Graphic representation aids greatly in determining the effectiveness of a treatment and of the rate of change of behaviors.

A nice addition to any frequency count chart is an accumulative frequency record. This is usually the last entry in the chart and represents the accumulative number of responses, lost pounds, etc. The cumulative frequency count chart allows you to determine how well you are doing over-all at one glance. Figure 4-3 represents a typical cumulative frequency chart that may be used to chart weight loss or gain.

MECHANICAL DEVICES

How in the world can a person possibly keep up with all these diverse behaviors? After all, one can't really carry a pad and pencil

FIGURE 4-2

A TYPICAL FREQUENCY GRAPH OF SMOKING BEHAVIOR

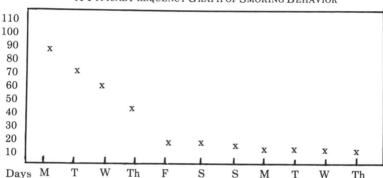

Note: Each gradation of 1 represents 1 puff. A graph such as this is constructed by first drawing the horizontal and vertical axes, placing the frequency of the behavior on the vertical axis using equal distances to represent equal frequencies of behavior, e.g., one inch might equal 20 puffs in this case, with each vertical inch always equal to twenty puffs. The horizontal axis is used to represent time, days in this case. Equal distances should be used to represent equal amounts of time, e.g., one inch might represent one day. The frequency of the behavior for each day is plotted by first finding the frequency along the vertical axis, and then taking this level and plotting it directly above the day in which it occurred. For example, on the first Tuesday, a frequency of 76 was found along the vertical axis and then plotted above the Tuesday. When the plotting marks (x's in this case) are connected, a graph of the levels of behavior results.

around all day making little slash marks, can one? We think a person could if the person was genuinely interested in changing some behavior. Luckily, there are devices on the market that eliminate the problem of carrying around paper and pencil all the time. Mechanical counters which may be carried in the pocket or purse are ideal for the purpose of a frequency count. There are several kinds. Some are extremely expensive, made from metal and designed specifically for the purpose of counting behaviors. For most purposes, however, a simple grocery money counter is an excellent alternative. These plastic counters cost about one dollar and they can record

FIGURE 4-3

A TYPICAL CUMULATIVE FREQUENCY CHART

Date	Weight	Amount Lost	Cumulative Amount Lost	Contingencies
10/7	140	0		
10/8	139½	½		
10/9	139	1		
10/10	138½	1½		

Note: Such a record may be kept for many different kinds of behaviors. The headings would have to be changed to suit whatever behavior was being changed. For example, if smoking behavior was being charted, the headings might read numbers of puffs, number of puffs less than the day before, cumulative change in smoking by number of puffs, and so forth.

numbers up to 999. One hopes the behaviors you intend to change will not be occurring more frequently than 999 times a day. At the end of the day the number visible on the face of the counter may be directly transferred to your frequency graph or your tally sheet.

A STEP FURTHER

As we continue with chapters dealing directly with the change in certain behaviors, we will mention over and over a particularly useful addition to a frequency count. The "awareness chart" is a chart so devised and constructed as to allow the individual to record several things at once concerning the behavior under question. An example of this is pictured in figure 4-4. In such a chart the individual must record the time at which the behavior occurred, the level of intensity of the behavior, who the individual was with when the behavior occurred, how the individual felt when emitting the response, and lastly, why the individual thinks the behavior occurred. These different bits of information provide the person engaged in keeping track of the behavior with information pertinent to the modification of the behavior. It may happen that certain times of the day, certain occurrences, or certain people tend to form discriminative stimuli that cause the person to emit the response more frequently than under other conditions.

The use of such a charting device should enable you to both analyze your behavior and to better adopt a "treatment" for the behavior.

There are several techniques available for comparing treatments. Some of the statistical designs are quite complex and suited more to the scientific community than the individual interested in changing his or her own behavior. Some of the simpler techniques used are typical behavior modification designs that allow a comparison of treatment effects.

A TYPICAL "AWARENESS CHART"

Time the behavior occurred	level of behavior	Who with	How felt	Why occurred

Note: This should be kept in close accord with the definition used in the frequency count.

The simplest is an ABAC design wherein A stands for the baseline period (that period of time wherein no treatment is being administered). B stands for the first treatment and C for the second treatment. A typical graph of such a design is pictured in figure 4-5. Such a design calls for first keeping a record of the behavior to be modified under "natural conditions," i.e., under no treatment. This, as we discussed above, becomes the reference point (baseline) for examining the effects of whatever treatments we introduce later. The first treatment is referred to by B and amounts to a record of the behavior to be modified under the conditions of the first treatment. The return to baseline, or the record A, is again a reference point for evaluation of the next technique.

This method of staggering treatments around non-treatment

FIGURE 4-5

A TYPICAL ABAC DESIGN

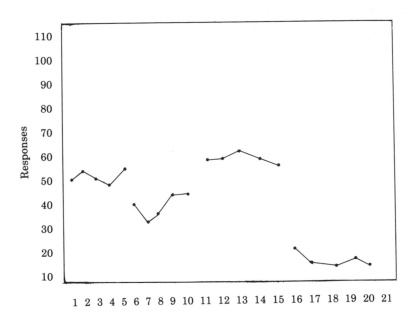

Note: A refers to the baseline or no–treatment period, B refers to the first treatment and C refers to the second treatment. In this particular graph, treatment C seemed to lower the level of responding more than treatment B.

periods is used to try to eliminate confusing effects of two treatments. Some behaviors can be fairly readily changed under appropriate treatment conditions but are extremely difficult to change back to their original levels of occurrence and, hence, confound the effect of a second treatment on the behavior. For example, once some treatment has raised a child's reading rate to a certain level, removal of that treatment is very unlikely to cause the reading behavior to return to its original state. For this reason the second baseline is used to facilitate the evaluation of a second treatment. The second treatment is referred to by C and is a record of the behavior under the conditions of the second treatment.

The problem with such a design is the cumulative effect on the second treatment caused by the first treatment. Generally more complex designs such as a ABACACAB etc., are used to alleviate such problems. Redundancy soon becomes a factor, however. One hopes it will not be necessary for the reader's purpose to enter an in-depth analysis of the effectiveness of two or more treatments. If such a situation arises, the reader should consult a good text dealing with such design problems. Such texts provide a wide variety of possible forms of analysis of two or more treatments.

Summary

In this chapter we discussed the usefulness of graphs, charts and good record keeping. If you are to start the change of some of your behaviors you should find them a useful tool.

A frequency count is merely a tabulation of the frequency of occurrence of some behavior. Extreme care must be taken to properly specify the behavior to be studied. A frequency graph often aids in the interpretation and evaluation of the effectiveness of treatments. A cumulative frequency graph aids in allowing you to see the total amount of change of the behavior.

"Awareness" charts allow for greater analysis of specific behaviors. There are several possible designs for the comparison of different behaviors but we suggest you investigate further when such problems are to be treated in depth.

5

Weight Control

One of the problems often encountered by people in the American culture is obesity. Estimates of the extent of the problem vary from author to author as do the criteria established for the achievement of overweight status. The persons we are directing our current chapter to are those who meet the following criteria.

1. You have been medically certified by a practicing, licensed, medical doctor as needing to lose weight.

2. You see a need for yourself to lose weight. Perhaps you feel uncomfortable, are worried about your future health, are under a doctor's orders to lose weight, would like to be more physically "attractive," or are generally convinced that maintaining a proper weight for yourself would be a beneficial goal.

3. You are willing to work for the change in your behavior.

4. Your goals are realistically set and you are aware of what to expect by changing your behavior.

5. You are willing to "play the game" and admit that your behavior can be governed appropriately.

6. You are willing to be consistent, organized, and persevering.

7. If you do not need to lose weight, you are in the position of wanting to stabilize your weight.

Before starting a weight-change process of more than a couple of pounds, consult a physician. The doctor should be able to determine how much weight you need to lose and prescribe a sensible diet. The problem with sensible diets has never been that they don't work—they do. The problem has been that very few of us are able to change our behavior patterns sufficiently to allow us to adapt a new diet into our behaviors. Changing your behavior patterns and losing weight will cause a change in your physical state. A complete physical checkup with regular visits to determine your health are necessary to ensure that you don't lose your resistance and become ill, and that you don't suffer a glandular imbalance and become seriously ill. Nutritional deficiencies can occur if you are fifty pounds overweight or more. For all these reasons, a doctor's help is necessary. We have only one life and we must safeguard it as best we can. After all, what good is losing twenty or thirty pounds if the "new me" is a me that is weak, ill, or suffering from nutritional deficiencies. Besides, it's a good idea to get a physical once in a while to make sure that the ol' body is still in good running condition. The funny thing is that most of us take better care of our cars with checkups and maintenance than we do of our bodies.

Overweight as a Behavior Problem

Not including glandular imbalances, overweight is the result of some very specific behaviors. Overweight is a condition but it is not a dynamic state, rather, it is the result of a series of conditioned responses. No one response, of course, could cause extreme gains in weight, but the cumulative effect of several thousands of similar responses will result in the condition. For us, then, overweight is the direct result of behavior. In dealing with excess poundage we will not address ourselves to the condition itself, but rather to the behaviors which have resulted in, and which continue to support a state of overweight.

Stimulus Properties of Food

In chapter two we delineated different kinds of stimuli, among them reinforcing stimuli. As you will recall, this was defined as a stimulus, that when applied after some response, caused that response to be strengthened. Further, an unlearned (innate or primary) reinforcing stimulus is one that has the properties to bring about reinforcement because of the biological nature of our organisms. One of the most powerful among these reinforcers is food.

Reinforcers are unusual stimuli. Through past experience we may learn that the attainment of reinforcers is the culmination of some successful behaviors. Further, we sometimes administer reinforcers to ourselves after trying or frustrating situations. One of the examples that we have commonly encountered includes buying new clothing (reinforcing stimuli) when feeling especially low. This attainment of a reward (reinforcer) has in the past often been associated with being a good person, with making correct decisions, or with being successful. The attainment of a reinforcer, although not directly related to the behavior that made the person feel "blue" or sad, is an overt attempt to provide the person with some reward and the feelings (positive, happy, etc.) that go along with achieving a reinforcer.

Food, used as a reward, more than other reinforcers, is often paired with many other reinforcing stimuli. (Note: The concepts of reinforcer and reward are very similar and need to be clarified at this point so that the reader will see what we are attempting to say. As previously stated a positive reinforcer strengthens the response it follows. This has nothing to do with the intentions of the reinforced organism, the environment, or a person within the environment. The positive reinforcing stimulus itself has the properties to cause such a change in behavior due to either the biological structure of the organism or the past experience of the organism. A reward, on the other hand, may or may not be a reinforcing stimulus. It is, however, some stimulus applied to an organism to attempt to reinforce the organism. Rewards may be overt—a parent hugging a child for being a "good child"—or covert—an action on the part of a child that results in a response by another person that is a reinforcer. Rewards, hence, are attempts by persons within the environment, either one's self or others, to try to reinforce some behavior.)

Food, a very accessible reinforcer for most Americans, is quite naturally used for more than the biological needs it should fill. Very often parents actively seek to reward "good" behaviors on the part of their children with food. For example, many of us remember doing something good and then receiving approval, attention, affection, and a cookie or a piece of fruit for being such a good child. "You've been such a good child, let me give you a scrumptious piece of this cake." This form of reward and reinforcement by parents is not at all unusual. This pattern emerges in infancy and continues well into adulthood. One spouse may greet the other at the end of a hard day and say something very much like this: "You've worked so hard today (been such a "good person") let's go out and get a steak to celebrate" (let me reward you with a cookie substitute). Well, there is nothing wrong with this kind of behavior unless it gets out of hand. After all, we all want to reward our children, spouses, and friends for doing "good" things. The problem sets in when it is overdone or when it becomes a self-initiated form of reward.

We all reward ourselves for many of our behaviors. Often we will have worked very hard on something and find that there is no external reward for it. We may be *reinforced* for the working behavior by self-satisfaction, completion of the work, or the actual solving of some problem, but it is easy to feel as though this is not enough and that we should really be rewarded overtly. Hence, we decide to reward ourselves by engaging in some behavior that has been reinforced in the past or we decide to obtain the reinforcers directly. The direct attainment of the reinforcer is often rewarding oneself with a good meal or a cool drink or a piece of cake. We may not actually physically need the reward, but we eat anyway. Why? Because we want a reward and this has been one very often in the past.

Why isn't self-satisfaction (the internalization of reinforcers) enough? For many people it is enough. For others it is not. This may be due to a common phenomenon that often occurs when reinforcers or some part of the reinforcers are removed from a behavior. Organisms in this situation will often start producing the previously reinforced response at a higher level in order to obtain the reinforcer that is now absent. On the part of humans, rather than repeating the same response, if some reinforcer is not present following a behavior and it usually has been in the past, (such as approval, affection, attention, food, etc.) the human can provide this external reinforcement himself or herself. Since it is difficult to provide an overt reinforcer like attention or approval, food is often the substitute.

What this can result in, in fact, what it does result in with many people, is the application of food as a reinforcer for many behaviors, even though the food is not needed physically.

FOOD PAIRED WITH OTHER GOODIES

As our discussion above stated, food is very often paired (associated with) many other kinds of reinforcing stimuli. In chapter two, when we described the process of the development of secondary reinforcers, we mentioned that a neutral stimulus, after having been paired with a primary reinforcer, obtained some of the reinforcing value of the primary reinforcer and eventually was reinforcing by itself. This same process, associative pairing, can work with the pairing of two or more primary reinforcing stimuli. For example, if food and affection are paired very often, food will eventually gain some of the reinforcing qualities of affection while affection will obtain some of the reinforcing properties of food. (We wonder if the statement "live on love" comes from this sort of associative pairing paradigm?)

There is no doubt that food is often paired with many forms of reinforcement, primary and secondary. Affection, attention, and approval, as previously noted, are often paired with food both in childhood and in adulthood. Food is also often paired with socialization, good company, happy times, and rest. It is no great wonder to the observer, then, that when people are unable to obtain satisfactory amounts (satisfactory to the individual) of reinforcers like approval and social interaction, that food is a stimulus that can be substituted for them. Again, there is nothing wrong with pairing food and other forms of reinforcers, but certain limits must be recognized. Food is not a suitable substitute for other forms of reinforcement. Awareness of this fact alone can help diminish some of the problems people have with overeating. Food is a biological necessity, but it, and other reinforcers, can become too heavily relied upon and cause more problems than they can solve.

EATING BEHAVIOR

In the next section of this chapter, we will examine several different kinds of behavior patterns (habits, if you will) that have resulted in overweight. We certainly do not expect the reader to "pick the one most like me," rather, we present them as a way of demonstrating how many different kinds of behavioral patterns can result in overweight. There should be no stigma attached to these behaviors. All of us have conditioned individual patterns of behavior that are not as successful or appropriate as they might be. Behaviors leading to inappropriate levels of weight, however, are more obvious and perhaps more uncomfortable than some others. In this section we will be looking at behavior from two points of view, that include different factors governing weight control.

There are two basic factors governing behaviors that effect the weight of any organism. (1) Food intake; the greater the amount of food intake, the greater the propensity for weight gain, and (2) energy output; given equal amounts of food intake for the same organism, weight gain will be directly affected by the amount of energy expended, i.e., the more energy that is expended, the lower the probability is for weight gain. These two factors seem extremely simple and are well known by anyone bothering to consider the problem of weight gain and loss. The series of behaviors governing these two effects, however, are less well understood.

All of us have some intuitive ideas concerning cutting back on food intake and increasing energy output as the means for losing weight. But how do these two things combine in the first place to bring about weight gain?

1. *Simple overeating.* Overeating amounts to eating more food than is necessary. This kind of behavior has several possible origins but we will attempt a general explanation, one much like the example we gave in chapter two of the girl who had become overweight because of the highly reinforcing characteristics of eating behavior in her environment.

Let us re-examine a similar situation, considering only the problem of overeating at mealtimes. Joe, our hypothetical overeater, doesn't snack much between meals, doesn't eat exotic or overly fattening foods, and doesn't drink or smoke. What he does do is eat three good meals a day, as he has done for years. However, this has resulted in a slow but sure increase in his weight. Joe shares (there could be hundreds of reasons, but ours will be a general one) a common malady with many post adolescents; he is continuing a food intake that he developed during his youth and continued into his adult years. His eating habits (good as they may have been during adolescence) have not changed while his other habits have changed. Joe has moved from the active life of an adolescent who, (by the way) needs a considerable amount of food/energy intake for growing and maintenance (Perkins, 1974) to the relatively placid and non-strenuous life of an office worker.

We can see that we are dealing with two specific behaviors in Joe's weight gain; eating behavior and energy output. Joe's eating behavior was developed during his adolescent years by some rather wise parents. He was permitted, in fact, encouraged, to eat very well at mealtimes, but was not allowed frequent snacks between meals. The reinforcers supporting his eating behavior were approval, affection and attention from his parents. Approval, attention, and affection were only necessary in a consistent fashion at first. After he learned the appropriate behavior by which he could obtain reinforcers from his parents, the reinforcers only needed to appear at infrequent intervals in order to maintain the behavior. In fact, after several years of being maintained on a reinforcement schedule of eating a certain amount of food three times a day, the process of reinforcement became internalized (in the sense that the performance of the appropriate eating behavior, after having been paired with other reinforcers for so long, gained some of the reinforcing characteristics of the affection, attention, and approval reinforcers).

Now that Joe is thirty, his behavior has not changed. Why should it? It has been successful for 18 years in garnering external reinforcers at first, and for the last few years has largely been self-reinforcing.

Joe's energy expenditure behavior (physical activity) however, has changed. Joe is probably aware that such a change has occurred, but he probably is not exactly sure why it has changed. change period. After all, many of the situations he has encountered large an amount of energy/food intake to support growth. Second, he has "given-up" the running, jumping, and other forms of activity during the day and replaced them with work in the form of cerebral (we hope) activity on the job. This has happened in a completely natural way. The contingencies (environmental sources of reinforcement and punishment) have changed rather drastically from the time Joe was in high school to the current time.

In high school Joe's environment (which, as we have pointed out, includes people in the situation) encouraged physical activity in athletics, physical education, after-school games, running in the halls and so forth. On any given day, Joe would expend considerable energy just performing activities that would gain reinforcement from his peers and teachers. In fact, running, jumping, and generally high levels of activity were accepted and encouraged behaviors.

In moving from high school to college (where many of the contingencies remain similar) and eventually (or immediately) to his job, the contingencies change. Running, jumping, shouting, and "rowdy" behaviors are no longer reinforced. Instead, competing behaviors such as walking quietly, sitting quietly, and speaking softly are reinforced. Joe probably knows that his behavior must be different and does not have to go through an extensive behavior change period. After all, many of the situations he has encountered earlier had similar contingencies, e.g., church and classroom behavior. The difference is that, to gain reinforcers (attention, acceptance, approval), he must now adhere to the contingencies in operation for eight or nine hours a day. The tensions and other variables that affect an office worker during the day insure that the worker is fatigued when he comes home. Irrespective of this, contingencies in the home supporting housecleaning, dishwashing, child-care, and other activities are considerably less physically rigorous than activities pursued before the onset of marriage and family life. Joe, then, has changed his energy output levels without changing his eating habits. It is no surprise that Joe's behaviors have led to the problem of overweight.

2. *Eating too much, too often and lousy eating habits.* Many of us cannot resist the urge for little snacks in addition to our regular meals. A doughnut with coffee in the morning, a candy bar in the afternoon and a cold beer and some nuts before bedtime. Well, chances are, unless you lead an unusually strenuous life, a continuous pattern of this kind of eating behavior will lead to overweight. By the way, snacking isn't always very obvious. Cooking in the kitchen can lead to a taste here and there. All this work leads to a soft drink which adds a little more. Alas, by the end of the day, these little tastes have accumulated and will eventually lead to overweight.

There seem to be basically two patterns of behavior that lead to this miserable eating habit syndrome. First, there is the snacker who is conscious of what he or she is doing; looking for a little reward for a hard day or a job well done. Reflection on the earlier discussion of the reward/reinforcement qualities of food should fit here exactly. The reward-oriented snackers may know that they don't need the food, but they have "earned" it (usually in lieu of other reinforcers) or one little snack won't hurt (I may not have earned it, but no other reinforcers are coming in and I could sure use some).

The second pattern of bad eating habits is apparent in those people who are really not aware that they are consuming any food (I'm just tasting the borscht) or are not aware that they are consuming a significant amount (Pshaw, it's just one little, bitty piece). Either of these or similar patterns of eating habits are the easiest to control, as we will demonstrate (hopefully) later.

3. *Lack of physical activity.* One common cause of weight gain, as we pointed out earlier, is the cessation or lack of enough exercise to burn away the calorie intake. Unless a diet is highly restricted and well planned, it seems almost a certainty that some moderate exercise (walking, jogging, yard work, etc.) is necessary to control weight. Obviously, exercise to many people has noxious properties (it is too much like work; it hurts; it takes up valuable time; "I'm already tired when I come home"; "exercise is for kids"; etc., etc., etc., ad nauseum). Exercise seems to be a health-promoting activity if properly administered. (Remember our caution to see your doctor? This also applies before you begin any kind of exercising if you have been relatively idle.) However, there should be some method to the madness of exercise. Developing a good exercise schedule is not particularly difficult.

4. *The boredom eater.* Food is a powerful reinforcer, and, as we have noted repeatedly, it often attains some of the reinforcing quali-

ties of other reinforcers. When boredom sets in and there is a lack of reinforcing stimuli (or any kind for that matter), many people fight boredom by participating in activities that have, in the past, led to reinforcement. This may include going out to a movie, going for a drive, reading a book, watching television, listening to the radio, and eating. Very often, if there is nothing else to do, we eat. This form of substitution can be fairly simply corrected as we will demonstrate soon.

5. *The I-love-to-eat eater.* Some folks, one of the writers included, love to eat, and perhaps overemphasize the process of eating. Meals become events that are looked forward to; meetings are conducted over lunch or over supper; good times (reinforcing activities) center around going out for supper; cookbooks are literally pored over; and a lot of thought goes into the choice of foods. This form of overemphasis on eating behavior may arise from frequent pairing of other forms of reinforcers (e.g., approval, good-times generally, business success, social interaction, etc.) with food. Eventually food and the process of eating food become more powerful reinforcers than they should, acquiring many of the properties of other reinforcers and generally becoming discriminative stimuli for the acquisition of other reinforcers. This is not a phenomenon limited to wealthy people. Rather it is common to many, especially when we consider that in many households, not only is mealtime the intrafamilial event of the day (the only time when all the family is together) but it is also the only thing many families really have to look forward to.

This kind of overemphasis may not necessarily lead to overweight if the eating behavior itself is carefully governed, but it is easy to consistently overdo a good thing and gain weight. We don't feel that it is necessary to eliminate or greatly modify the importance of eating behavior, but it is necessary to modify any overindulgence in such settings.

Not to be left out of this "classification" is the person who has very little else to look forward to except eating. We do not like to think of these kinds of problems, but they are real enough.

6. *Problem eating.* So far we have mentioned five rather common kinds of problem behaviors related to weight control. There are serious problems, however, that are neither easy to deal with nor safe to deal with in cookbook fashion. These include the substitution of food for other needed reinforcers such as love, affection, esteem, social interaction, attention, and so forth. Our general feeling is that many people can overcome what is commonly referred to as compensation via behavior modification. Others may need the help of specialized personnel, such as counselors, psychologists or psychiatrists. We will not try to oversimplify a very complex and very difficult topic. Compulsive eaters, compensatory eaters, people with glandular disorders and other serious psychological and physical disorders have problems more serious than simple maladaptive

behavior patterns. It is possible that the eating behavior patterns can be changed, but there may be other more serious problems that cannot be dealt with by reading a book.

7. *The beer drinker and snacker.* Excessive consumption of beverages seems to be limited only to alcoholic beverages. We cannot recall hearing of many instances of people consuming too many fruit juices, too much milk, or too many soft drinks (although it is certainly possible). The problems of over-consumption of alcoholic beverages may be tied to overweight. Obviously, there are many more problems tied to the over-consumption of alcoholic beverages than a mere pattern of behavior. We are not directing ourselves to any of these problems, only to the modification of behavior patterns that result in the consumption of a drink or two in the evening along with some munchies.

How does this start? Well, aside from the reinforcing properties of alcohol on the body system, a drink or two are often associated with other reinforcers, such as socialization, approval, attention, prestige, celebration, etc. And as with all the behavior patterns we have so far described, overdoing it will lead to over-consumption and ultimately overweight. The behavior pattern becomes fixed after several reinforcing situations whenever the consumption of a couple of drinks becomes a normal way to unwind or relax.

The problem of a few drinks, given no compounding problems beyond the scope of this book, may be changed much as the other behaviors we have mentioned and will be described below.

The few examples we have given are certainly not all-inclusive. They were presented as general examples and will be referred to as we describe the process of extinguishing inappropriate eating behaviors and replacing them with appropriate responses. Before we move to our "how-to-do-it" section, however, we do need to review two previously mentioned concepts (chapter 2) and relate them to food consumption.

Discriminative Stimuli and Eating

If the reader will harken back to chapter two, and re-read the definition of a discriminative stimulus, he or she will find that it reads as follows: "A discriminative stimulus is a stimulus in whose presence you have been reinforced for certain behaviors in the past and, hence, are likely to perform those behaviors again when you again perceive that stimulus." (This was included here for the benefit of those folks who skipped over chapter two. If you are one of these people, go back and read it before you go further. Shame on you!)

Discriminative stimuli govern all our operant behaviors. The examples in chapter two should bring to mind discriminative stimuli in whose presence you have been reinforced for eating. There are many possible different discriminative stimuli for eating behavior including the time of day (it's six o'clock and time to eat), certain kinds of socialization (sitting at a table and playing cards may start one to thinking of snacks), smells (the odor of frying bacon is likely to make one ready to eat even if he or she is not hungry), the sight of someone else eating, and so forth. Awareness of the effect of discriminative stimuli is probably the best defense against responding in their presence. What must be done is to stop the reinforcement of the unwanted response (eating) while reinforcing only a competing, appropriate response.

As long as eating occurs, it is unlikely that reinforcement can be denied the eater, but the suppression of the eating response and replacing it with a competing response is possible. A competing response is one that cannot go on at the same time as the response it competes with. For example, it is impossible to not eat and eat at the same time. Eating responses and non-eating responses are incompatible, competing responses. In the re-conditioning process the appropriate responses must be continually reinforced (we will describe how this is done below) while the inappropriate responses receive no reinforcement. Eventually, the discriminative stimulus will no longer evoke the inappropriate responses, but will evoke whatever appropriate response we have replaced it with.

CONTINGENT AND DEPENDENT RELATIONSHIPS

So far we have used the words contingent and dependent several times without fully clarifying the difference between contingencies (contingent relationships) and dependencies (dependent relationships). When an environmental event is said to be dependent on a behavior we mean that the environmental event does, in fact, follow the behavior and must, by the nature of the event, do so (Reynolds, 1969). Examples of dependent relationships include the behavior of jumping out a third-story window which is followed by falling to the ground. If you jump out the window, you're going to fall to the ground and there isn't anything you can do about it. This is a dependent relationship. If you hold a pencil at arm's length over the floor and release it (your response), it must, by the nature of the event, fall to the ground. This, too is a dependent relationship. If you turn off the radio, it does not play. These examples are frivolous but we offer them as a contrast to examples of contingent relationships below.

When an environmental event is said to be contingent on a behavior, we mean that the environmental event does, in fact, follow the behavior, but does not of necessity have to. For example, if the reader claps his or her hands every time a comic on stage tells a good joke, the reader has devised a contingent relationship. The environmental event does, in fact, follow a behavior (the good joke) but it need not do so (the reader need not clap hands if he or she does not want to do so). Other contingent events include giving a child a hug for straightening up his or her room (it need not happen, but it does), smoking a cigarette after drinking a cup of coffee, thanking a youngster for hand-delivering the newspaper in a rainstorm, buying a friend a drink after a particularly hard day, etc. etc.

Contingent events occur constantly and govern many of our behaviors. The majority of our operant behaviors are predicted on the contingent reinforcement of these behaviors. One of the best ways to change behaviors, then, would be to change the contingencies supporting the behaviors. Oh, don't get us wrong, contingencies can be negative, some punishment could follow a behavior, but it is not necessary to have negative consequences to change that behavior. It is only necessary to remove the reinforcing contingencies and develop contingencies to support the incompatable, competing responses we mentioned earlier. Keep the idea of contingent relationships in mind, as we will be referring to them frequently in the next few pages.

CHANGING THE BEHAVIOR

In this section we will first delineate a general procedure for changing eating behavior and then we'll address ourselves to more specific problems. The first step in any behavior change process is an assessment of the current situation; an analysis of the behaviors and their supporting contingencies. Why do this? Isn't it going to be obvious what behaviors I want to change and how they are supported? Not necessarily. It is quite possible for the problem-behavior to be a matter of overweight as in the "simple-overeater's" case or in the "snacker's" case. In these instances, we do not want to change the entire behavior; rather, we want to modify only parts of the behavior pattern.

Where to Start? The first place to start is with keeping a daily log for a couple of days. In this daily log, keep track of every item that is tasted, eaten, drunk, or in any manner placed in the mouth. While you are jotting this down, note how you feel at that moment. Think about what you are expecting from the consumption process. Write these thoughts down. Then, while and after you've eaten, jot down any contingencies that are in effect (how did you feel while or after you had eaten; what were the reactions of other people; what seemed to be paired with the consumption process and so forth). Whew! Isn't this a lot of work just to get ready? Yes, it is, but it is a process that will become easier and faster as the days go by. Besides, we've cautioned you over and over that this business is hard work. Note: A caution should be taken not to behave differently than "normal" while you are doing this.

During these same few days, think about those things you do (besides eating and drinking) that you very much enjoy or anticipate doing. List these in order of how important they are to you.

The list may include reading, watching television, tending to a hobby, fishing, knitting, or crocheting, talking with friends over the phone, etc. When you have completed these initial steps you are ready for the initiation of behavior analysis (See figure 5-1).

Behavior Analysis. Now that we know how often eating occurs, what the consequences of eating are, (both internal feelings, and external environmental contingencies which include the reaction of other people) and those stimuli that eating is paired with, you will be able to develop a rationale for why you eat, how much you eat, and what the goals of eating are (i.e., what contingencies are expected from eating).

You may find that you snack or eat from boredom, to "relax" yourself, because others expect you to, or because you feel that good things will happen if you eat. We will come back to this phase of behavior analysis after we examine one rather important principle.

The Premack Principle. The Premack Principle, first articulated by David Premack (1959), amounts to holding a high-frequency behavior contingent on the performance of a low-frequency behavior. Quite literally, this means that some frequently occurring behavior is controlled by someone and is not allowed unless some low-frequency behavior occurs first. Stated another way, behaviors that you enjoy very much are held contingent on the occurrence of behaviors that are not enjoyed.

Does all this sound familiar? It should. Many of us had parents who applied the Premack Principle to our behaviors, although probably without knowing that Premack had ever had anything to say about the matter. For example, "Susie, you can't go out and play (a high-frequency behavior) unless you make your bed (a low-frequency behavior) first." How about the following: "You can't have any ice cream to eat (a high-frequency behavior) unless you eat all your broccoli" (a low-frequency behavior)? One last example would be: "You can't go on a date (a high-frequency behavior) unless you do your homework first" (a relatively low-frequency behavior).

Articulating this in the form we used in chapter three, we are assuming that some behavior that occurs frequently will be a potent reinforcer for the performance of a lower-frequency behavior. Well, isn't all this kid stuff? After all, we're adults now and we all get to do pretty much what we want to do. We certainly do not feel that the Premack Principle is kid stuff. As a matter of fact, most of us govern a lot of our behaviors with this principle, or something very similar to it. How often do you delay the enjoyment of some very gratifying behavior until you have finished something that you do not enjoy, but feel must be done? For example, you may decide to finish reading the remainder of this chapter before you take a

FIGURE 5-1

A TYPICAL CHART FOR KEEPING TRACK OF EATING BEHAVIOR

Time	What eaten	With who	Felt how	Expected what	Reaction	Paired w/
10:10	candy bar (3 oz.)	George & Sally	happy	more talk	seemed happy	socialization
12:15	soup, sandwich, coffee	Sally	happy	talk & relaxation	talked	socialization & relaxation
3:10	doughnut & coffee w/cream	alone	sad	a "lift"	-----	-----
6:15	beef (6 oz.) mashed potatoes (4 oz.) salad, tea	George	at ease	attention, relaxation & affection	pleased, attentive	socialization, attention

Note: This chart represents a typical day's consumption of food. From such records kept over a brief period of time, a week or so, quite a bit of information regarding eating information can be gathered.

coffee break. Or, you may delay taking your vacations until you have completed some work around the house. We all set up little tasks like these for us to complete before we relax or before we stop to enjoy ourselves. This informal use of the Premack Principle helps us govern our behaviors as we strive to set up rewards for our behaviors.

Contingencies and Weight Loss. Now that we've mentioned a couple of things, it's about time that we explained how to use them in attacking the problems of overweight. You've certainly figured out by now that that list of highly enjoyable behaviors is going to be held contingent on weight loss. The actual problem in determining what behavior to attack (i.e., smoking, eating the wrong things, eating too much, etc.) is highly complex, so we offer what has been a very successful technique in the past: holding the enjoyable behaviors contingent on some daily weight loss. There are some steps to follow in this procedure below:

1. Determine with a doctor's aid a realistic amount of weight to be lost every day. This should be some amount that you can reasonably expect to lose with effort (don't make it easy) but an

FIGURE 5-2

A TYPICAL WEIGHT CHART FOR A PERIOD OF TWO WEEKS

Date	Weight	Amount Lost	Cumulative Loss	Contingencies
2–3	190	0	0	
2–4	189	1	1	+
2–5	188½	½	1½	+
2–6	188	½	2	+
2–7	187½	½	2½	+
2–8	186½	1	3½	+
2–9	187	+½	3	−
2–10	186½	½	3½	+
2–11	186	½	4	+
2–12	185	1	5	+
2–13	184½	½	5½	+
2–14	184	½	6	+
2–15	183½	½	6½	+
2–16	183	½	7	+

Note: This is a typical weight chart kept for a period of two weeks. A plus in the contingency column denotes that contingencies were obtained on that day. A minus sign denotes that contingencies were not met.

amount that you can accurately measure with your bathroom scale. We generally suggest one-half to one pound as a reasonable amount that can be accurately measured.

2. Weigh yourself accurately in the morning before breakfast of the first day you begin to institute the weight-loss process. Record this on a chart and on the corresponding graphs (see figures 5-2 and 5-3).

FIGURE 5-3

A CONVERSION OF THE WEIGHT CHART INTO A WEIGHT GRAPH

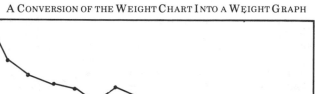

Note: This graph uses the same data that appeared in figure 5-2.

3. Determine what reinforcers you will hold contingent on the weight loss. Here is where your stick-to-itiveness will be tried. You must promise not to engage in certain enjoyable behaviors unless you meet the criteria for performing the undesirable behavior as measured by your daily weight loss. It is important for you to choose a valuable behavior to hold as a contingency, one that you truly enjoy. If you choose something that you can readily do without, you will have defeated yourself early in the game.

Don't Cheat. If you want to lose weight you've got to play fair. If you have made watching television contingent on losing one-half pound, you must not watch television. After all, the purpose of developing contingencies in the first place is to cause you to lose something (punish you) if you do not achieve your goal and to reward you (reinforce you) for meeting your goal.

Now, if you're leaning back and laughing at this, and have decided it is a form of mechanistic childishness, think again. If you want to lose weight, you must do something about it. We can't do it for you. If you perceive that, indeed, your weight is a problem, you have two alternatives: (1) do something about it or (2) do nothing.

Many people "go on diets" and achieve no results. However, their guilt concerning being overweight is mollified because they rationalize that they are at least doing something about it. Well, don't approach this program in that manner. If you do, you're not going to lose one ounce. There is absolutely no reason, unless there is an organic problem, why you cannot lose weight if you adhere to a good program. If you are not willing to follow through ("I don't have the will power," or "it's so childish") with a weight-loss program, why not save everyone concerned a lot of headaches and admit that you don't want to lose the weight in the first place?

4. Write your contingencies out and post this agreement with yourself, as well as the two charts, in a conspicuous place.

5. Refer back to your behavior analysis and note those discriminative stimuli that evoke unnecessary eating. Keep your log up and note every act of consumption. Purposely inhibit eating at inappropriate times. You may substitute if necessary. Have some water or coffee instead of that doughnut and milk. Chew gum instead of eating a candy bar, etc. At meal times take special note to take in only as much food as your diet (as prescribed by a doctor) recommends.

You should now be aware of environmental contingencies that support eating. Do not comply with these; rather, emit other behaviors that are appropriate, e.g., gum-chewing or reading. Well? Is that all there is to it? Yes. However, the process is more difficult in practice than it is to read about. For instance, if you analyze your behaviors in the next couple of days and pick some of the contingencies supporting your eating behavior, you will not find it easy to change your habits. But you will understand how your behaviors are supported and this should enable you to make some changes. Further, as we pointed out earlier, you must structure your contingencies supporting your weight loss in such a manner that the deprival of activities (or things) for not losing weight is a really noxious experience and that gaining those privileges for losing weight is highly rewarding.

Example 1

Mrs. T had been concerned with her physical appearance for some time. At the time of our first conference she weighed a not unpleasant 142 pounds but expressed a high degree of concern about regaining her youthful figure at 120 pounds, the weight she had maintained at the beginning of her marriage two years previously.

We instructed her to start keeping an accurate account of everything she ate. We further explained our views of behavior patterns and suggested that keeping an account of how she felt and thought before, during, and after she ate would be helpful, as well as describing the situation (this was for the discriminative stimuli and environmental contingencies). She was also to consult a physician for a checkup and a reasonable diet to follow.

On her return in a week, we discussed her records of eating behavior and became convinced that most of her superfluous eating was due to boredom. Actually, just keeping an accurate record of her eating behavior had brought about a noticeable drop in her food consumption during the period of one week. (We find often, that keeping accurate records of eating behavior causes the person to stop cheating himself or herself. In fact, seeing in black and white exactly what you have been eating can be a very punishing experience, especially if you value honesty with yourself and others, and the idea that you have self-control).

We then demonstrated the graphing techniques we presented earlier in the chapter and had her list her four most desired activities in order. These turned out to be:

1. watching television
2. knitting
3. reading
4. listening to music

At this point we described the Premack Principle and set each of these activities totally contingent upon the loss of one-half pound a day. In other words, no television, knitting, reading (even the paper or bubble gum wrappers), or listening to music unless a half-pound a day was lost.

Well, it took some convincing, but Mrs. T was determined to lose weight and agreed to go on the wagon. We didn't see Mrs. T again until two months later, but did have a couple of phone calls. Below is the result of her weight change in graph form (see figure 5–4).

Some interesting things are pertinent to note about the weight loss program:

(1) The graphing procedure, especially after some headway had been made, became a real source of pleasure for Mrs. T. (We would say that this very visible process became a positive secondary reinforcer). In fact, the process became exciting to the point that she no longer worried about the consequences of her weight gain or loss in terms of the Premack Principle, but rather began to work hard for the change in the graphs.

(2) After the process began, many social reinforcers were brought to bear on her weight loss. Comments concerning how well she looked, how attractive, how small, how much weight she lost, etc., were all highly potent reinforcers for her weight-loss behavior.

(3) She felt better physically. (This, too, is a form of reinforcer.)

(4) Mrs. T's appearance to herself was highly reinforcing during

FIGURE 5-4

MRS. T's WEIGHT LOSS RECORD

Date	Weight	Loss	Cumulative Loss
4–1	142	0	0
4–2	141	1	1
4–3	140½	½	1½
4–4	140	½	2
4–5	140*	0	2
4–6	139	1	3
4–7	138½	½	3½
4–8	138	½	4
4–9	137½	½	4½
4–10	136	1½	6
4–11	135½	½	6½
4–12	135½*	0	6½
4–13	135	½	7
4–14	134	1	8
4–15	133½	½	8½
4–16	133	½	9
4–17	132	1	10
4–18	131	1	11
4–19	131½*	+½	10½
4–20	131	½	11
4–21	130½	½	11½
4–22	130	½	12
4–23	129	1	13
4–24	128½	½	13½
4–25	128	½	14
4–26	127	1	15
4–27	126½	½	15½
4–28	125½	1	15½
4–29	125	½	16
4–30	124	1	17
5–1	123½	½	17½
5–2	123	½	18
5–3	123*	0	18
5–4	122	1	19
5–5	121½	½	19½
5–6	121	½	20
5–7	121*	0	20
5–8	120	1	21

Note: This graph represents the weight loss of one individual over a period of 38 days. Her maintenance is not included.

*On those days marked with asterisks, no contingencies were earned. On 5–9 contingencies ceased.

the change, as was the amazing (to her) fact that she could now wear all her size-ten clothes again.

(5) New clothing in a size ten was a potent reinforcer as was her husband's delight with the return of her very attractive shape.

Some less than positive things occurred too. We will list these too, as possible outcomes of a weight-loss program:

(1) On some days she did not gain her reinforcers. She (as do many folks) reported feeling very silly about just sitting there and was sorely tempted to dismiss it all as nonsense and return to her old habits.

(2) There was a strong sense of futility when progress became slow.

(3) She threw out all the candy and other snackable goodies from her house, this being the easiest way to avoid snacking. This brought about some inconvenience for others in the house.

(4) At first, the record-keeping process was a dreaded experience. In fact, she finally enlisted the aid of her husband to ensure that she would not cheat.

(5) Cheating was a very strong temptation during the first two weeks.

Mrs. T was extremely pleased with her weight loss and has continued to check her weight daily, determined to stay at or under 120 pounds. In the last six months she reports that she has not deviated more than two pounds from her desired weight. It's not always this simple for all folks, so we will talk about maintaining a desired weight later in this chapter.

EXAMPLE 2

Mr. W, a 210-pounder employed in an office situation came by our office on a whim. He professed a longing to return to 185 pounds, a weight he had held during his college days. After we had explained the process to him, he expressed considerable skepticism but "since nothing else worked," he agreed to keep a log of his eating behavior according to our previous descriptions.

Two days later he returned with a truly incredible list of food stuffs he had consumed. The fact that he was only thirty pounds overweight seemed amazing. Again, we explained the graphing process and the concept of the Premack Principle. He agreed to set watching television, reading and his evening drink contingent on losing one-half pound a day. He was to obtain a complete checkup from his doctor and plan a reasonable diet.

Two weeks later Mr. W returned. He had gained a pound and was determined to rub this fact in. In discussing the matter with Mr. W, we were able to determine that he had cheated by watching television "because I didn't want to be away from my family." We pointed out that the problem was not necessarily something wrong with the technique, but rather his refusing to follow it. Drastic measures were called for, so we got Mr. W to list the three most noxious things he could think of to do, i.e., those things he disliked doing more than anything else. He listed these as follows:

1. sorting the garbage
2. walking to work
3. fixing the family meal

We left the original contingencies intact but added some negative consequences (punishers, we hoped) for failure to lose at least one-half pound a day. On any day that he did not lose one-half pound, he would have to sort the garbage and walk to work. To avoid this nasty business, he would have to lose the weight. To add to the validity of the process, Mr. W agreed to explain the process to his spouse and have her check his weight in the mornings so that no cheating could go on.

Well, to make a long story short, Mr. W lost his thirty pounds although he occasionally missed his favorite activities and had to perform those that he did not particularly relish. He claimed that losing the last fifteen pounds was much easier than losing the first fifteen. Generally, all those effects (social reinforcers, etc.) mentioned in the previous example also held true for Mr. W. He had a more difficult time with weight loss than Mrs. T but found it just as rewarding.

Now that we have given two rather typical examples, let us go over the outline of steps to follow in developing your own program and lastly, relate this set of steps back to our descriptions of types of overeaters.

(1) Quantify your eating behavior.

(2) Determine the contingencies supporting your eating behavior along with the discriminative stimuli that evoke it.

(3) Consult a doctor and obtain a physical examination, determine a reasonable amount of weight for you to lose each day and set up a nutritious diet.

(4) List your three favorite activities (bar none) and set these contingent on your daily weight loss.

(5) Make out your table and graph for recording daily and accumulative weight change.

(6) Post your contingencies in a conspicuous place.

(7) Change your eating habits to meet your criteria for obtaining your reinforcers.

(8) If things aren't going too well, set up punishment contingencies for yourself, setting some very undesirable activities contingent upon not losing your quota of daily weight.

(9) Still fudging? Have someone check your weight daily so that you cannot cheat, even just a little.

CONTINGENCY MANAGEMENT AND KINDS OF WEIGHT LOSS

The nine steps we outlined above, if adhered to, will work regardless of the form of behavior that brought on overweight in the first place. The only step that will vary will be step seven above. As the reader, no doubt, can visualize, each person will have to modify a unique set of behavior patterns that will be relatively unlike any other behavior pattern. This can range from merely restricting food intake at certain meals to substituting other behaviors for eating in the presence of discriminative stimuli.

MAINTAINING WEIGHT

We have often come in contact with people who can lose weight but gain it back in short order (no pun intended) after their "diet" has stopped. The best technique for maintaining weight amounts to a continuation of the weight-monitoring process we discussed above with reintroduction of contingencies if weight falls outside some given parameters. For example, if you have lost twenty pounds and now weigh 180 pounds, we suggest you continue to weigh yourself daily and plot this. If you exceed 182 pounds at any time, reintroduce the contingencies that helped you reach 180 pounds in the first place.

If you did not use the technique described in this chapter to lose your weight, we feel that developing a contingency management program for your weight maintenance should help considerably in controlling your weight. The only difference in maintaining weight as opposed to losing it is that the criteria in each morning's weighing will be to be under a certain weight rather than losing a certain amount.

EXERCISE

The reader has certainly noticed that so far we have not described specific methods for developing a good exercise schedule. The reason for this is that much of the same program that we developed for controlling weight loss can be applied to the development of a good exercise regimen. As with weight loss, the first place to start is with a thorough physical checkup. One should never start a physical exercise program without first determining that the old body is up to it. Second, a set time of the day should be set aside for the exercise. (We are not going to argue about the comparative strengths and weaknesses of various forms of exercise. We would assume that the reader is highly capable of making such judgments based on age, physical factors, availability of equipment, etc.) Third, a set location for the exercise should be selected so as to make the new habit easier to form. Fourth, high-frequency behaviors should be held contingent upon the successful completion of the day's exercise. (Again, we do not feel that it is necessary to discuss the amount of exercise that should be attempted, as each reader's circumstances are unique. We do feel that a doctor or a physical-education specialist can set some optimum level of exercise for each person. This could be walking a mile each afternoon, jogging a mile, lifting so much weight, etc. Again, each reader will want different results from the exercise regimen.) Once the exercise has become a regular part of the day, it should be a very enjoyable and rather brief interlude in the day. We had one friend who ran one mile every morning at ten o'clock during his coffee break. He was able to change, run, shower, and return to the office in his street clothes within twenty minutes daily. Certainly an afternoon stroll or a swim can also become a highly anticipated part of the day.

The Residue

What happens to all those old eating behaviors that I used to exhibit now that I have ceased to emit them? Well, they have been extinguished if they no longer occur and are likely to have been replaced by some other behaviors. Remember, a behavior is extinguished when it ceases to be reinforced and drops in frequency to a level of relative inoccurrence. Spontaneous recovery, however, lurks right around the corner. Spontaneous recovery, you will remember, is the process of inadvertently reinforcing an extinguished response and its subsequent return to full strength. We suppose one could say, then, that no response ever becomes completely lost as spontaneous recovery can very easily occur. The wise contingency manager remains aware of this and takes precautions not to allow the return of inappropriate behaviors.

Summary

Overweight is the result, in most cases, of inappropriate behaviors that have led to an over-accumulation of food, and, hence, weight. There are many different behavior patterns that can lead to overweight.

Analyzing your eating behavior by quantifying it and determining the discriminative stimuli that evoke the eating behavior and the reinforcers for the behavior should allow the reader to modify these behaviors appropriately.

The Premack Principle, wherein a high-frequency behavior is held contingent upon a low-frequency behavior, allows the novice contingency manager to hold preferred activities contingent on weight loss. Further, negative consequences (punishing activities) can be included in addition to the deprivation of preferred activities as consequences for not losing weight. Weight may be maintained with the same procedures used for weight loss. Care must be taken to avoid spontaneous recovery of inappropriate eating behaviors. Above all, the person must want to lose weight. No techniques are ever substitutes for the proper motivation.

6

Smoking

Smoking is one of the most common behaviors in American culture, yet it is one of the most unnecessary behaviors. An entire industry has grown up around the smoking habits of America. If everyone in America were to quit smoking tomorrow, we would undoubtedly face a grave economic setback on an international level. To keep this kind of tobacco manufacturer's nightmare from occurring, millions of dollars are spent annually in hawking the advantages of tobacco consumption to Americans.

We all recognize the problems of smoking, both socially and in terms of national health. We will not spend a great amount of time and effort trying to pile up vast amounts of evidence concerning the bad effects of tobacco. That has been done over and over again since the early '60s and has had seemingly little effect. If this sort of "logical" approach worked, no one would be smoking now at all. Instead, let us look at three sources of supportive contingencies for smoking behavior. Later we will examine more carefully the apparent reinforcers for smoking behavior, and lastly, we will suggest a general procedure for attenuating smoking behavior, which, incidentally has worked for a wide variety of people including the authors.

SOURCES OF CONTINGENCIES SUPPORTING SMOKING BEHAVIOR

The most obvious source of contingencies supporting smoking behavior comes directly from the tobacco industry itself through the advertising agencies that they retain. Cigarettes (and pipes, cigars, snuff, and chewing tobacco) are a big business predicated on the habituation of the consumer to smoking (or other consumption) behavior, an absolutely unnecessary behavior. There is absolutely no physically sound reason for anyone to consume tobacco. Since both the industry and its advertising agencies are aware of the total lack of need for the product, advertising is so structured as to avoid mention of the inherent worth (or lack of it) of tobacco. A lot of this kind of advertising, which will be detailed below, goes on in the sales of other items as well, but tobacco has the unique properties of seeming to cause a health problem that necessitates an investigation. You may not need a new car, but you may need a car. You may not need a new shirt, but there may be advantages in buying one. Generally speaking, most consumable items have some value and the advertising is slanted toward convincing the consumer that the product is good enough so that the consumer will want to purchase a new one, or to purchase a certain brand.

An examination of some of the techniques used by advertisers seems to be one pertinent way of helping the reader develop his or her own analysis of the contingencies.

Modeling. The one technique most frequently used to attract established smokers, or new smokers, to a certain brand is modeling. We are all familiar with the various kinds of modeling that goes on. Brand A is smoked by rugged outdoorsmen. The implicit message in this advertisement is that if you see yourself as similar to the model, you will also have to smoke the same brand of cigarette so that you, too, will be a rough outdoorsman. The point isn't that the average American can't see through this business, but rather that if you're going to smoke, and you see yourself in a certain way, you will smoke brand A.

Brand B models a different form of behavior. The "liberated," "now" woman smokes brand B. Again, most folks can see exactly what is going on, but as we pointed out in our modeling chapter, given the right circumstances, the viewer will be apt to produce the smoking behavior provided by the model.

We don't feel that we need to examine this modeling business over and over until we run it into the ground. Merely being aware that modeling is occurring should help the reader inhibit these inappropriate responses.

If You're Going to Smoke Anyhow. Of the more palatable kinds of advertisements is the "if you're going to smoke anyhow, you'll be safer smoking brand C" advertisement. These advertisements are generally aimed at incorrigible smokers who are urged to be safe and smoke a less nasty brand. The problem here is that these cigarettes are represented as relatively safe when, in fact, no evidence exists that really demonstrates this to be the case (Gary & Glover, 1975). Certainly, these kinds of advertisements do not discourage new smokers from starting out with a "safer brand."

Paired Association. Some of the most repellent (to us) advertisements pair smoking behavior with fun, sex, success, and other neat goodies. These are in modeled form, and the intent is to convince the consumer that a good sex life, a good time, or business success is tied directly to smoking brand D. These advertisements are aimed at both the smoker and the non-smoker.

As the reader has certainly noticed, these advertisements are almost unavoidable. It is, perhaps, only necessary to remember that they are not a true picture of life, but rather a picture of how life is presented in a way that is intended to maximize cigarette consumption. If these advertisements are placed in the frame of reference that we normally place fantasy stories and non-factual television programs, the behavior that is modeled can be inhibited. The reader, for example, is not likely to rob a bank in the way he or she has just seen it done on television. Instead, this behavior is inhibited, although it may well have been learned. The same frame of reference should be superimposed on cigarette advertisements.

Peer Pressure: Social Reinforcers. Most smokers acquire their smoking behavior during their adolescence or during early youth. Why? Generally, because a high degree of reinforcement value may be attached to smoking behavior. Adults smoke. Hence, smoking is an "adult behavior." (This kind of fallacious logic can easily be countered but still produces reinforcement from peers for smoking, i.e., behaving in a manner perceived as "adult".) Smoking is also generally a no-no for adolescents and they are able to gain prestige from peers, attention from adults, and a feeling of adultness by smoking. Adolescents want very much to be treated like and seen as adults. Not always, but much of the time (Glover & Gary, 1975). Unfortunately, smoking has been paired over and over with adulthood, independence, rebellion, and so forth. It has been paired with adult-like behaviors so often that it has become an almost irresistible behavior for many adolescents. The problem is that if an adolescent does not smoke, it is far harder to obtain the reinforcers from one's peers that go along with smoking. Smoking is an easy behavior to perform, one that takes no maturity, self-control, or special talent, and yet it gains a high degree of reinforcement in terms of prestige and other social consequences.

Self-Administered Contingencies. As we pointed out earlier, smoking behavior seems to be very closely associated with "adult behavior," at least from the vantage points of many young people. Evidently, "adult behavior" is a highly reinforcing behavior for many young people and smoking, as pointed out earlier, is an easily attainable "adult behavior." Aside from the external contingencies supporting smoking behavior once smoking behavior has been established, there are many factors contributing to the continuation of smoking behavior.
Physical addiction. Anyone who has smoked for a lengthy period can attest that smoking is physically addictive. It is not so addictive as other drugs, but definite signs of addiction exist. Smoking to avoid "withdrawal symptoms" certainly is a form of negative reinforcement, i.e., smoking a cigarette stops or avoids the feelings generated by a cessation of the intake of nicotine and other chemicals and, hence, postpones bad feelings.

Associative pairing. An inveterate smoker will have conditioned smoking behavior to many different situations through associative pairing. The most common situation is a cigarette after meals, with a cup of coffee, while solving a problem, or while relaxing after a hard day. Associative pairing after a long time will, of course, result in smoking behavior acquiring some of the reinforcing characteristics of the reinforcing activities it has been paired with. Eventually, smoking behavior can become a substitute for many other forms of reinforcing behaviors.

Superstitious behavior. Superstitious behavior is behavior that has been accidentally or vicariously reinforced and, hence, fixed into the behavioral repertoire of a person (in other words it has been learned). If a person is emitting smoking behavior and is accidentally reinforced for smoking during some activity, chances are that in the future the smoking behavior will appear again under the same circumstances. Hence, we have smoking while in an argument. If smoking in a previous argument was reinforced inadvertently by winning the argument, it is likely that smoking will occur in future arguments. What we're saying is that smoking in any number of situations in which reinforcement occurs is likely to increase the probability of smoking behavior under similar circumstances in the future.

Smoking and Boredom. Once smoking behavior has acquired the reinforcing properties of other kinds of reinforcers via associative pairing, people are likely to seek reinforcement in relatively stimulus-free conditions (conditions that induce boredom) by smoking.

Taste. A lot is made of the taste of different brands of cigarettes in advertisements. While we doubt that many people smoke to obtain the taste of smoke, it is possible that some people find the taste of smoke highly pleasant, and hence, highly reinforcing.

A Crutch. Very often, people who have already established smoking behavior in their behavioral repertoire will emit smoking behavior in strange or uncomfortable situations. This is probably due to the search for some kind of reinforcing stimulus during the new situation. Hence, we often see people smoking when meeting someone for the first time. Such smoking also goes on during exams, periods of extreme tension, and periods of high anxiety.

As can be seen from the brief discussion above, there are many possible sources of reinforcement for smoking behavior. To the smoker attempting to extinguish his or her smoking behavior, in fact, it may seem that the whole world is organized to keep one smoking. It matters little whether there is any "truth" attached to the various ways smokers are reinforced for their smoking behavior, the effect of the reinforcers is the same at any rate.

TECHNIQUES FOR EXTINGUISHING SMOKING BEHAVIOR

There are several possible ways to adapt learning theory (behavior modification) to the extinction of smoking behavior. (Glover & Gary, 1975; Horn & Waingrow, 1966; Keutzer, 1968; Bernstein, 1969; etc.) We will discuss two of them, those that are most generally applicable, and offer an example of a person who has extinguished the smoking behavior in each instance. It is well to keep in mind that the "strength" of smoking behavior varies from individual to individual with some people experiencing relative ease in the extinction of their smoking behavior while others seem to suffer a great deal. There are certainly differences in reinforcement history to account for this and probably differences in biological functioning as well.

The Punishment of Smoking. One of the techniques we most frequently hear of being adapted to the process of extinguishing smoking behavior is the so-called punishment or avoidance technique. This technique is usually built around having the smoker ingest some substance that will make the process of smoking a cigarette a punishing behavior. Various kinds of chemicals are used for this purpose and their effects range from causing the cigarette to taste bad to causing violent sickness in the person consuming the cigarette. Occasionally, electric shock is used in the same process, but this is a technique that is almost wholly restricted to clinical usage (Gendreau and Dodwell, 1968).

Such techniques do work if the noxious stimulus is powerful enough to be a punisher. Remember, the definition of a punishing stimulus is a stimulus that when applied to some behavior, causes that behavior to weaken. Side effects such as high anxiety and toxicity, however, do cause problems. The whole process can become so nasty that the smoker will opt to stop the extinction process altogether rather than continue. Cheating, that is, the cessation of consumption of the drugs that cause the reactions to smoke, is also a problem.

The process centers on altering the immediate effect of smoking, i.e., substituting a noxious stimulus for what may or may not have been a pleasant one. The idea is that a person will be conditioned to avoid the noxious stimulus by not smoking. The drawbacks, however, are readily apparent. First, the noxious stimulus may not be powerful enough to outweigh the reinforcement value that smoking has attained. Second, the smoker, even if he or she initiated the extinction process, may feel that someone is out to hurt them, manipulate them, or force their behavior into some pattern against their will. Lastly, the experience, if not properly conducted, can cause the smoker to give up his or her plans to quit smoking.

This technique can be successful, however. The following example should help facilitate the reader's conceptualization of the process.

EXAMPLE

Joe B, a graduate student in psychology was a four-pack-a-day man. For various reasons, not the least of which was his health, he decided that his smoking behavior had to stop. Joe was able, through a prescription from his physician, to obtain a chemical that would cause nausea upon the inhalation of smoke. Joe, after a few bouts with violent stomachaches, was able to stop his smoking behavior entirely. Smoking, for Joe, had become such a noxious experience after repeated pairing with physical illness, that he avoided it like the plague. Joe did report to us that he experienced a high degree of anxiety about smoking for some time after the "treatment" was instituted. In fact, he could not stay in rooms where other people were smoking without becoming highly anxious. Luckily, Joe was willing to put up with some nauseous feelings or this process might have had the best of him.

Well, it's obvious from our discussion that we do not particularly care for this method of extinguishing smoking behavior.(Quite a play on words, don't you think?) Other psychologists, however, report a high degree of success with such methods and feel that, properly administered, they can shorten considerably the process of unlearning an inappropriate behavior (Grimaldi & Lichenstein, 1969; Franks, Fried & Ashem, 1966; Lublin, 1968; Ober, 1968; Powell and Azrin, 1968; etc.). Johnston (1972) certainly makes a good theoretical case for the efficacy of punishment as a behavior change technique and points out that, in fact, punishment should work just as well or better than any kind of reinforcing contingencies. This may very well be the case but we feel considerably more comfortable dealing with techniques that are not as unpleasant as the punishment technique.

SMOKING AND CONTINGENCY MANAGEMENT

Those of you who read the chapter on weight-loss will find the techniques discussed below to be very similar to those developed for weight control. The idea behind our program, generally, is to use the Premack Principle, described in the previous chapter, to modify smoking behavior. Certain high-frequency behaviors will be held contingent upon the appearance of low-frequency behaviors; in this case, the low-frequency behavior being not smoking. Homme (1965) was the first of several experimenters to test this technique.

Since the procedure has been very well described in the previous chapter, let us here outline the steps to follow in extinguishing smoking behavior. We will do so for two forms of the technique.

1. Keep a daily log of your smoking behavior. Record each cigarette you smoke, the discriminative stimuli that evoked the smoking behavior (the conditions that seem to "touch off smok-

ing"), how you felt as you smoked, and the external reinforcers (reactions from the environment that seemed to support the behavior). From this daily log, determine the causal relationship between the environment and your smoking behavior. After doing this, you should be able to exert far greater control over your smoking behavior. It is likely that this alone will lower the level of your smoking behavior.

2. List the three absolutely favorite behaviors you emit, not including smoking.

3. Determine some daily level of smoking behavior that is acceptable to you. Set the three behaviors you listed above contingent on smoking at or below the level you have determined.

4. Gradually decrease this level of acceptable smoking behavior to zero while holding your contingencies constant.

5. Reinstitute the contingencies if smoking re-occurs.

Sounds easy, right? It sounds easy, but believe us, it is very difficult for the first two weeks or so. After that, the process is very easy. One of the writers quit smoking by this method. Below is an analysis of the smoking behavior and a description of the contingencies and a graph representing the smoking behavior (See figure 6-1).

On examining the writer's smoking behavior for a period of three days, a pattern of behavior began to emerge. About twenty cigarettes a day were consumed with one after every meal and one with each cup of coffee or other liquid refreshment. This accounted for eight or nine cigarettes a day plus twelve others smoked at times when there were lulls in the day's activities. The basic forms of discriminative stimulus were meals, liquid consumption, and engaging in relaxation from the day's activities. Armed with this information (the writer probably could have guessed at it, but several cigarettes were actually never smoked because of the process of keeping a log of the smoking behavior), the writer set out to eliminate the smoking behaviors. The high-frequency behaviors to be set contingent to not smoking were (1) reading, (2) watching television, and (3) listening to music. These reinforcing activities were contingent on smoking behavior decreasing as pictured in figure 6-1.

The reinforcing behaviors were earned as long as the frequency of smoking behavior remained under the line denoting the acceptable levels of smoking behavior. Incidentally, any lit cigarette was counted as one cigarette, whether one or twenty puffs were taken from that particular cigarette. Hence, the "game" could not be beaten by smoking part of a cigarette, stubbing it out, and relighting it later.

After the smoking behavior had reached the level of non-occurrence, the contingencies were kept in effect for a period of two weeks. The hardest part of the entire process was the last week of smoking and the first week of non-smoking. The writer spent considerable time trying to determine whether or not to cheat on the

FIGURE 6-1

A GRAPH OF THE WRITER'S SMOKING BEHAVIOR

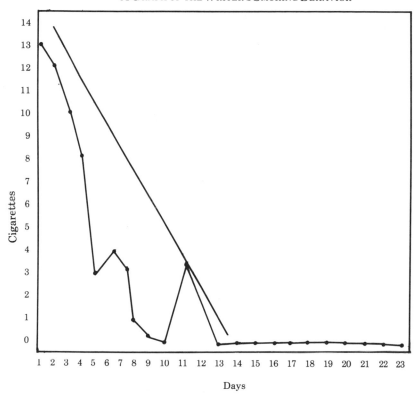

Days

Note: The solid line denotes that level of smoking behavior that was acceptable during the treatment phase.

process. Unfortunately, this did happen once and the writer lost all his high-frequency behaviors as a result.

Well, all this sounds pretty neat while reading about it, but what about the inveterate smoker who is willing to give up his or her high-frequency behaviors to continue smoking? Ah, ha! In such an instance, it is time to determine what noxious behaviors the person is least likely to engage in. These can include things like sorting the garbage, working in the garden, doing the dishes, etc. This most noxious behavior should be contingent upon smoking behavior, i.e., if smoking occurs above the acceptable daily level, then the person must perform the noxious behavior.

This technique is predicated on one very important variable: the person must want to quit smoking more than he or she wants to continue smoking. No technique can be any better than the person administering the technique. Behavior change is hard work; there is no easy way around it. To get something, you've got to give something. If you are unwilling to give up your reinforcing activities if you smoke too much, then you are not willing to give up smoking, either. The only way to be absolutely certain a person will quit smoking is to place the person in a situation where smoking is impossible and keep the person in such a situation. Short of that, the person must be willing to work at changing his or her behavior or there will be little or no effect.

COLD TURKEY

The same techniques described above can also be used to help facilitate a person "going cold turkey" or quitting absolutely without some gradual decrease from high-frequency levels of smoking behavior to low levels of smoking behavior. Both the application of high-frequency behaviors as reinforcers and the application of noxious behaviors as punishment would continue in the same way. Many people find it easier to break completely with smoking while others find the gradual approach more comfortable.

EXAMPLE

Mrs. Jones became convinced that she should stop smoking. It seems that her cigarettes didn't taste good like a cigarette should, and anyway, she was a newly expectant mother and wanted to rid herself of what she felt to be an inappropriate habit to be modeling. We explained the process of keeping a diary of smoking behavior to her and suggested that she record the level of her smoking behavior, the discriminative stimuli that seemed to evoke the smoking behavior, and the reinforcers that were obtained by the smoking behavior. She agreed to do this for a week and then check back with us.

A week passed rather quickly and Mrs. Jones returned with a veritable logbook of smoking behavior. In fact, during the week her smoking behavior decreased in frequency from about twenty-six cigarettes daily to fourteen (again, we defined the process of lighting any cigarette or any part of a cigarette as the consumption of a cigarette). She informed us that the process of keeping track of her smoking behavior in diary fashion alone caused her to delete "unnecessary cigarettes." Further, it seemed that most of her smoking behavior could be considered to be social in nature, i.e., all but three of her smoking behaviors began while she was engaged in talking to someone else. The two occasions when she smoked without speaking to someone both occurred in the morning with her first cup of coffee in the office.

Her reinforcers included the physical pleasure of inhaling smoke on some occasions, while on others, the reinforcers seemed to be directed at her social behavior and not her smoking per se. With this information, as we pointed out above, she had already cut her cigarette consumption in half.

We then asked her to list her three favorite behaviors. She listed, in order of preference, reading, window-shopping, and watching television. From this, we explained the idea of contingency management and convinced Mrs. Jones to commit herself to holding these three highly enjoyable behaviors contingent on her meeting the acceptable levels of smoking behavior as pictured in figure 6-2.

To gain her reinforcers, her daily level of smoking behavior would have to fall below the line on the graph that represented the acceptable level of smoking behavior. As can be seen from the graph, her smoking behavior dropped off to zero within fourteen days. During this time, she exceeded her limit and forfeited her reinforcers only twice. Unfortunately, maintaining her smoking behavior at a non-appearance level was more difficult. After reaching the zero level, smoking behavior was erratic, some days she smoked a couple of cigarettes while other days she did not smoke at all. After a phone conversation about this problem, we instituted some noxious consequences as a result of her inappropriate smoking behavior. Every day that she smoked led to her scrubbing out all the fixtures in two bathrooms. Since smoking did not occur again, we can only assume that the behavior of cleaning toilet bowls and sinks was so noxious that they remain dirty while her lungs are clearing up.

Is It the Person or Is It the Technique?

Both. A technique will not do anything for you. You must still do the work. The technique we have described is one that makes the process of extinguishing a behavior more orderly and somewhat easier. More than anything else, it makes the negative contingencies of smoking more apparent and helps reduce the behavior more rapidly.

Summary

Extinguishing smoking behavior is hard work. Smoking behavior is supported by three generally recognizable forms of contingencies: those generated by the tobacco industry; peer and social contingencies; and personal contingencies. Smoking behavior may be attenuated by pairing noxious consequences with the ingestion of smoke (punishment) but this technique has the drawbacks of possible anxiety, toxicity, and giving up the effort to quit smoking. The Premack Principle, wherein a high-frequency behavior is held contingent upon the appearance of a low-frequency behavior, may be adapted to the management of smoking behavior. Negative consequences may be added to the process if the reinforcers contingent upon not smoking do not prove to be sufficient.

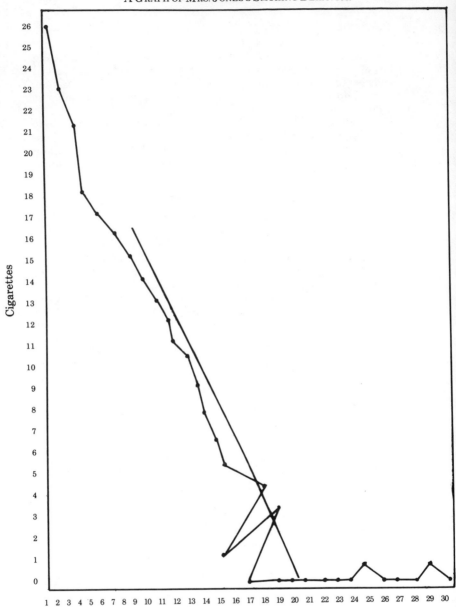

FIGURE 6-2

A GRAPH OF MRS. JONES'S SMOKING BEHAVIOR

Note: The solid line denotes that level of smoking behavior that Mrs. Jones was not to exceed in order to gain her reinforcers. As can be seen, Mrs. Jones only lost her reinforcers twice during the extinction process, but emitted erratic smoking behavior for some time after extinction.

70

7

Speech Habits

In the course of the last several years we have had the experience of helping several people change what they felt to be inappropriate speech habits. These ranged from incessant use of "you know," "uh" and "er-ah" to poor grammar, and inappropriately high levels of cursing. During these years we have developed three techniques which have been highly successful in remediating speech problems. Rather than spend a large amount of time delineating how such inappropriate speaking behaviors are learned and supported, we will go directly into the techniques used to extinguish them. In each instance we will offer a specific example, but our discussion will be rather general to encompass all the various kinds of inappropriate speaking habits in which the reader is likely to have an interest.

A considerable amount of research has been done by psychologists in the area of speech therapy, the change in speech habits. Unfortunately (depending, of course, on the point of view), almost all of the research has been aimed at pathological problems such as stuttering, aphasia, and language development among the severely disturbed. A good summary of the kinds of work done appears in Sloane and MacAulay (1968).Guess, Sailor, Rutherford, and Baer (1968) have probably come closest to the techniques we will describe here.

BASIC PROCEDURES

In this section we will describe some basic procedures common to all our approaches to behavior change in speech and then deal specifically with our favorite. As the reader has no doubt discerned, we have stressed in each technique discussed so far the process of quantifying the behavior to be changed. This is also the case in modifying speech habits. To quantify the level of occurrence of an inappropriate form of speech, it is first necessary to adequately define the part of your speech that you want to modify. It may be that a statement of an over-used term such as "you know" will be enough, or it may be necessary to define the problem at greater length. For example, any inappropriate grammatical usage of the word was: e.g., we was, they was, etc. To borrow a thought from Malott (1972) "think small." By this we mean that only one behavior at a time should be modified and usually only a small bit of that behavior. It is fairly easy to modify small bits of behavior at a time, but biting off more than one can chew will not result in any kind of effective process. Rather, it generally results in confusion and headaches, because of the overly complex problems involved.

How should speech habits be recorded and placed into appropriate form? The technique that we have found to be the simplest, easiest, and yet still effective, is a simple frequency count of the behavior. In this manner one may either record the behavior in a log kept for that purpose or use some form of counter similar to the ones described in chapter four. Incidentally, the process of taking a frequency count of such behavior often results in rather impressive decreases in the frequency of the behavior even without any kind of treatment. A typical frequency count chart and graph is pictured in figure 7-1.

FIGURE 7-1

A TYPICAL FREQUENCY COUNT CHART AND CORRESPONDING GRAPH

MONDAY																							
TUESDAY																				
WEDNESDAY																			
THURSDAY															
FRIDAY													
SATURDAY											
SUNDAY									

Note: This graph corresponds to the levels of inappropriate speaking behavior recorded above.

Note: Each slash mark corresponds to one inappropriate speaking response

The frequency count of such a behavior must be kept accurately and consistently. The person wishing to make the change should not "put off till later" the process of recording the behavior. The behavior should be recorded immediately after it occurs. This serves a two-fold purpose. First, it makes the person highly sensitive to the behavior in question and, second, it makes for much more accurate records.

Reasonable consequences should be developed to facilitate the change in behavior. This is the part of our process that forms the major difference between the techniques that we will discuss.

Immediately after the inappropriate response, re-respond and do so correctly. In other words, if you inadvertently say a sentence interspersed with "you know," record this inappropriate response and then repeat the sentence without using the inappropriate term. People around you may think that you are slightly daffy, but we believe that this is a necessary procedure to help the person develop appropriate speech patterns.

THE WORSER I TALK, THE RICHER I GET TECHNIQUE

Our favorite technique is one that is rather easy to perform and has the added advantage of setting the consequences of inappropriate behavior in a position that immediately follows the behavior. These immediate consequences should facilitate the learning process (Reynolds, 1969; Mikulas, 1970; Williams and Anadam, 1973; Malott, 1972, etc.). In this technique, all the steps outlined above are followed. The consequences in this case amount to the person placing some small amount of money in a container each time the inappropriate response occurs. For example, a person might place a nickle in the container each time the term "you know" is used. The trick is that this money is to be placed out of reach of the person so that it cannot be spent. The money may be given to charity, deposited in savings, given to a spouse, or saved for some use for which the person seldom sets money aside. In this fashion the consequence immediately follows the behavior, and while the consequence is somewhat unpleasant, it is a constant reminder that the behavior was inappropriate.

This technique can be strengthened, if necessary, by adopting one of Malott's suggestions (1972) by having the person give the money collected to whatever agency or cause that the person most greatly despises. This should result in an added incentive not to cause the money to be "lost" by making the inappropriate response.

EXAMPLE

Mr. Roberts was an intelligent young man who became aware that his oral communication with other people was greatly hindered by his incessant interjection of the terms "you know" and "like." He felt that ideas he wished to convey were often obscured by his seeming inability to verbalize effectively. He dropped by our office one afternoon with the idea that there had to be one good technique for alleviating his constant use of inappropriate terms. Since he was a student currently enrolled in the writer's behavior modification course, he had a firm grasp of the concepts that would be employed in the behavior change process. We discussed keeping track of his behavior and he settled on using a pad of paper to tabulate his behavior, placing a slash mark on the sheet for every use of the term "you know." We decided to postpone working with the term "like" until the response of "you know" had been extinguished. He was first to tabulate and graph his inappropriate speaking behavior for a week before instituting the behavior change process.

On his return, one week later, he presented us with the results of his data-gathering process. This is pictured in figure 7-2. After examining Mr. Roberts' baseline data, he agreed to continue to keep

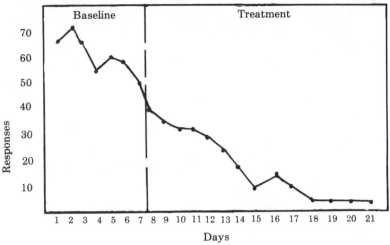

FIGURE 7-2

A GRAPH OF MR. ROBERTS' INAPPROPRIATE SPEAKING BEHAVIOR

track of his inappropriate speaking behavior (by the way, notice how the frequency of occurrence of the term "you know" had dropped off by the end of the week) while adding the consequence of dropping a nickle into a piggy bank he would carry around with him for every appearance of the inappropriate term. He would further re-respond in appropriate fashion after every instance of inappropriate responding. By the way, Mr. Roberts had decided to really "beef-up" his consequences by donating the "proceeds" of his behavior to a political party that was not in his favor. Judging from the rather high level of the occurrence of the inappropriate behavior, we felt that Mr. Roberts might either go broke or donate a very large sum to someone he disliked.

Note: Speaking behavior is a highly variable kind of behavior. Obviously, if you are engaged in conversation all day long, it is much more likely that inappropriate responses will occur more frequently than if the person does not converse with anyone all day. There are means whereby this can be controlled, but we feel that they unnecessarily confound the issue and make the behavior-change process much more difficult and confusing and probably decrease its effectiveness.

At any rate, most people do not want merely to lower the levels of inappropriate responding; they want to extinguish the behavior entirely. So, for most purposes, ignore the variability factor. However, if you are going to do an experiment, or if you are going to try to set up a complete behavior modification design, you really should familiarize yourself with techniques for developing behavior modification designs. (For a more thorough discussion of this, see Glover and Gary, 1975; Williams and Anadam, 1973; or Bandura, 1969. Titles and other pertinent information are in the bibliography.)

In referring again to figure 7-2, we see that Mr. Roberts' inappropriate behavior diminished at a rather rapid rate until it approached non-appearance levels. Mr. Roberts then proceeded to modify the response of saying the word "like" too frequently. Mr. Roberts reports that the second behavior was much easier to change than the first. This, of course, is in accordance with the conditions that affect extinction, noting that the more frequent the number of previous extinctions, the easier the current extinction should be to perform (Reynolds, 1975). This phenomenon should hold true for the reader too. Pictured in figure 7-3 is the record of Mr. Roberts' frequency of saying the word "like" inappropriately.

FIGURE 7-3

A GRAPH OF MR. ROBERTS' USE OF THE TERM "LIKE"

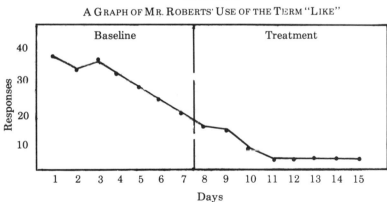

I'M A GOOD BOY/GIRL; I SAID IT RIGHT

In many instances, the behavioral problem is of a nature that cannot adequately be modified by use of the simple but powerful technique just discussed. For these kinds of problems, we take a different approach, one that relies more heavily on the concepts of shaping and fading rather than that of avoidance. In this technique we are dealing with a specific behavior that appears very infrequently, rather than one that appears frequently as before. Further, rather than provide noxious consequences, we want to provide positively reinforcing stimuli after the appearance of the behavior. This positive reinforcer may be a pat on the back, a cookie, an apple, a point that is earned toward some later reinforcer, etc. The reader will recall from chapter two that a positive reinforcer is a stimulus that when provided after some response, causes that response to be strengthened. Oh, yes, all the other conditions that we described at the outset of the chapter also hold true with this technique.

An illustration of the technique before we move to our example should help clarify the issue. Let us suppose that a student has difficulty speaking in complete sentences, i.e., much of his or her speech is in broken phrases that do not contain both a noun and verb. In such a situation, some highly reinforcing activity, goal or object (this could be reading that evening, watching television, having a good dessert and so forth) is held contingent upon the appearance of the appropriate behavior (properly defined and behaviorally specified, naturally) at some predetermined, acceptable rate.

This can be facilitated by keeping track of the number of correct responses with either a counter or a check sheet as in the first technique we described. If enough of these checks (which are immediate, secondary reinforcers) are obtained, then the student gains the goal of the contingent relationship (which is a delayed primary or secondary reinforcer). It may also be necessary, if the behavior is not appearing at all, to go through a procedure of reinforcing approximations of the behavior, gradually shifting the kind of behavior until it more and more closely resembles the correct behavior. The final goal, of course, is the complete, correct behavior. This procedure was described in chapter two and is referred to as shaping.

EXAMPLE

Mr. Brown was an undergraduate student at the university who had come to study in the United States from a foreign country. Mr. Brown was a highly intelligent young man who was having trouble communicating effectively in English. He felt that his lack of oral expression was hurting his classroom performance. He understood English very well, and was aware of the rules of English grammar. Unfortunately, he tended to speak in only nouns and basic verbs, disregarding tenses and leaving out anything besides nouns and verbs. On hearing the description of the problem (and observing it first hand at the same time) we described the process of reinforcing appropriate responses and described the technique of developing a contingency management program.

Mr. Brown's first task was to decide what aspect of his speaking behavior to work on (think small, remember?). He settled on using the appropriate tenses at the appropriate times. (It seems that he knew which tenses to use but had a high degree of difficulty in implementing his knowledge correctly.) After this determination was made he was to spend a week keeping an accurate record of the number of times appropriate tenses were used in his speech. This data was to be tabulated and converted into a graph for easier interpretation.

As the reader has observed, we almost always suggest a week as a reasonable length of time for a baseline. This is for two reasons. First, it acclimates the person to the process of keeping track of his behaviors and secondly, it is a convenient length of time for the baseline and is apt to provide an accurate assessment of the behavior under scrutiny.

On Mr. Brown's return, we went over his data and talked about what level of correct speech he should try to settle on for the purposes of developing his contingencies. There are many problems with speech because of the high degree of variability in terms of how much speaking behavior is emitted, and so we decided to deal with a percentage rather than the total number of correct speech behaviors on any given day. Figure 7-4 represents the speaking behavior of Mr. Brown during the four-week period we worked with him, expressed in percentages of correct responses. This complicated the technique somewhat as we pointed out earlier, but Mr. Brown was quite adept at computing the percentages.

(The procedure, by the way, is to divide the total number of responses into the number of correct responses and then multiply this figure by 100. Hence, if you spoke thirty times in one day and you spoke correctly fifteen of these instances, your percentage of correct responding would be $15/30 \times 100 = 50\%$. We feel that such a technique is acceptable in developing a new set of responses, but do not think that it belongs in the extinction process described earlier.)

We also set a level of progress for Mr. Brown to meet to continue to gain his contingent reinforcers which he had decided would be watching television and reading for pleasure. The results are pictured in figure 7-4 where the solid line represents the acceptable level of progress.

Not everyone can expect to have the same kind of success that Mr. Brown achieved, as he worked very, very hard at changing his speech habits. Incidentally, Mr. Brown went on to change many of his other speech habits by applying the same technique.

The reader can see that such a technique has more problems than the first technique we described, but we feel that it is a technique that if properly carried out, will result in the correct responses.

FIGURE 7-4
A GRAPH OF MR. BROWN'S SPEAKING BEHAVIOR

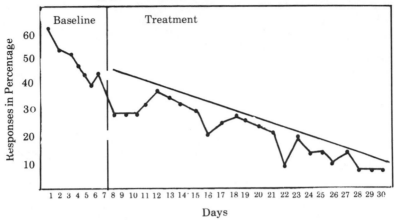

Days

Note: The solid line represents that percentage of correct responses that had to be reached in order to gain the reinforcers held contingent upon correct responding.

UTILIZING THE PREMACK PRINCIPLE

Our third strategy is one that is highly similar to techniques that we have previously discussed with respect to eating and smoking behavior. In fact, it is an adaption of this technique to the modification of speaking behavior. All of the general methods presented in the first part of this chapter should be adhered to: (1) the behavior must be recorded accurately, (2) the behavior must be properly defined and the results should be immediately recorded, (3) reasonable consequences should be developed and (4) the appropriate response should follow immediately after the inappropriate response.

In utilizing the Premack Principle, some high-frequency behaviors (highly desirable behaviors) are held contingent upon the performance of low-frequency behaviors (the correct form of speech). This technique is a good one, but has some drawbacks when compared to the coin-loss technique. The reinforcer that one is working toward is quite a distance away in time from the appearance of the behavior. Only secondary reinforcers (in the form of slash marks) are provided after the inappropriate responses, and only two or three positive reinforcers are held contingent on the non-appearance of some behavior rather than on the appearance of some behavior.

EXAMPLE

Mrs. Adams wanted to stop using the phrase "uh" with which she constantly interspersed her speech. Her typical sentence would contain from one to several "uhs." As per our usual procedure, we had her spend one week keeping a frequency count of her inappropriate speaking behavior and had her convert this into a graph. Inappropriate, in this case, was defined as any utterance of the interjection, "uh." On her return a week later, we described the process of contingency management and had her choose her three favorite activities and set them contingent upon her saying the term "uh" less than thirty times a day to start with. Gradually, this level of occurrence was decreased to zero. Figure 7–5 pictures the results of Mrs. Adams' behavior change.

FIGURE 7-5
A GRAPH OF MRS. ADAMS' SPEAKING BEHAVIOR

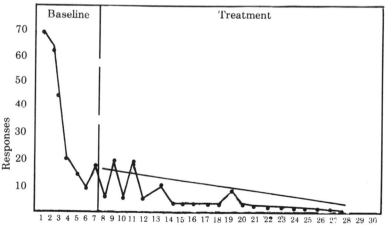

Note: The solid line represents the number of incorrect responses allowable.

As can be seen, on several different days, Mrs. Adams did not meet the criteria for gaining her reinforcers. She did, however, lower very drastically the levels of her inappropriate speaking behavior. Interestingly, the greatest amount of change in her speaking behavior occurred during the baseline period, rather than during the treatment phase, again demonstrating that merely heightening the awareness of the person to some behavior along with accurate data keeping will often result in a change of behavior.

Summary

In this chapter we applied some of the techniques of behavior modification to the problem of changing inappropriate speaking behavior. First, it is necessary to adequately define the behavior. Secondly, the behavior must be thoroughly quantified. Third, immediate recording of the behavior enhances the behavior-change process. Fourth, reasonable consequences must be developed for the behavior, and lastly, a correct response should always be made to follow the inappropriate response.

We described three distinct forms of contingency management to modify the inappropriate behaviors. All had certain limitations. Certainly any of the three techniques, if properly administered, will help the behavior-change process. As with all behavior-modification procedures, however, changing patterns of speech is hard work.

8

Budgeting Your Time Wisely

One of the most common problems that face us all is the problem of budgeting our time wisely. "I would go to the library but I just don't seem to have the time." "I would really love to exercise but I just don't have the time." "I would have done much better on the test if I had just had the time to study." All of us could probably list a whole series of activities that we would like to engage in if we could just somehow find the time for them. This chapter is a compilation of those things we have found to be helpful in working with people to develop systematic approaches to the budgeting of time.

SOME ISSUES

It seems that Western people are slaves of the clock. At 8:00 A.M. we must be at work. Our lunch is from 12:30 to 1:00 and we leave work at 5:00 P.M. If we are to see the news, we must be seated in front of the television at 6:00 P.M. If we are to go shopping, we must be in and out of the store before 8:00. The children must be in bed by 9:00, and when have we had supper? Our purpose in writing this chapter is not to make you more of a slave to someone else's time schedule or to make you a slave of the big hand and the little hand. Rather, it is our purpose to help you do those things you want to do, not to develop obeisance to other's goals or needs. If there are things during the course of a day that you feel you should be able to do but somehow cannot find the time for because things get in the way and time is frittered away doing things that you did not expect to have to do, or alternatives arise without being expected (for example, an all-night beer bust the night before an exam) then, perhaps, this is the chapter for you. Our approach is designed to help you do what you want to do and to avoid engaging in those activities that you "don't really want to do."

Below we will outline the steps we suggest you follow in changing your time-consumption behavior whether it be studying, gardening, hiking, or merely taking a daily nap.

1. *Think Small.* Think small has been our watchword throughout this book. Think small again will be our governing concept for time budgeting. The majority of us are awake and doing things for

sixteen hours a day or more, and even if we are just considering those hours of the day before and after work, the simplest, easiest, and likely the most successful technique is to pick just one small bit of behavior at a time, master it, and then go on to the next.

2. *Define the behavior.* Before going off half-cocked in the pursuit of modifying some behavior, you really should determine what, exactly, the behavior is you want to change, and at what level, if any, it is occurring now. (If you have waded through this much of our text, you should certainly know that if anything, we are sticklers for determining the behaviors to be studied and the frequency of occurrence of these behaviors.)

Defining your behavior may be simple but it may not be realistic. Suppose you want to increase your levels of jogging. This may be a very admirable goal, but don't go overboard. If you haven't been jogging lately, you might be surprised at your physical state if you try to jog for two miles the first time out. (At first you might be afraid you were going to die. Later you might be afraid you wouldn't die.) While such a variable may not be as critical with other behaviors, e.g., reading, writing, etc., you should formulate in your definitions how much is enough. We also feel that the more specifically you define behaviors, the more likely you will be to achieve success. So, if gardening is what you have in mind, perhaps it would be a good idea to describe exactly what kind of work it is you expect to do and how much of it you expect to do. More about this later, though.

Once you have defined a behavior, e.g., reading twenty pages of Glover and Gary, walking one mile without stopping, etc., you are ready to take a baseline of your current behaviors. In other words, you are going to determine at what level your behavior is currently occurring.

This is not particularly difficult since we are only going to be working with one behavior at a time. (All right, admit it. How many of you are still thinking of tackling more than one behavior right off the bat?) The best way we know of to handle this problem is for you to record the occurrence, duration and numbers of times the behavior you are working toward appears every day for about one week. No fudging now. If you start jogging at 4:10 in the afternoon and knock off at 4:12 for six minutes and then jog for four more minutes, record six minutes of jogging time, not twelve. Accurate and thorough records are an absolute necessity. It is too easy to "fudge" if you do not stick to a thorough and systematic approach in recording your behavior. After all, you're the one that wants to perform the behavior, not us. If you're not going to be honest with yourself, then who can you be honest with?

Your daily charting of behavior will probably also be enhanced if you note how you felt at those times you performed the behavior, e.g., bored, tired, sleepy, angry, etc. Figure 8-1 represents a com-

FIGURE 8-1

A TYPICAL CHART FOR QUANTIFYING BEHAVIORS

Time	Behavior	How Felt	Duration	Contingencies Gained	Lost
3:30					
4:00					
4:30					
5:00					
5:30					
6:00					

Note: The above chart represents a typical chart for quantifying behaviors.

FIGURE 8-2

AN ACCUMULATIVE FREQUENCY GRAPH OF READING BEHAVIOR

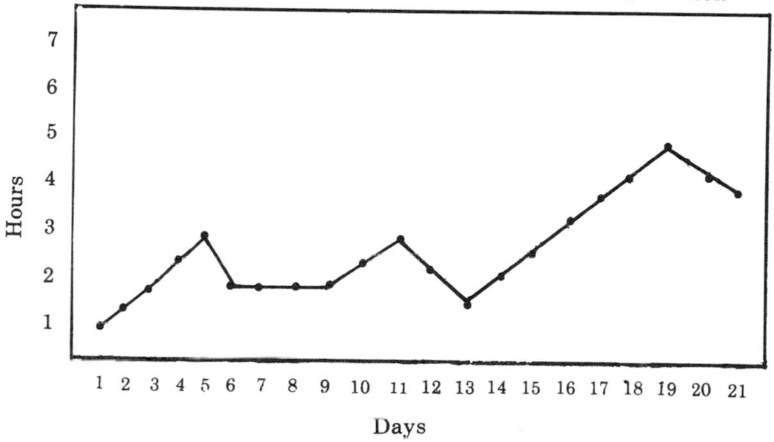

Note: The graph above pictures one person's reading behavior over a period of three weeks in terms of daily time spent in reading.

mon chart used to record behaviors such as we have discussed. Figure 8-2 is a graph of reading behavior that has been drawn from a series of daily charts.

Finally, we suggest that you post your daily charts and your graph in a conspicuous place, such as your bedroom door. This should serve to remind you what your tasks are and that you should keep track of them daily. Keep a baseline of your behavior for about one week.

3. *Set a time for the behavior.* Remember how we hammered away at consistency earlier in the book? The best approach to ensure that some behavior (e.g., jogging, reading a chapter of a book, gardening, etc.) is performed is to set aside a time of the day for this behavior. (If you will refer back to our definition of discriminative stimuli, you will see that time certainly can be part of a discriminative stimulus and that we are beginning to develop discriminative stimuli here). This should also greatly facilitate your record-keeping behavior, allowing you to zero in on a certain set time every day.

4. *Set a permanent place for your behavior* (more of the discriminative stimulus). The authors of some recent research in this area (more specifically in study habits) have demonstrated that restricting your behavior to one location will increase the likelihood of that behavior increasing (Beneke and Harris, 1972; Briggs, Tosi and Morley, 1971). If you are going to be studying, pick one place where you will do this and stick to that place. This could be a quiet room visited on the same time every day or a quiet nook in the library or perhaps a comfortable spot under a particularly shady tree. If you are going to jog, run at the same location every day, the same track or around the same block. Picking a spot and sticking to it has been demonstrated to be one way of increasing the levels of appearance of these behaviors you want to develop.

5. *Remove distractions.* This, of course, is going to vary as the different kinds of behavior you approach vary. If you are going to try to study at 4 o'clock in your bedroom, you should sit so that you are not distracted by things outside; place out of sight tempting novels or magazines; turn off the television; and generally depress the levels of noise around you. Music may or may not be a distraction depending, we suspect, on the kind of studying you are doing and on your personal characteristics. Several investigations have been made on the effects of music on studying behavior (Freeburne and Fleischer, 1952; Kirkpatrick, 1943; Schlichting and Brown, 1970; etc.) and the results of these investigations have been inconsistent, some finding that music is helpful, others that it is highly distracting. You certainly wouldn't want to listen to music that stirred you sufficiently to stand on your desk performing gyrations. You will have to determine for yourself, depending on the kind of quiet behavior in question (i.e., studying, reading, preparing tax returns, etc.) whether or not music bothers you and more specifically, what kind of music.

Jogging, exercising or other more physical activities, have different kinds of distractions that you should avoid if possible. The purpose behind the removal of extraneous variables is to lessen the chance of your veering off the straight and narrow. Consider how difficult it might be to perform gardening behavior if you have brought a portable television set outside and are absorbed in the latest escapades of a daytime serial's heroine.

6. *Consequences of the behavior.* While keeping accurate records of a well-defined behavior and performing this behavior in the same place at the same time without distractions are certainly steps in the right direction, there still may not be enough "motivation" to perform the behavior consistently. The best laid plans of mice and men do flounder if not supported by powerful enough contingencies. Hence, the sixth step in our approach is to devise a set of realistic consequences for engaging in the behavior. Since we have previously discussed the Premack Principle, we will dispense with a thorough discussion of it here and move directly to your implementation of it.

First, list the three behaviors that you perform during the day that are your favorite activities, that is, those three that occur most frequently. These can range from sewing, knitting, watching television, reading, or sitting around the student center, to jogging, or building models. Whatever your three favorite behaviors are, list them. Now, set the performance of these behaviors (that's right, all three) contingent upon the performance of the behavior you are working to modify. Specify in advance how long the behavior to be changed must last (e.g., running two laps, reading one chapter, reading twenty minutes, gardening for thirty minutes, etc.). Write down this agreement with yourself and post it above your daily time charts and your accumulative graph. You can now add the final two columns to your daily chart, contingencies gained or lost (see figure 8–1).

What you have done now is to provide consequences for the behavior (no wiggling out of it) in such a way that you gain the right to perform your favorite activities only if you perform your predetermined task for the length of time (or amount) called for in your agreement with yourself. Isn't this silly or childish? "After all, I can watch television whenever I blessed-well please." Sure, you can. But if you are serious about making a change in your behaviors, you will live up to the consequences you have settled on. Setting up contingencies and then living up to them is no more childish than not being able to manage the time to study or read or garden. Remember, our technique is one designed to let you gain the control over your time that you want. It is not as though we were "Big Brother" and forcing you to do something against your will.

If you do not meet your goals, you lose the right to engage in the behavior that you have set up contingent upon meeting the goals. No television, no reading, no listening to records tonight if you don't jog for twenty minutes. The idea is that you will work to avoid this loss of your enjoyable activities.

7. *Noxious consequences.* Well, let us suppose that a week has gone by and you still are not meeting your goals for this one behavior. You are forfeiting your favorite activities every day but are

still coping. "No crummy behavior modification program is going to get the best of me." If you have this attitude, it never will get the best of you, but we still have one card in the hole. If the consequences of gaining favorite behaviors by performing a less favorite behavior does not seem to be working, list the three most noxious behaviors you can imagine. These may include sorting the garbage, cleaning the cat litter, walking to work, eating spinach and liver, doing the dishes or whatever. Of these three terrible things, pick the worst (you may not always be able to do all three in any given day, so we will have you do whatever is available) that is available each day and perform this behavior if you do not meet your goal. Add this to your agreement. To keep yourself honest, inform your spouse or friends and have them check to see if you are following up on your task. You may find that pressure from these people may be enough to help you meet your goals.

Now, if you do not meet your daily goal, not only do you have to miss your three favorite behaviors, you also have to perform a noxious behavior.

There are some general things that we really should mention. First, be realistic. Do not set your goals so low that meeting them is meaningless. Neither should you set them so high that you cannot attain your goals with more than a reasonable effort. After all, if you haven't been reading at all, four hours of reading a day seems a bit much but ten minutes a day seems a bit too little. Pick some goal that you can reach but one that will necessitate some work. After all, you do want a feeling of accomplishment.

Second, don't fall in the trap of cheating yourself or "beating the system." No one suffers but you if you do this. We understand that it can be highly reinforcing to foil our process, but what purpose does it serve? In the end, you are responsible for what you do. No system that you could employ can possibly do more than set up guidelines for you to follow. We can't do it for you. You can only take our program and do it for yourself.

AN OUTLINE

At this point, let us list the steps we have just discussed that you should follow in developing your new behaviors.

1. Think small, pick only one behavior.
2. Define your behavior and keep accurate records of the behavior.
3. Set a regular time for the performance of the behavior.
4. Set a regular place for the performance of the behavior.
5. Remove all possible distractions.
6. Develop consequences for the behavior.
7. If necessary, develop noxious consequences for failing to meet your goals.
8. Continue to keep accurate records.

PHASING OUT: PHASING IN

As you master each small bit of behavior you want to add to your daily schedule, you may choose to repeat the process we have just outlined to add still another behavior. Questions that we often hear about this process include: "When should I add a new behavior?" "Do I have to keep track of all these behaviors now?" "What if I want to increase the levels of the behavior that I have been working on first?"

We suggest that you not add a new behavior (the second one) until the first occurs automatically, i.e., until after the first has become a regular part of your day. A more concrete answer might be that you shouldn't try to add a second behavior until you have demonstrated about three weeks of maintenance of the first behavior without losing your contingencies or gaining noxious consequences. Each individual, naturally enough, will feel the need for different lengths of time to fully establish the first behavior before going on to a second.

How long should you keep accurate records of a behavior once it has been fixed into your daily pattern? This answer, too, varies with individuals. We suggest that you continue to keep a daily log of behaviors in a form shown in figure 8-3 until you are convinced that you will not slip from the wagon. After all, you can always start over. You can probably dispense with the contingencies though, after three weeks or so of adequate performance, i.e., not suffering the consequences. As you add a new behavior, you will merely pencil the first one in on the chart shown in figure 8-3 as well as the new one, but you will be going through the entire process again with the new behavior. Each added behavior, by the way, should take less effort than the preceding one to fix into your repertoire.

FIGURE 8-3

A CHART FOR MANAGING MORE THAN ONE BEHAVIOR

Time	Behavior #1	Behavior #2	How Felt	Duration	Contingencies Gained	Lost
3:30						
4:00						
4:30						
5:30						
6:00						

Note: For the behavior that has already been mastered, a checkmark will suffice to determine that it has been completed. The other behavior should be recorded using all the columns in the chart. Other behaviors may be added as they are mastered by adding additional columns.

What about lengthening the time spent in cert. in activities? All you really need to do here is to change your goals on a regular basis and set your contingencies up around the new goals. In other words, if you want to read forty-five minutes a day now instead of thirty, set your contingencies up for the new goal. This may be done in a gradual manner or in a step-wise manner. Figure 8-4 pictures the gradual increase in goals for jogging behavior. Remember, moderation is important. Do not overextend yourself.

FIGURE 8-4

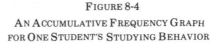

AN ACCUMULATIVE FREQUENCY GRAPH
FOR ONE STUDENT'S STUDYING BEHAVIOR

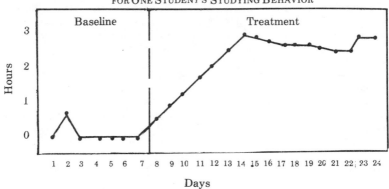

Days

Note: This student's studying behavior increased dramatically after the onset of treatment conditions. Her behavior stabilized at three hours a day after the introduction of the treatment.

EXAMPLE 1

One of the undergraduates' most common laments is "I didn't (or don't) have the time to study." Honestly, we can say that about fifty percent of all our students make this claim. One of these students was a particularly bright individual who would on some occasions perform at extremely high levels of competence on examinations, but on other occasions she performed miserably. Engaging her in conversation after a particularly dismal test performance, we evoked the old "I just really don't seem to have the time to study enough."

We decided that given her obvious concern, and the potential that she had shown, that we would try to convince her to keep a time check of her behavior. So, by mentioning a few goodies like "how would you like to try a new technique that could really help you use your time wisely" and other professorly statements, we maneuvered her to our office where we explained the concept of keeping a daily log of behaviors and how this could be checked for a week to determine how much time she now spent studying. We defined studying behavior as reading, writing or other forms of direct work involved in studying. Just sitting and thinking didn't count. She estimated that day that she probably spent an average of fifteen to twenty hours a week studying. We sent her away armed with an example of a time log and a frequency graph of studying behavior with the expectation that we would meet back in one week and go over her actual studying behavior.

After one week, she popped into our office before class and presented us with the baseline of her studying behavior. This is pictured with a frequency graph in figure 8-4. Much to her chagrin, she had determined that rather than studying fifteen to twenty hours a week, she was actually only studying about four to five hours a week. A lot of her time, she admitted, was spent in "phony studying," i.e., organizing books and papers, worrying about studying, talking about studying, sitting and listening to the radio, watching television, looking at magazines, in fact, almost everything that can be done in a dormitory room except study.

Faced with all this information, she had increased her study time somewhat during the week but was now very eager to pursue our "new technique." Following the outline we developed earlier, the first thing we did was set a time every day for study. Our student's schedule was such that the hours of two to five were free and after some hedging around, we all agreed that two o'clock should be the starting time daily for her study sessions. Next, we discussed the places where studying should occur. The student center was discarded immediately because of the tremendous level of noise, disturbance and general diversionary nature of the place. Her dormitory room was considered and then discarded after we determined that her roommate watched the daily adventures of various folks in daytime serials during most of the afternoon in her room and was not likely to move to the dormitory lobby. Several other places were considered before she settled on a table hidden in the stacks of the library that she visited and felt would not be very open to diversions. After settling on a spot, we reminded her to avoid all possible distractions such as magazines, chatting, or novels. A lot of this problem had already been solved by picking a comfortable, but relatively distraction-free environment in which to study. We agreed to start with two hours a day of studying behavior, seven days a week. "Phony studying" would not count.

For the enjoyable behavior to hold contingent upon her studying behavior, she decided on watching television, listening to records and using the telephone (evidentally a highly desirable behavior since young men seemed to call frequently). She also agreed to keep up her daily log and frequency graph and check back with us in two weeks. She decided to post her logs and frequency graph on the door of her dormitory room as a likely spot where they would not be ignored. Figure 8–4 (treatment) shows the result of her treatment.

Two weeks later she checked back and reported that she now had more than enough time to study all her courses at a rate that would allow her to perform at her potentially high level of achievement. In fact, she had added reading books that she felt to be important (Freud, Riesman, etc.) each day when she had finished her assignments. Interestingly enough, after the first day, she did not once spend less than three hours either reading or studying, seven days a week. She reported that after she became accustomed to the process, it seemed to leave her more free time during the rest of the day and made this free time far more enjoyable because she was not constantly worrying about studying. She decided to keep up her program indefinitely because she was convinced that it significantly contributed to more than just the academic part of her life. As an aside, she never fell below an "A" on any of her tests or assignments at any time during the rest of the semester.

EXAMPLE 2

An acquaintance of ours had fallen into the habit of constantly griping about how he never had time to work in his garden, except, it seemed, for those days when it was raining or when he had other things to do. Well, after the umpteenth time he brought this up, we mentioned that we had a technique that worked well for other people having trouble budgeting their time. We related to him that this method seemed to be just about what should fix him up. After convincing him we were serious, we explained the premises underlying the keeping of a time log of daily behaviors and how this could be converted into a frequency graph. He agreed to really keep track of his behavior during the week just to demonstrate to us how little time he had in a week to do any gardening. He agreed to meet us in a week with all the evidence necessary for his argument.

One week later, a very chagrined acquaintance dropped by at lunch with a frequency count showing no gardening behavior at all on any day. His time logs, however, were complete and showed that after work he spent between three and five hours watching television, talking, playing, eating, and generally goofing-off. All of the behaviors were worthwhile, more or less, but he was really surprised at how "unbusy" he was. In fact, only about three hours were spent with his wife and family. The rest was spent in "generally goofing off."

After talking about the state of his behaviors, (we must say that we were severely tempted to say, "I told you so.") we discussed the times of day that he felt were most convenient for gardening and settled on 4:30 to 5 in the afternoon as a starter. Further, since he wanted to avoid "phony gardening," he listed those tasks that needed to be accomplished around his yard and divided these up into daily tasks. Gardening was then defined as actually performing those tasks he listed (e.g., turning over the soil in the vegetable patch, pruning several trees, seeding and fertilizing the lawn, etc.). Gathering tools, getting dressed, resting, and other activities that usually accompany gardening were not included in the definition of gardening behavior.

At this point we already had met the first four criteria for our method of developing time budgeting. We had thought small and chosen only one behavior that would have only a short duration. Our gardener was keeping accurate records of his behavior and would continue to do so. He also decided that he would post his records on the kitchen door so that he could not possibly avoid them. A regular time (4:30 to 5:00) and a regular place (his yard) had been set. Our next step was to remove all possible distractions. In discussing the problem, he agreed to avoid the two major sources of distraction by informing his children that he would be unavailable to play until five, and he would ask his wife to set aside various other chores that she had in mind for him until after five.

In developing the consequences for his behavior, he decided that watching television, reading the paper, and working on his children's and his model railroad were his favorite activities. He would set all three of these preferred behaviors contingent upon his gardening one-half hour a day. Because of the nature of gardening, rainy days were

FIGURE 8-5

AN ACCUMULATIVE FREQUENCY GRAPH
OF ONE PERSON'S GARDENING BEHAVIOR

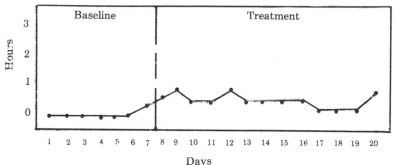

Note: The graph above represents defined gardening behavior for one person over a period of twenty days represented by daily amounts of time spent gardening. Notice the increase and stabilization of gardening behavior during the treatment phase. Those days marked with an asterisk are Sundays or rainy days.

thrown out of consideration. We realized, of course, that a sprinkle at seven in the morning might dry by noon but still be cited as a reason for not gardening. While this could have been adjusted by finding alternate activities or devising some objective measure of ground and weather conditions, this seemed a bit much to pile up on a beginning behavior modifier. Our acquaintance decided that he would check back with us in about two weeks to see what kind of change had been brought about.

Figure 8-5 represents the gardening behavior of Mr. Smith over a two-week period. As can be seen, he did garden ten days out of sixteen, with no gardening on Sundays or rainy days. He was pleased with this slight change in his behavior, especially since he did not ever forfeit his other leisure-time activities.

Not all adjustments of how people use their time are as successful or as easy as these two examples we have just presented. Generally, the desire to make the change in behavior must be stronger than the desire to avoid the task. Although neither of our examples included the use of noxious consequences for not performing the task (studying, gardening), they can be instituted rather easily and add strength to the behavior change process.

Summary

Time budgeting is a common problem but one that lends itself easily to change via contingency management. The important steps to follow are:

1. Think small
2. Define the behavior and keep accurate records
3. Set a regular time for the behavior
4. Set a regular place for the behavior
5. Remove distractions
6. Develop consequences for the behavior
7. If necessary, develop noxious consequences for failing to meet the goal
8. Continue to keep accurate records

Appropriate time budgeting will lead to more, not less, leisure time and will help you do those things that you just haven't had the time to do. The person making the change, however, must want to do it. Not following through with the entire procedure is a guarantee of failure.

PART II
Emotions and Their Control

Introduction

The next two chapters are closely related. In chapter nine we discuss fear, anxiety, phobias and their reduction. In chapter ten we talk about tension and its reduction and the control of nervous habits. Before entering either chapter it is necessary for us to discuss our general views concerning emotional behavior and to describe the process of classical or respondent conditioning.

Emotion, as Isaacson, Douglas, Lubar and Schmaltz (1971) point out, is an extremely difficult concept to define in adequate terms. Most of us make gross or broad distinctions between emotions such as anger, fear, joy and so forth. The difficulty has been in pinning down specific emotions and making fine discriminations between emotions, such as a feeling of well-being and a feeling of contentedness. Semantically, and perhaps cognitively as well, we can differentiate between emotions at this level, but scientifically it becomes far more difficult. This problem, differentiation between highly similar emotions, could be an insurmountable problem for us as it is still being debated by psychologists of many persuasions. We, however, approach emotion from the point of view of behaviors which we outline below.

THREE COMPONENTS OF EMOTION

We feel that all emotions have three basic components: a respondent component, an operant component, and a label (Reynolds, 1975). Further, we believe that there are only two basic forms of the respondent component: pleasurable (e.g., contentment, joy, happiness, a feeling of well-being, love, affection, etc.) and an unpleasant form (e.g., anger, fear, hatred, contempt, sadness, frustration, etc.). We tend to feel that the human at birth possesses only an overall series of reflexive responses that constitute emotion with little or no differentiation between pleasure and discomfort. Morgan (1965) describes different internal reactions among adults for pleasant and unpleasant emotions. Evidently, soon after birth the human infant develops the two basic forms of emotional responses, pleasant and unpleasant. Whether this is "learned" or "instinctive" is a debatable point.

Beyond the two basic forms of emotion, we believe that all other emotions are learned via generalization of the original two components of the respondents. (Note: The term respondent refers to a response that is reflexive in nature that has been conditioned into the repertoire of the organism.) Since we do not recall, offhand, anybody concerned about "feeling too good" (unless they were inebriated) we will examine the formation of unpleasant feelings and how they come to be associated with situations that cause a person to feel unpleasant. Another reason to concentrate on the unpleasant emotions is that the two chapters that follow deal specifically with them. The reader should keep in mind that the processes to be described would be highly similar for pleasant emotions.

We think that in humans there are two basic sources of unpleasant feelings: pain situations from which we believe fear, anxiety and sadness are generated and anger or attack situations from which are generated feelings of frustration, tension, resentment and contempt. Both these situations bring about the same reflexes within the organism, evidently to prepare the organism to flee or to do battle. No distinction between the reflexes of fear and anger are possible. What is possible, however, is to induce the emotive state in the organism that prepares it for flight or fight and then to place the organism (that has been artificially "energized" by way of injecting adrenalin) in different situations which then seem to provide the description or label for the emotion. For example, a person injected with adrenalin who is placed into a theater showing a horror movie may ascribe the feeling of readiness (called fear by the person) to the movie. Similarly, a person injected with adrenalin or another energizing substance and placed into a debate may ascribe the same bodily responses (now called anger) to the debate.

This summation of Schachter's (1967, 1963, 1962) arguments demonstrates that only one unpleasant emotional bodily state is generated regardless of whether it is generated by fear or anger. Hence, the *respondent* component of emotion is the series of bodily reflexes that are elicited by stimuli that are perceived as threats to the organism. It makes no difference whether you are angry, afraid, anxious, tense, sad, etc., your body will respond in the same way. We tend to believe, however, that while the same reflexes are elicited regardless of the stimulus, the strengths of the reflexes may be different for different stimuli. We could say that extreme fear may have a greater *response strength* than a minor feeling of anxiety, that is, the *relative strength* of the stimuli that elicit the respondent components of emotion determine to a large degree the *strength of the emotional response.*

To make the going easier, we will refer to reflexes as respondents, since the body's reactions are all respondents, that is, responses to the environment.

The various stimuli that elicit the respondent component of emotion (i.e., fear stimuli, anger stimuli, etc.) may be learned through the operant component of emotion or through "classical" (respondent) conditioning. The classical conditioning of a fear response to a stimulus that does not ordinarily elicit the respondent component of fear can easily be understood after we consider four points. First, since all the unpleasant respondents the body brings forth are actually the same respondent, there must be many eliciting stimuli capable of bringing forth this respondent. Second, we believe as Schachter (1967) has demonstrated, that the label or the organism's interpretation of this respondent is due to the condition you find yourself in. Your respondent (your body's reflex) is fear if the situation is one which you "think" should produce fear and it is anger if it is a situation that you "think" should produce anger. It really makes no difference as the respondent is the "same" in either case. Third, the vast majority of stimuli that elicit emotional responses are learned. Only a few stimuli, evidently instinctual in nature, can produce the respondent of emotion during the first few days of an infant's life. Other stimuli that eventually produce unpleasant emotions are learned. Fourth, and last, emotional respondents are learned and unlearned throughout life and do not cease at any time.

Those eliciting stimuli (stimuli that bring forth reflexes or respondents that produce unpleasant emotional respondents in infants include loud noises, pain from external sources including heat and is cold, bodily discomfort, hunger, falling, losing physical support and bright lights (Bridges, 1932). Other stimuli that elicit the respondent component of unpleasant emotions have also been observed but there is some ambiguity as to whether the respondents were the result of maturation (enhanced visual ability was most often cited) or of learning. We favor the learning position.

From this basic discussion, consider the following "classical" or respondent conditioning paradigm.

Several Pairings

Pain of hunger (an unconditoned or "natural" stimulus)	respondent (release of adrenalin, increase of blood pressure, heart rate, etc.).
+	
Sound of bell (a neutral stimulus)	
After a few trials	
Sound of bell (now a conditioned stimulus)	respondent (same as above, now called a conditioned reflex).

This simple associative pairing paradigm, we feel, is the source for much of the "learning" of "what to fear" or "what to feel frustrated" about. The astute reader will notice that the associative pairing paradigm is identical to the associative pairing technique that results in the learning of conditioned reinforcers. In this way, literally hundreds of stimuli can be paired with those unconditioned stimuli that elicit the emotional respondents. This, of course, does not explain totally how unpleasant emotions are learned. We believe that a tremendous amount of stimulus generalization occurs in emotional behavior. That is, an organism is highly likely to respond the same way in the presence of stimuli similar to the ones that were originally learned. Using the pictured paradigm as an example, once a person has "learned" (become conditioned is really more appropriate) to respond in the presence of a bell, similar respondents can be brought forth by stimuli that are similar to the bell that was originally paired with pain (e.g., bells of different sounds and tones, buzzers, clanging, etc.).

In adult life, stimuli that elicit emotional responses are generally far more complex and subtle than a bell, although many stimuli that simple do elicit emotional respondents. If experiences in a boss's office have produced fear, the experiences may be paired with some other fear-provoking stimuli and eventually elicit fear by themselves. Generalization to other, similar stimuli, of course, also occurs. In this manner, with a considerable number of pairings between the boss's office and fear, other offices will generate the same sort of fear response through stimulus generalization.

The *respondent component* of emotion, then, consists of the body's involuntary response that was originally elicited only by a very few stimuli and those stimuli which have been paired with them and the resultant stimulus generalization.

We have given a case for how emotions are conditioned, and how more and more stimuli can elicit various emotional states through associative pairing and stimulus generalization, but we have not yet described how the emotions become differentiated from each other. We believe that the basic division in unpleasant emotions, that between fear and anger, can be traced directly to the situations that elicit them.

The reader will have noticed that we have used the term "elicit" to describe the causation of a respondent by an eliciting stimulus. *Elicit* is always used with respondent behaviors while *emit* is always used with operant behaviors. In one case the *environment* elicits the respondent from the organism, that is, it causes it directly. In the case of operant behaviors the *organism* is said to emit a response, that is, the organism acts on the environment rather than the environment acting on the organism.

Fear, we believe is a result of pain stimuli. Anger, we believe is a result of frustration stimuli, such as hunger or discomfort, rather than pain. Remember, though, the respondents are the same, only the names and the organism's perception of the emotions are different.

(A note to the reader concerning our use of the terms "the same" and "similar": No two respondents are ever absolutely identical. When we speak of "similar" or the "same," we mean that all the same functions within the organism are occurring and that the same effects will transpire. There are some physiologists who disagree with Schachter, most notably Ax (1953) and Funkenstein (1955). They did determine differences in bodily excretions between states of anger and fear. However, as Isaacson, et. al., point out, these two studies supply the strongest evidence to contradict Schachter's position. For the purposes of most readers, it can be given that all unpleasant emotional states have the same internal changes.)

Well, if the respondent is the same regardless of the form of unpleasant emotion, how are the emotions different? As we have mentioned, we feel they are different only in how we perceive them, that is, how we interpret the emotion. How we interpret the emotion is the *label* component of emotions.

LABELING

Labeling is the process of learning the name for something. We call a dish a dish but we could just as well refer to it as a "knard" or a "doofus" or a "chang." The name of an emotion is learned in much the same way we learn the name for anything else, by modeling at first, and later, reinforcement of the use of the "correct" term. Once we learn that when we feel a certain way that this feeling is called "bitterness," for example, we will continue to refer to it in the same manner in the future; it has become part of our vocabulary and has also become a concept that we understand (the feeling we had, the situation we had the feeling in, etc., all form the concept of "bitterness"). (Symbol and concept formation are extremely complex topics far beyond the scope of the current book. For a discussion of symbol formation we refer you to Werner and Kaplan, 1967. For a discussion of concept formation, we refer you to Saltz, 1971).

There are still factors in emotion that need to be accounted for before we can say that we have adequately described how emotions are learned. First, how do we account for the fact that you really "feel" differently when you are experiencing different emotions? Secondly, why do emotional behaviors continue to appear far longer than they should, since they appear without the original eliciting stimulus? Lastly, aren't there other reasons why some emotional behaviors are maintained in the apparent absence of unconditioned eliciting stimuli?

In answer to our first question, we believe that humans are operantly conditioned as to how to "feel" during a given emotion. An operant conditioning approach based, of course, on the consequences of behavior would suggest to us that somehow the consequences of "feeling a certain way" during a period of emotional energization are positive reinforcers. This is not too difficult to conceive when we consider that "correct responding" is a highly powerful source of reinforcement, i.e., knowing that we have done the right thing is highly rewarding. This process is easier to picture when we consider a hypothetical small child and how she learns how to "feel" anger.

Let us assume that our hypothetical child wants her older sibling's candy bar. Denied this and she will respond emotionally with something that an adult would call anger. She does this through either stimulus generalization, i.e., generalizing from real hunger pains to the prospect of eating her brother's candy, or associative pairing, i.e., having had the denial or inaccessability of food paired with hunger feelings. The child has the same internal response that she would have if she were afraid, but she is about to learn some subtle differences. This emotional response will be interpreted by the adult and bring on the adult's reaction: "You're very angry because you didn't get the candy," or "The way you feel must be a feeling of anger," etc. What has happened here is that the adult has provided certain information about the feeling the child has had and given a label to the feeling. Whether or not any reinforcement occurs at this point is immaterial. What is important is what happens when this procedure is repeated in the future.

Two days later the little girl is again denied something of her brother's. One or two things will fix the "feeling of anger" into the child's repertoire. First, she could say, "Boy, am I angry at you," and if she got some reinforcing reaction from her brother, (a scared look or the candy, etc.) not only would the state of anger be reinforced and strengthened in this situation, (which incidentally answers our second question) but the "feeling" that she had corresponding to the actions that she called anger has also been reinforced and fixed so that it will be more likely to appear in the future. After a few "correct" responses (if I am angry, I should feel this way) the "feeling" occurs simultaneously with the body's internal changes.

The second way that a "feeling of anger" could be fixed into our child's repertoire of behaviors would be for one of the parents to ask the girl how she "feels" during a series of responses that the parent interprets as anger. If the child responds, "I am angry" or its equivalent, the child will have given the "correct" answer and obtained reinforcement by way of confirmation from the parents. (They may not actively approve, but it is highly likely that if the child had said, "I'm joyful" that the parents would have corrected her with a response something like, "No, you're not joyful, you're angry, aren't you?") It is very interesting how we train, very purposely, the way children should feel. It is one of the most important things we teach, along with language and behavior, a part of the overall socialization process. Well, this reinforcement of a verbal response also reinforces all the other responses that happen to be paired with the overt signs of anger. After a few trials like this, the child will know which feeling is "covert" for which emotion and feel that way.

Obviously, there are literally hundreds or thousands of possible ways that the "feeling" you have during different emotional states could be reinforced and fixed into your repertoire of behaviors. This "feeling" is something we are all aware exists, but as has been pointed out by several authors, cannot be adequately identified, observed, measured, or defined to allow any usefulness in its study, at least currently (Bem, 1968; Holland and Skinner, 1961; Schachter, 1970). We believe that this "feeling" certainly exists, but it just is not available for us to study. We know that it is learned and we know you feel it, but that is as definite a statement as we can make.

MAINTAINING EMOTIONAL BEHAVIORS, THE OPERANT COMPONENT

Emotional behaviors are maintained beyond the level of strength we would normally expect from a response learned through associative pairing by the consequences of these responses. That is, emotional behavior is successful behavior or it would not continue to appear. The consequences of emotional behavior are positive reinforcers. Perhaps not for every response, but frequently enough to maintain them. Consequences such as our hypothetical young lady obtaining her brother's candy via anger responses reinforce the appearance of the anger behavior. If we examined any other emotional behavior, joy, fear, etc., we would find the same result for the behavior. Any emotional behavior that you exhibit has a history of reinforcement whether or not you can "remember" it. The reinforcement may consist of attention, a positive reaction from another person, problem solutions, etc. Because emotional behavior is highly successful behavior we tend to exhibit it at highly frequent levels (like it or not, folks, little girls and boys learn that sadness or fear will get attention and that anger or hostility often gain results).

MODELING

Our last question has been partly answered by the discussion above, i.e., since emotional behaviors are highly successful, they are supported for very long periods between reinforcements, in fact, nearly indefinitely. Modeling, previously mentioned throughout our text, is also a major source of the learning of the overt, external components of emotion. We learn to frown, grit our teeth, mash up our eyebrows and clench our fists by watching other people who are angry or by obtaining reinforcement for such behavior from parents and other significant people in the environment. There is a tremendous amount of information (Bandura, 1969; Bandura and Walters, 1963; etc.) concerning the learning of emotional responses via modeling.

The fact that the individuals in our society show such tremendous similarities in the overt, observable responses for different emotions (e.g., fear, joy, etc.) without any genetic or biological bases for such behavior demonstrates to us that the external signs of emotional behaviors are learned in the same ways as any other behaviors, i.e., modeling or operant conditioning.

In summary, then, we have discussed how emotions are learned, and more specifically, how the three components of emotion—respondent, labeling, and operant—are developed. Our discussion was specifically limited to the unpleasant emotions but exactly the same processes can be applied to pleasant emotions. Emotional behavior is necessary behavior in many instances, during periods of threat or in periods of great joy. The problem with emotional behavior is not one of occurrence or non-occurrence, since emotions must always be present for us to be human. The problem lies in the over-arousal of human beings to the point of causing physical or psychological harm. Emotions cannot be destroyed or totally stifled (prefrontal lobotomies and other similar surgical procedures do lessen emotion, however) without destroying the organism. What can be done for those who suffer from high degrees of anxiety or tension is to develop techniques for managing these emotions so that they cease to have debilitative effects. The next two chapters discuss how this may be done. In Chapter 9 we concentrate on fear, anxiety and phobias. The current discussion of how emotions are learned is expanded there to include specifically those fear states. Since the discussion of how tension states are learned would be highly redundant, Chapter 10 does not discuss this matter, leaving the reader to recall the material from the discussion of anxiety.

Importantly, because of the high degree of similarity between anxiety and tension, the techniques for controlling both forms of emotion are discussed in Chapter 10. Chapter 9 is concerned directly with those emotional states that can be identified readily as fear states. Anxiety and tension are taken together in Chapter 10 and considered to be so similar as to obviate the necessity of discussing the matter twice. Nervous habits, whether ascribed to tension or anxiety, are also discussed in Chapter 10.

9

Fear, Anxiety, and Phobias

In this chapter we discuss how fears, anxiety, and phobias are learned, what environmental components control them, and how they may be treated by behavior modification techniques designed for self-administration. It is extremely important to note that since there is a great deal of overlap between anxiety and tension, we discuss the primary treatment of anxiety in the next chapter in combination with the treatment of tension. People may or may not perceive anxiety and tension differently. While we sometimes do not know whether we are tense or anxious, we usually ascribe our feelings to the context in which they occur. Anxiety is primarily a generalization of fear responses while tension is primarily a generalization of anger responses. Since the body's internal responses are so similar as to be identical in both states, and since we have more and more frequently used the same treatments to attenuate both feelings of anxiety and feelings of tension, we have combined them in the next chapter.

In this chapter we are primarily concerned with responses that are clearly associated with fear states. We will describe rather thoroughly how fears are learned. This description of the specific learning of one form of emotion can be easily transferred to account for the learning of any other emotion. Hence, we do not go through the process of discussing the learning of anger and frustration responses in Chapter 10.

LEARNING FEAR

The human infant is a nearly fearless creature with only a few stimuli that can elicit generalized states of emotion. During the first two years of life, infants learn through experience the difference between anger or frustration feelings and those of fear. As we have pointed out, the body's responses are highly similar in either instance. Learning the difference between fear and anger amounts to discriminating between those situations that elicit the two forms of unpleasant bodily responses.

Fear. Fear is an objective, realistic recognition of threats (the imminent occurrence of pain or damage) and the corresponding bodily changes that are brought about by the fear state. Fear is a legitimate and realistic response to threat. Once a child discriminates between fear and anger (whether this is through shaping or modeling matters little) fear becomes a state (a way of feeling) that is associated with the situation (the stimuli) that elicited it. In other words, the feeling of fear is associated with those situations which have in the past elicited fear. This could be a loud noise, falling down the stairs, having a big dog run up while barking furiously, and other unpleasant situations. The child learns, literally, that when he or she feels fearful, something bad is going to happen. Fear, as we will discuss later, becomes a discriminative stimulus itself, giving rise to responses which alleviated fear in the past, e.g., crying, running to a parent, etc.

Fear, as all emotions, is learned for different situations through two basic processes: respondent conditioning, i.e., associative pairing with fear-eliciting stimuli and stimulus generalization and operant conditioning, i.e., shaping and modeling. By these techniques, children may learn to fear water, if immersion in water is associated with fear-eliciting stimuli or the fear response can be generalized to immersion in water from other similar experiences. Fear of water can also be learned by observing a person who is fearful of water. If the parents, for example, are afraid of being immersed in water at the lake or at a pool, the child may learn this fear by observation without ever experiencing the situation personally. Fear responses, of course, can be reinforced for certain stimuli so that a fear response is learned (shaped) in much the same way as any other operant behavior.

Appropriate and Inappropriate Fears. Fear is a necessary response to some situations. Being afraid of people with guns, wildly careening cars and falling from high places, for example, are useful fears in that such responses are likely to keep a person from harm. If we did not fear such situations, we might be shot, run over, or carelessly fall from a skyscraper. There are many obvious physical dangers that we should fear. The fear of these dangers is one way we manage to survive in a highly complex and threatening environment. How long might someone live commuting back and forth to work if the person had no fear of other cars on the road or of colliding with them? Besides the obvious physical dangers that we could point out as being situations that should be feared out of necessity, there are also many situations that are sanctioned by society as fear provoking. In the Western culture such fears include the fear of failure, the fear of embarrassment, etc. In other cultures such fears could include the fear of loss of face or the fear of transgressing upon religious tabus. While these kinds of things do not actually constitute physical dangers, they are mandated by various societies as necessary situations which should provoke fear. All these kinds of fears, socially enforced and physical, are appropriate fears and are necessary to life. Unfortunately, not all fears are appropriate.

Inappropriate fears (including anxieties and phobias) are fears of situations which should logically not be feared. (Logic, incidentally, is defined as whatever society says you should fear in addition to physical dangers. Logic in its correct definition, may or may not have anything to do with society's determination of what to fear.) For example, if a person is afraid of a thermos bottle, this is an inappropriate fear. No doubt there are good reasons for such a fear, as we will point out later, but thermos bottles by themselves are not threatening to human beings. Not only are fears inappropriate in terms of what is feared, but also in the amount of fear. Most of us might fear having an airliner fall on our house, but we do not ordinarily give such thoughts much notice. If we built our house underground to protect us from falling planes, however, we might be considered to be somewhat eccentric because of an overreaction to a fear. Another example is a fear of being mugged. Most people would take precautions to avoid such a situation by walking only in brightly lit areas. An inappropriate fear would be to never leave the house.

Both appropriate and inappropriate fears are learned in the same ways. A person has no reason to fear snakes if snakes are never encountered either directly or through the observation of others who have encountered them. A fear of snakes is learned only by encounters with snakes either directly or vicariously, i.e., being told stories about snakes, or observing extreme fear of snakes in others. A fear of snakes, of course, could be generalized from a fear of other, similar objects. A person also has no reason to fear thermos bottles unless the person has associated thermos bottles with other fear-eliciting stimuli, generalized a fear learned from other similar stimuli, or observed a person who is fearful of thermoses. There is just as much reason to fear thermos bottles as there is to fear snakes if the person has not directly encountered either object. Some snakes are poisonous and should be feared, but some thermoses can be broken and cut your fingers. The learning to fear objects or situations is a highly complex problem with many anomalies when it is restricted to vicarious learning.

Direct experience with objects or situations without any form of vicarious experiences can also result in the learning of both appropriate and inappropriate fears. If you fall out of a tree and are hurt, you should learn to be afraid of high places and the situation which led up to the fall. It is also possible, though, to learn to be afraid of trees.

In this chapter we will be primarily concerned with inappropriate fears, inappropriate anxiety and phobias, which are irrational fears.

ANXIETY

Anxiety is a fear, unrealistic in form, of threats that may or may not be real, but are not directly perceived. All the bodily reactions are the same as in fear. The difference is that no real or objective source of threat can be found.

Anxiety, a pervasive feeling of unease, a feeling of free-floating fear, is the source of many complaints from people of all walks of life. In a way, anxiety can be seen as a low-grade form of fear that can either help or harm our bodies, our psychological state, and our activities. Prolonged anxiety can lead to physical illnesses, such as hypertension, heart problems, ulcers, and severe headaches. Prolonged anxiety can also result in psychological damage, by inhibiting the enjoyment of life, frustrating the accomplishment of daily tasks, or just getting in the way of living.

We have defined anxiety. At this point we need to determine how anxiety is learned, what environmental factors control anxiety, and how anxiety can either be beneficial or harmful.

Anxiety is learned in two basic ways, operantly and respondently. We will examine the respondent form of learning first. In the respondent form of learning certain objects, people or situations become paired over time with fear-producing stimuli. Eventually the fear-producing stimuli may be absent, but the new, conditioned stimuli will elicit a fear state independently. (The kinds of things that can become conditioned, eliciting stimuli for anxiety are, as Baughman and Welsh 1965, point out, uncountable. People, places, situations, concepts, etc., all can become conditioned stimuli for anxiety.) The majority of these sources of anxiety are not recognized by the anxious persons. The conditioned stimuli elicit the fear response but they cannot be identified.

Such learned anxiety can develop through one to several experiences. An example of such learned anxiety would be the anxiety many people feel when entering auditoriums or places similar to auditoriums such as theaters, playhouses, and churches. One of the ways in which this is learned is through a series of noxious experiences in similar circumstances, e.g., the classroom. If a person has had a series of unpleasant experiences in classrooms, the fear-eliciting stimuli (the teacher, a bully, etc.,) are paired over and over with classrooms. Anxiety produced by auditoriums, then, is a result of stimulus generalization. Of course, this was just a hypothetical situation, but we believe that it is similar to many common sources of anxiety.

Anxiety can be learned for any stimulus or set of stimuli, including thinking about something. Our anxieties can be attached to anything that can be perceived or imagined. The difference between anxiety and fear is the lower strength of the anxiety response and that the source of the anxiety often is not recognized or understood. Anxiety can vary from feelings as powerful as the most terrifying experience possible to a slightly annoying sense of unease. The strength of the anxiety seems to be governed by the strength of the original fear stimulus, the number of times the fear-eliciting stimulus was paired with the anxiety-eliciting stimulus, the length of time since the pairing has ceased, the number of trials the anxiety-eliciting stimulus has been "run" without the original fear stimulus, the general emotional state of the organism, and the whole host of operant concepts that affect behavior.

As in the case of fear or anger, anxiety can be produced by stimulus generalization, much like the example of the anxiety surrounding auditoriums that we presented earlier. It is difficult to determine after the fact whether anxiety is due to direct pairing of stimuli or whether the anxiety is due to stimulus generalization. In fact, the conditioned-eliciting stimuli for anxiety may never be determined in many instances. Behavior, life and learning are just too complex for us to make accurate *post hoc* determinations of the elicitors of behavior.

The operant component of anxiety can be discussed at four levels: vicarious learning, avoidance learning, direct instruction and modeling. In vicarious learning of anxiety, the response is almost always inappropriate. This form of learning amounts to discovering (without meaning to do so) that anxiety is a behavior that leads to reinforcement under certain circumstances. This is appropriate only when the anxiety is managed in a way that is not harmful to the individual. We are aware, for example, of students who purposely try to induce feelings of anxiety (one student calls this "getting psyched up," another refers to this as "hyping up") before taking examinations in their courses. These students tell us that they perform better in test-taking situations when they are moderately anxious than when they are calm. This so-called facilitative anxiety will be discussed later in the chapter.

Operantly-learned anxiety for the most part is an inappropriate response. We have encountered people who have learned that they could gain attention, prestige, affection and other interpersonal goodies by responding with anxiety. We don't wish to say that you should ignore anyone experiencing anxiety, but we feel that anxiety can become a highly paid-off (reinforced) behavior that becomes a more and more frequently appearing device used to gain attention, sympathy, affection, etc. if other behaviors are not more successful in obtaining these same reinforcers. This vicariously learned anxiety is controlled in the environment by discriminative stimuli (discriminants) that are stimuli in whose presence the anxiety has been reinforced previously. Anxiety, a rather common response, can be vicariously reinforced one time with the result that it is likely to occur more frequently under the same or similar discriminative stimuli in the future. If anxiety is successful in gaining those reinforcers that other behaviors do not obtain, then very likely the person will develop considerable amounts of anxiety behavior in order to continue to be paid-off via stimulus generalization to the point where anxiety becomes a serious problem resulting in physical and/or psychological damage.

One example of this form of learned anxiety can be illustrated by a five-year-old male who learned that anxiety responses led to more attention, affection and sympathy than any other responses in his behavioral repertoire. He had to compete for attention with two older brothers and two younger sisters and he succeeded dramatically. He also made himself very ill and made his parents nervous wrecks. The process could have been avoided if the parents had provided him the attention and affection he needed for appropriate responses and denied him these reinforcers for the inappropriate behavior. This is very much like giving children candy to get them to stop crying. If that works, guess what the children will do next time they want a piece of candy? Cry, naturally. It works.

Most of us have some vicariously learned anxieties that can easily be extinguished. This form of learning anxiety, though, can lead to highly debilitating effects if it is not stopped quickly.

ESCAPE OR AVOIDANCE BEHAVIOR

Escape behavior is a behavior that removes an organism from the presence of a noxious stimulus. Avoidance behavior is one that an organism has learned to avoid a noxious stimulus before it is encountered. Anxiety is a response that can be used successfully as either escape or avoidance behavior. It is learned in the same manner as the vicarious anxiety, i.e., it appears once and is reinforced by escaping or avoiding a noxious stimulus. In the future, then, anxiety is more likely to be the response brought forward to escape or avoid similar noxious stimuli.

This form of the learning of anxiety is very common. We see it frequently among students who "become ill" the day of an examination and successfully avoid an exam. Some students actually become so anxious before examinations that they do become physically ill. The student is not lying when reporting a violently upset stomach. The student most certainly was ill. The illness, however, was induced by the state of anxiety. In this manner anxiety leads directly to successful avoidance behavior. Much the same kind of example could be made for escape behavior. The difference is that in escape behavior the noxious stimulus must already have contacted the person. Anxiety could produce test-escape behavior by inducing illness in a student five minutes after the onset of an examination.

Anxiety as a form of avoidance or escape behavior is inappropriate behavior. Not only can such high levels of anxiety (the result of its previous successes) actually cause illness to gain the escape or the avoidance of one situation, but they can also easily be generalized and used to escape and/or avoid more and more unpleasant situations. If such behavior proliferates without control, it can result in seriously debilitating effects both physically and emotionally. Interestingly, people suffering from problems with anxiety are generally aware of the anxiety and often can identify those situations that generate the anxiety, but seldom link their physical illnesses or bad feelings to the anxiety.

DIRECT INSTRUCTION

Many of our anxieties (and our fears, too, for that matter) are learned by direct instruction from others. We are literally taught by parents, siblings, peers or other significant persons that certain things should provoke anxiety. As with all teaching, our responses are shaped by other persons until we develop the correct or appropriate response, in this case, anxiety. This may be "unconscious" on the part of the person that is teaching the anxiety. He is aware of what he is doing but not aware of the consequences of what he is doing. In other words, parents or other people who teach anxiety are generally not aware that they are doing anything but teaching caution or care. It is also possible, by reinforcing "appropriate" responses and ignoring or punishing "inappropriate" responses, to teach purposely anxiety. If parents decide that certain objects, situations, or people should be sources of anxiety for their children, it can certainly be taught.

MODELING AND ANXIETY

Modeling, learning by observation, is also one source of learned anxiety. Without redescribing the modeling process, we need only point out that we can learn to be anxious concerning certain things by observing others behave anxiously in various situations. For example, if you have no experience with postmen and you observe some person over a period of days behave in a very anxious way around postmen (giving overt signs of anxiety) it is possible that you will imitate this behavior. As with all modeling situations, though, there are manifold variables that affect the actual performance of modeled behavior.

ENVIRONMENTAL CONTROLS OF ANXIETY

To sum up the various kinds of learned anxiety we will describe the environmental control of anxiety. Anxiety can either be learned respondently or operantly. Respondent anxiety is controlled by unconditioned-eliciting stimuli, conditioned-eliciting stimuli and generalization to other conditioned-eliciting stimuli. As we shall note later in the chapter, it is possible to extinguish respondents in the presence of conditioned-eliciting stimuli.

Operantly-learned anxiety is controlled by discriminative stimuli, that is, stimuli in whose presence we have been reinforced for being anxious. Operant responding to discriminative stimuli can also be attenuated or extinguished.

What are these conditioned-eliciting stimuli and discriminative stimuli that control anxiety? They are unique to every person. While there is always the possibility of making general statements about various stimuli that provoke anxiety, e.g., the sound of a wailing siren, standing in a high place, the sight of an injured person, etc., it is wise to remember that each person has had an absolutely unique set of experiences that has led to the learning of those stimuli that control anxiety. Further, it is often not possible to identify these stimuli clearly and your own conscious control of anxiety must often proceed without the knowledge of exactly what in the environment has provoked your feeling of anxiety.

ANXIETY, FACILITATIVE AND DEBILITATIVE

Several investigators (Palermo, 1957; Castenada and Lipsitt, 1959; Lazarus and Erickson, 1952, etc.) have reported that some people believe anxiety is a facilitative or helpful state on certain occasions. We know students, for example, who report to us that they do not perform well on examinations or out of class assignments unless they are somewhat anxious. That is, unless they feel somewhat afraid or "hyped-up" as one student puts it. One young man explained it by saying that he really did not feel that he was making a maximum effort unless he was nervous and anxious. He told us that he purposely delays working on out-of-class assignments until there is just enough time, in his estimation, to barely complete the task before it is due. We know others who actively try to "work themselves up" before an examination so that they can perform at their optimal level.

Anxiety in this frame of reference is useful and facilitative. In fact, people sometimes actively seek the feeling of anxiety to help their performance. The concept that certain individuals function best while under "pressure" is supported by the work of Worthy (1971, 1974).

Other examples of facilitative anxiety can be seen in athletic events. Coaches and athletes often report that they and their teams perform better when they are highly emotionally charged rather than when they are relaxed or "flat." Many of us force ourselves into feelings of anxiety to heighten our ability or our productivity. The question arises in view of the many who seek anxiety as an aid in different tasks as to whether their behavior is superstitious behavior or whether the bodily changes during anxiety really facilitate the performance of these tasks.

The answer is both. Undoubtedly, if you are highly successful on examinations while you are highly anxious, not only will the behaviors that led to the success be reinforced, but also the state of your anxiety reaction. In this way anxiety is learned and seen as important to adequate performance in examination situations. Whether this was true or not, naturally, does not matter; it is like learning that chain-smoking while you study leads to better studying. The smoking or the anxiety may have nothing to do with eventual success but they are learned anyway.

The anxiety state is also an energized state for the organism. The person who is anxious is breathing somewhat faster than normal, the blood pressure is higher than normal, the pupils of the eyes have dilated, a whole series of internal reflexes, in fact, are in operation to help the person deal with some threat. This energization probably does lead to better athletic performance and perhaps to better academic performance as well. These effects, however, are not helpful or facilitative in all people.

Debilitative anxiety is a tremendously large topic that has an equally large bibliography. Literally thousands of reports have been made concerning the debilitative effects of anxiety. Rather than list an exhaustive review of all forms of disabling anxieties, we will describe three ways in which anxiety can be harmful. First, extended periods of anxiety can lead to physical damage or illness. The results of extended anxiety range from overweight to ulcers and hypertension. Evidently, too much anxiety is never good for the body ("too much," by the way, must be individually determined). Secondly, several authors have demonstrated that anxiety can have harmful effects on task completion (Sarason & Sarason, 1957; Hilgard, Jones & Kaplan, 1951; Korchin and Levine, 1957; McCandless and Castenada, 1956; etc.). This includes all of those tasks we discussed earlier that could be facilitated by anxiety. Evidently, anxiety has quite different effects on different people. Not only do we know students who want to be anxious to complete certain tasks, we also know students who report that they cannot do well in any form of activity if there is too much pressure or anxiety. We are aware of several students who had learned material for examinations but then "choked" under the pressure and anxiety of the test situation and did not perform at all well. In their cases, the anxiety was a debilitative state.

Lastly, anxiety can be harmful to the psychological state of persons. Anxiety, you see, becomes a discriminative stimulus by itself, a condition in which certain responses have been reinforced and punished in the past. The reader may remember being more easily upset by others during anxiety states and more likely to lash out against them because of the anxiety. Anxiety and its effects on psychological functions is another topic which has its own overwhelming bibliography. We will not here go into the many possible effects of anxiety on the psychological state as it is a topic that is far beyond the scope and purpose of this book.

PHOBIAS

Phobias are overwhelming, irrational fears directed to specific stimuli. The fear is of a compulsive nature and a tremendous overreaction to objects which should produce little, if any, fear. Phobias are irrational, that is, they are not based on a logical consideration of the situation. Phobias are differentiated from fears by the strength of the fear and their inevitable irrationality.

Phobias can be directed at many sources. Mussen, Conger and

Kagan (1974) mention school and death phobias as among the most common for school-aged children. Other common phobias include fear of heights, fear of heart attacks, fear of strangers, fear of water, and fear of being alone. Phobias are frequently given names to represent each of these fears. For example, acrophobia is the name given a fear of heights; aquaphobia is the fear of water, and so forth. Learning the terminology of phobias seems to be a task that is also beyond the bounds of this book. We refer the reader to Ullmann and Krasner (1969) for a basic description of various kinds of phobias and their correct names.

Phobias are fear responses and are learned in the same way as anxieties and other fears. However, several authors (Sutton-Smith, 1973; Stone and Church, 1973; Mussen, et. al., 1974; Heine, 1971; McNeil, 1970; McNeil, 1967; Ullmann and Krasner, 1969; etc.) describe the learning of phobias from a single traumatic event early in childhood and the subsequent generalization of this overwhelming fear to other objects encountered later in life. This is one-trial learning at its best, or worst, depending on your point of view.

Phobias are controlled by the same environmental stimuli as are other fears. The only difference is the strength of the response and its apparent irrationality.

An example of a phobia, one which we describe the treatment for later in this chapter, is a phobia of heart attacks. One gentleman we worked with developed an extreme and irrational fear of heart attacks in his early forties. We could not identify how his phobia was learned. Hence, the euphemism "developed." It had, in fact, reached the point where he was constantly monitoring his heart beat and the "way his chest felt." He was so aware of the beating of his heart that he often could not sleep for listening to it. This seemingly simple fear had in the space of two months almost immobilized a healthy adult male who professed to have few, if any, fears.

Not all phobias are as debilitating as this one was. All are irritating and unpleasant. Imagine avoiding elevators when working on the twentieth floor of a building due to a phobia of enclosed spaces. Imagine someone refusing a good job because the office is located on the twentieth floor of a building and the person has a phobia about heights. Phobias broadly can be managed as all fears can. In fact, we believe that phobias are often easier to treat than anxiety.

TREATMENTS

In this section we describe three ways in which a person can modify personally-held anxieties or phobias. We will describe each one and outline the steps to be followed and then present an example of individuals who have used the treatment to overcome their problem.

Paradoxical Intention. Paradoxical intention is a concept and a treatment form developed by Vicktor Frankl (1958, 1969, 1957) to treat phobias. Although Frankl is a psychoanalyst rather than a behavioral psychologist, we feel that this particular treatment can be described in behavioristic terms. We might add that we feel no qualms in borrowing what we think are highly successful and useful treatments or ideas from people who are not behaviorists. We certainly would be very narrow if we refused to include powerful techniques generated by those outside our field.

Paradoxical intention amounts to intending to do exactly what it is that you fear most. After doing this several times, you should be convinced of the illogical nature of your fear and be relieved of it. In other words, this technique from logotherapy, amounts to the person actively trying to do that thing that the person most fears (Tweedie, 1961). If, for instance, a person was extremely afraid (phobic) of blushing, then the person should try as hard as possible to blush. When the person discovers that it is not possible to control blushing behavior, the illogical nature of the fear is understood and, ultimately, controlled.

In operant terminology, we would describe paradoxical intention as a de-conditioning or desensitization process. The person is literally confronting the conditioned-fear-eliciting stimulus over and over without any unconditioned stimulus to support the fear respondent. What happens is the same thing that happens in any classical conditioning extinction process. When the conditioned-eliciting stimulus is called upon over and over to elicit the respondent (fear in this case) without the unconditioned stimulus to support it, the respondent will lose strength and gradually be completely extinguished. When extinction has occurred, the conditioned-eliciting stimulus no longer brings on (elicits) the fear response. It has once again taken on (or been assigned) the properties it had before the fear was learned in the first place.

Adapting Paradoxical Intention. Paradoxical intention may be adapted to attenuate any fear although it has most frequently been used to extinguish phobias (Gerz, 1966). For more serious fears, it is a good idea to build up the intent in imagination only at first and later move to the actual situation that provokes the fear. In this way the phobia is first discussed and imagined and then actually confronted. A phobia, remember, is a terrible and horrifying fear. If you have never observed a person with a phobia, it is difficult to imagine how terrifying merely discussing or imagining the fear can be. The steps to follow in applying paradoxical intention to a fear are listed below:

1. Identify the fear. (This is a rather ridiculous step to follow given one, overwhelming fear, but many individuals suffer more than one source of fear or anxiety. Think small, remember?)

2. Force yourself to intend to do exactly that which you fear.
   (a) If necessary, start with imagining the situation which is fear-provoking and then move to discussing it with someone.
   (b) Think about the result of your experience in terms of the logic of your behavior. List the fallacies of your fears.
3. Continue the confrontation process until the fear has been attenuated.

Only three steps. A very simple process, indeed. Or is it? The basis of paradoxical intention is the cognitive process within the individual, the recognition that the fear is illogical and useless. Once this point is reached, the fear is nearly overcome. The problem is getting this far. Paradoxical intention has been a recognized technique but implementing the technique is the problem. Fear can be such an overwhelming emotion that an individual often cannot confront it without tremendous support from family, friends, and a therapist. (More about this later.)

It is important to note that phobias or fears of some things can be damaging if the person goes out and directly confronts the source of fear! A phobia of falling out of a moving car can be overcome by eventually riding in a moving car—not jumping out of it. Of course, fears of uncontrollable situations or conditions, e.g., blushing, fainting, heart attacks, and so on, can be directly attempted. It is patently impossible to induce these in oneself without external intervention.

Example 1

The man we described earlier who had the phobia of heart attacks overcame his fear with the direct application of paradoxical intention. It was not difficult to identify the fear. In fact, it had become an obsession with him; he could think of almost nothing else. In talking with him we were informed that he had had a thorough physical examination within two weeks and that the doctor had judged him to be in excellent health. This, of course, did little to assuage the fear. From his constant stream of talk that dealt only with his fear of heart attacks, it was clear that there would be little purpose in having him further imagine a heart attack or to discuss the problem. Instead, with the supervision of a physician, we had him actively try to induce a heart attack. After much convincing, he did indeed try to induce a heart attack. He held his breath, jumped up and down and generally went into a rage for thirty minutes. When he was exhausted, he laughed long and hard. He couldn't do it! He had no control over his heart, other than to exercise or rest to alter the heart rate. His wife later told us that this was the first time she knew of his laughing at anything for more than six weeks. Furthermore, he was visibly relaxed, although tired.

We spent about thirty minutes discussing with him the physical impossibility of consciously starting or stopping the heart or of causing or avoiding heart attacks. After his experience, he agreed with us that his fear had been irrational. In fact, at that moment he could not quite understand why it had seemed so important only moments earlier. We instructed him to repeat the procedure, that is, to confront the fear of heart failure whenever his fear returned and to check back with us in a week. At the end of the week he returned and reported that he had beaten his fear. He found it necessary to go through the paradoxical intention routine only once during the week. On that occasion he had felt so silly that he again broke out laughing and had startled his wife to the point of asking what was wrong. He replied that nothing, nothing at all, was wrong.

Paradoxical intention was successful for this man because he was (1) convinced to try to do the impossible and (2) he saw the absolute illogic in his fear and then dismissed it. This is akin to being afraid of a big dog until you find that the dog is not harmful and, as a matter of fact, is a fine animal. The fear was pointless. This process, however, never deals with how the fear was learned or any underlying causes of the fear, if indeed there are any.

Our point is that fears often have no underlying cause other than the experiences that led to the fear. In cases where phobias or anxieties are symptoms of other disorders, we believe that removing one fear will not relieve the person and he will have to seek professional, clinical help to remove the causes of the fears. By the way, once a fear without some underlying cause (e.g., a psychotic or neurotic disorder) is unlearned, there are no loose ends left. The stimuli that elicited the fear are now neutral and there are no stray stimuli left around.

One note of caution to the reader: A thorough physical examination is in order before paradoxical intention should be attempted without supervision. Severe fears, fears that are so disabling as to be beyond what can be personally dealt with, must be treated by professionals. It is possible to cause damage if the problem is of a greater magnitude than that which could be considered to be a problem or fear of "normal" people.

Removal of Reinforcing Consequences. A large number of fears are supported in our repertoires of behavior by the consequences that these behaviors gain. Fear or anxiety can be highly reinforcing behaviors gaining attention, affection or more physical reinforcers such as cookies or candy. The extinction of operant-fear responses is highly similar to the control of any other operant behavior, although it is difficult sometimes to determine whether fear is operantly controlled or not. The most effective way to determine this is with a behavior analysis that is made during a baseline period of observation. This can be done by the individual, but is is highly unlikely that an individual with such a highly successful behavior (fear or anxiety) will be able to objectively determine the effects of the anxiety on others. What can be done, instead, is to remove all the possible reinforcers from other people during and after the fear responses and concentrate solely on appropriate behaviors.

An example of this is the small child who has discovered that fear or anxiety can be a great attention getter, a source of affection when the parents' energy is lagging, and often a source of overt goodies such as candy, milk or cookies. This behavior is learned very easily. If the parents ever provide attention, affection or physical reinforcers for anxiety or fear responses in the child, they increase the likelihood that such responses will occur more frequently in the future under similar circumstances. Alleviating a small child's fears is necessary but it must be wisely managed or the child will soon learn how to control the parents! The parents can control the inappropriate fears or anxieties but still support necessary fears by reinforcing only the appropriate occurrences of the responses and withholding reinforcement for inappropriate occurrences of the fear responses. From this, if a child is using fear as an attention getter, two things need to be considered. First, is the child obtaining enough attention and affection for appropriate behaviors? That is, is the fear or anxiety behavior necessary just to meet the child's needs or is it a source of extra, unnecessary goodies? Second, if the child is not receiving enough attention in other areas, the parents must see to it that this situation is remedied. All that is necessary to modify a child's inappropriate anxiety or fear behaviors is to totally ignore the behavior. It will eventually cease to appear. We encourage such parents, however, to increase their attention toward the child's appropriate behaviors.

On a more personal note, it is possible to eliminate the reinforcers a person has been obtaining from others for inappropriate behaviors. The steps to follow in developing such a treatment are listed below.

1. The inappropriate behaviors must be clearly defined in observable and unambiguous terms.
2. Once the behavior is defined, accurate records of the levels of occurrence of this behavior must be kept to determine the effectiveness of the treatment.
3. Instruct "significant" persons in the environment who may provide reinforcement for these inappropriate behaviors to ignore them totally and completely. This should include whatever family and friends are likely to provide the reinforcers in the form of sympathy, attention, affection, or encouragement.
4. Instruct them to reinforce non-anxiety or non-fear behaviors only.
5. Allow the re-learning process to take its course while continuing to maintain accurate records of the process.

Again, this seems to be a very simple program that can be outlined in five easily understood steps. It is very difficult to administer properly, though. It is necessary to obtain the complete cooperation of the others in the environment and this is not easily done, especially when their feelings and "common sense" tells them that the anxious or fearful person needs comforting. You must convince them that they will do much more to help you by ignoring your fear responses than they possibly could by attending to them.

EXAMPLE 2

Bobby, a nine-year-old fourth-grader, was suffering from severe anxiety, seemingly directed at everything and anything. He was a moderately bright boy but did not function well in school because of his frequent absences. His parents reported that Bobby was "a ball of nerves" and that he became ill very easily and could not be blamed for his lack of school achievement or his lack of friendship with boys his own age. Talking to Bobby, we were told that he did not always like being afraid and couldn't understand why so many things made him cry or upset him so. Of course, when he left our office and snuffled a little in the hallway, at least some of the reason for his high level of sustained anxiety became apparent. When he emitted a few shallow breaths and started to sob, his mother immediately stopped walking down the hall, went through the "mean old psychologist" routine, and paid strict attention to Bobby. Incidentally, Bobby managed to cop a new model airplane from his visit to our office. We were amazed at how well a little bit of anxiety worked. It provided attention, affection and model airplanes. A successful behavior if we had ever seen one!

The next day we scheduled a conference with the parents and Bobby. We talked to the parents first and pulled no punches about the whole business. We told them that we believed that *their* behavior was the reason for Bobby's high level of anxiety and further discussed how attention, affection and other goodies should be directed only toward appropriate behaviors. We don't need to discuss the emotional outburst, and the long argument. In the end, the parents agreed to ignore his inappropriate behaviors from that point forward. After nearly an hour of haggling, we asked Bobby in and discussed the approach with him. He agreed immediately, much to our surprise and helped all of us in the next hour by specifying exactly those inappropriate behaviors that were to be ignored. (Note: Bobby had been examined by a medical doctor and declared to be free from any form of physical problem prior to our first visit with him.)

We also developed a frequency count similar to those we have presented throughout the book and had the parents keep track of a general category called "anxiety responses" and graph this. We were in contact with the parents over the phone only for the next three weeks and on their next visit they presented us with the graph pictured in figure 9-1. Not only were the parents extremely happy about the change in Bobby's behavior; Bobby was happy. It had been

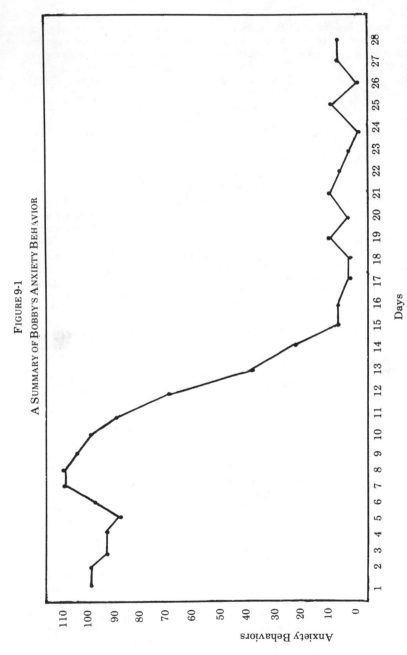

FIGURE 9-1

A SUMMARY OF BOBBY'S ANXIETY BEHAVIOR

Note: The graph above represents the frequency of occurrence of Bobby's anxiety behaviors as recorded by his parents over a 28-day period. There was no separate baseline period.

rough for the first week and a half. The complete dedication of the parents was necessary for the successful application of the treatment. The parents shifted their reinforcers to appropriate behavior so as not to be ogres and to make sure that Bobby had enough reinforcers, but the process was extremely difficult.

This extinction process of operantly-controlled fears is a very powerful technique but it depends almost completely on the kinds of cooperation that the person wanting to make the change can obtain from family and friends. These friends and family members must be highly disciplined and totally committed to making the change because the person may literally try anything to obtain the reinforcement that is being withheld.

Lastly, we do not feel that it is necessary to explain again how different forms of anxiety responses can be defined so as to allow a frequency count to be made. This is the same process as has been followed throughout the book.

Desensitization. There are many forms of desensitization that are practiced with varying degrees of success (Oliveau, 1969; O'Neil and Howell, 1960; Rachman, 1965, 1966a, 1966b; Rachman & Hodgson, 1967; Meldman and Hatch, 1969; etc.). We present here one form that is adaptable for self-administration. All desensitization processes are similar to the paradoxical intention procedure we introduced earlier. The nature of the desensitization process is to literally make the person less sensitive to those stimuli that have elicited fear responses. In desensitization, it is necessary to identify the stimuli that elicit the fear and then gradually approach this stimulus until the fear response has been extinguished. We believe that desensitization can overcome fears that are either respondent or operant in nature. The steps to follow in a desensitization process are as follows:

1. Identify the fear-eliciting (or evoking) stimulus. This could be high places, airplanes, crowded rooms, snakes, or almost any set of stimuli.
2. Determine how "closely" you can approach the stimuli. (This is not necessarily close in a physical sense although that will ultimately be a part of the process.)
3. Start at the closest approach you can make to the stimuli and gradually work your way closer and closer to the threatening stimulus, always going no further than you can comfortably advance. Set a goal for each day that will be an advancement and meet this goal.
4. Remove any possible sources of external reinforcement for your fear responses, e.g., sympathy and other reinforcers from friends and family.
5. If necessary, pair your closer and closer approaches to the fear stimulus with positive reinforcers.
6. Reach the stimulus (or as close as is logically feasible).

One of the things to be considered in dealing with the idea of "closeness" is that the word is here used as a psychological term, not a real measure of physical proximity. In determining how close you can come to an object, you may find that you can imagine being near the threatening stimulus, read about the threatening stimulus, talk about it or look at pictures of it. All of these are gradual steps closer and closer to the actual stimulus. In gradually approaching the threatening stimulus, care should be taken to go only so far each day as can comfortably be managed to be a step closer than the previous day. Reinforcers that could be paired with such an activity may be social or physical and should be used as rewards for more and more closely approximating the goal behavior. (Note: The term day is used as one convenient length of time between approaches to the threatening stimulus. We would suggest a time period no longer than two days and certainly no shorter than several hours between approaches to the threatening stimulus.)

EXAMPLE 3

A young man, who by the nature of his work, had to spend a considerable amount of time in the outdoors was extremely afraid of snakes. While a healthy respect for snakes, if not some fear, is necessary in working outdoors, a phobia of snakes that reaches debilitating levels is anything but a desirable state. In discussing this fear with the subject, we explained the desensitization process and encouraged him to give it a try. Identifying the threatening stimulus was not difficult: snakes, thoughts of snakes and areas where snakes were likely to appear. We believed that areas that were associated with snakes, such as thickets or swampy patches had become fear-eliciting stimuli by way of association with snakes and that we should work directly with the source of the fear, the snakes.

Our geologist agreed to a daily regimen of thinking about snakes once a day. At first he was to think about snakes and, as his fear diminished, he would follow the process of approaching the source of the fear. He rank-ordered the level of threat in snake-associated things in order of least threatening to most fear provoking thusly:

1. thinking about snakes
2. reading about snakes
3. talking about snakes
4. looking at a picture of a snake
5. looking at a real snake at a distance with the snake in a cage
6. moving closer to the caged snake
7. looking at a real snake at a distance with the snake outside a cage
8. standing within three feet of a snake

The geologist would go through these steps in desensitizing his fear. He decided that he needed no reward for his behaviors (in fact, he rewarded himself with feelings of accomplishment). He would put himself through the steps, availing himself of some snakes that were kept in the biology department of the university.

In a matter of four weeks he had reached the goal of standing within three feet of a snake without being more than "moderately" fearful. The self-administered desensitization process was a long and arduous ordeal but it did result in considerably diminished levels of fear for this man. We believe that the same kinds of fear control can be developed by others with reasonable amounts of effort. This process of desensitization of a stimulus is hard work and demands a full commitment. Initially, the geologist was extremely afraid of even talking about snakes or looking at pictures of them. He had to force himself through his behavior-change process.

Control of Generalized Anxiety. In the next chapter, we present a very thorough discussion of how both tension and generalized anxiety may be alleviated. We have already discussed the high degree of similarity between anxiety and tension. Our treatment of generalized anxiety and tension are identical. For generalized anxiety, anxious habits and so forth, we refer the reader to our discussion of tension.

SUMMARY AND FINAL COMMENTS

Fear is a learned emotion that is necessary to our survival. Fear has three components, as do all emotions: a respondent component, an operant component and the label. Inappropriate fears learned through respondent conditioning, stimulus generalization or operant conditioning can have very debilitating effects. Since fears are learned, they can be unlearned.

Anxiety is an irrational behavior that can be extinguished in the same manner as any other learned behavior. There are, however, some people who find anxiety to be a facilitative state leading to higher productivity.

Phobias are irrational fears learned in the same way as any other fears. Single traumatic events are often cited as the cause for phobias. Extinction of phobic behavior follows the same treatment as other fears.

The eliciting and discriminative stimuli in the environment control fear responses. Neutralization of these stimuli will reduce the fear behaviors.

Three treatments that can be adapted to self-administration for controlling fear are: paradoxical intention, a non-behaviorist technique; the removal of reinforcing consequences, a treatment for operantly controlled fear; and desensitization, a direct application of the typical respondent paradigm.

All three techniques have been used successfully.

It is important to remember that fears that are the result of other, underlying factors should be treated by specialists. Further, no treatment of fear responses should begin until the person has had a thorough and complete physical examination. The techniques included in this chapter were given for those persons we might call "normal," that is, persons who on occasions have high degrees of anxiety or fears and who need a little help in working through these fears. If there is any reason to believe that the problem is more complex than those described in this chapter, we refer the reader to the interlude following Chapter 10.

Chapter 10

Tension, Generalized Anxiety, and Nervous Habits

In this chapter we discuss the control of tension and generalized anxiety. Although tension is learned from anger or frustration responses rather than fear, from which anxiety is learned, we will treat them simultaneously in this chapter. The major reason for this is that the reader may have considerable difficulty in discriminating between tension and anxiety. The second reason is that we have commonly used the same treatments for both of the conditions. Hence, while the major thrust of this beginning section discusses tension, the reader should be aware that we are, for the purposes of treatment only, discussing tension and anxiety as synonymous conditions. In fact, as we have previously discussed, the internal bodily changes in both conditions are identical. The real difference is the label attached to the emotional state from the setting in which it occurs. That is, we may call the emotional state anxiety when we are in a position that we have learned should provoke fear, while we might refer to this same state as tension if we are in a position that we have learned should provoke anger.

The last section of this chapter details how "nervous" habits are learned and how they may be easily extinguished. Again, there is little purpose in assigning a particular emotional state to these habits, tension or anxiety, as the habits are likely to appear in either state and furthermore the treatments would be the same regardless.

TENSION

A considerable amount of attention has recently been drawn to the phenomenon of hypertension. Hypertension, in simple terms, merely means too much tension. Hypertension (which is variously defined by different authors) has been linked to strokes, heart attacks, and other forms of cardio-vascular problems (Young 1952). The distinction between tension and hypertension is difficult to ascertain and we feel that it probably must be made on an individual basis.

Tension (and generalized anxiety) is a condition in which the body is ready for action and no action is foreseen in the future. In other words, the heart rate is higher than if the person were at rest; the muscles of various parts of the body (primarily hands, jaws, neck and shoulders) are "made tense," i.e., are contracted, as though awaiting some shock; the eyes dilate somewhat to allow more light to pass (generally resulting in more acute vision); most of the other senses are also more acute; and the individual is less aware of pain.

Some of the bodily responses we listed above, primarily the tightening of muscles, are not automatic responses but are learned ones. The reader should soon see, however, why these responses were included. Although a precise physiological outline of all the bodily processes that occur during times of stress would be far longer than our brief description, we are here dealing with the personal control of such a state and not the specific bodily functions.

Generally, tension is the function of the human body under prolonged stress in which the body reacts to various environmental cues (discriminative and eliciting stimuli) as though maximum strength were necessary to meet environmental threats. Your body is reacting to stimuli that *do not* require physical action in a way that prepares the body *for physical action*. It is as though you were led to a boxing ring and told that you would fight the heavyweight champion of the world. Your body prepares itself through reactions of fear and anger. But if the actual physical release does not occur—you are just kept waiting and under the stress—your body will eventually exhaust itself with results that are highly unpleasant.

Considerable evidence exists that tension or prolonged stress can actually be useful in certain situations (Lazarus and Erickson, 1952; Hilgard, Jones and Kaplan, 1951; Korchin and Levine, 1957; etc.). For the most part, however, tension has results that most of us do not find gratifying: tremendous headaches, "nervous" tics, physical exhaustion for little discernable reason, grinding teeth until they break, emotional instability, or needing a few drinks every evening to "unwind."

Most of the people we have worked with in dealing with tension have wanted only to remove tension because of its debilitating effects. In the remainder of this chapter we will discuss the general treatment of tension, how it can be quantified and lastly, we will present two successful cases of clients who were able to reduce their levels of tension. The astute reader will notice that we are, as usual, approaching tension as a learned behavior (see the development of anxiety in Chapter 9) and describing methods that lead to unlearning tension behaviors and learning new responses. We will not specifically attempt to develop the pattern which describes how tension is learned since it is highly similar to the learning of anxiety responses. The major difference is that tension is generalized from anger responses, while anxiety is developed from fear responses. The processes of learning either emotional response are essentially the same.

BASIC PROCEDURES

Throughout our book we have stressed the importance of quantifying, defining and identifying those behaviors that are to be modified. It should come as no surprise to the reader that this is exactly what we believe to be the most important part of tension reduction treatment. We are convinced that if you can successfully learn to define, identify and quantify tension (generalized anxiety), that you will be very near to having control over the tension state.

Defining Tension and Generalized Anxiety. The most common characteristics of a definition of tension coincides with what you will use to identify anxiety. We frequently use various recognizable physical reactions as a means for identifying tension. In line with this, let us describe some general things that can be determined by observation to be a part of tension and then suggest how you can modify this to fit your situation.

The physical responses that we have found to be most clearly associated with tension and generalized anxiety are clenched teeth, tightened jaw muscles, tightened and strained neck muscles, compulsive flexing of various muscles, squinting and the general feeling of body "tightness." How often have you listened to presentation of a problem or considered a troublesome situation when you noticed that your teeth were tightly clenched, perhaps to the point that your jaws ached? Have you noticed that after some extremely harrowing days that your jaws or neck and shoulders ached? How about a headache that seems to be located at the base of your skull (your upper neck) and is also painful behind your eyes and low on your temples? These are most certainly the result of high, prolonged tension in the muscles in your neck, jaws and eyes, which incidentally restricts the flow of blood while other physical responses heighten your pulse rate and blood pressure, all of which combine for those terrible headaches. Have you ever been extremely angry or worried and found yourself clenching and unclenching your fists (flexing) or perhaps blinking your eyes very powerfully over and over? All these responses are signs of tension, or anxiety, leading us to define tension or anxiety as the appearance of any of these responses. Prolonged tension or anxiety, of course, generally produces more than one of these responses.

What has tension to do with headaches? This is a highly complex question and is really the province of your physician or a medical source. There are many reasons besides tension for headaches and if you are suffering from recurrent headaches, your first move should be to obtain a thorough examination from your physician, who can best guide your treatment. If tension is the cause of your headaches, though, we believe that you will find that your headaches will decrease as your levels of tension are reduced.

Self-defined Tension and Anxiety. Just because the responses we have listed are frequently the kinds of responses of many people who are tense or anxious is no reason to believe that any or all of these responses will describe your case. How can you determine what physical responses occur during periods of tension or anxiety for you? Well, ask yourself. Sit down and list those responses you remember emitting when you are tense. (Note: We are assuming that the reader has already determined when tension occurs and can identify, broadly, this occurrence.) If you have a hard time doing this, one simple technique we have employed is to suggest carrying a notepad along during the day and jot down how you felt and what was happening when in a state that you would identify as tense or anxious. Almost inevitably, the identification of "feeling tense" will lead to the identification of those physical responses during tension.

Identifying Tension and Anxiety. Now that we have defined tension and anxiety by the appearance of those physical responses that normally occur during tension or anxiety (e.g., tightened neck muscles) or if you have defined it for yourself, we need to attend to identifying tension or anxiety. First, the sooner you can identify the onset of tension or anxiety, the sooner you can deal with it and the less effect it will have on you in terms of wear and tear on your body, headaches or exhaustion. Second, as you become more and more familiar with the identification of tension or anxiety, you will become more adept at recognizing the symptoms before they take effect.

Identifying a behavior (a series of responses) such as tension or anxiety is far more difficult than identifying an overt behavior, such as smoking or eating, but it can be done in similar fashion. We have generally recommended two ways of identifying tension, each of which works well with different people. In cases where the problem of tension or anxiety is extreme, we generally suggest checking your physical state for signs of tension (those responses previously identified as part of the tension state) at periodic intervals throughout the day.

We have varied time intervals from fifteen minutes to an hour. In this kind of technique we recommend keeping a running diary of behavior during the day by making entries in the appropriate spaces during the predetermined time intervals. Figure 10-1 represents a typical chart for this form of logbook, which is usually very successful in helping the person identify those times at which tension or anxiety occur.

Another technique, which we have used less often, is carried out with the same form of logbook, but in this case we do not set predetermined times for entries. Rather, the person is to make entries at any time the onset of tension or anxiety is felt. Some individuals have done very well with this technique, but the problem exists of not identifying tension or anxiety until it has been present for several hours. We recommend the use of the logbook with reasonable time intervals at first. Later, when we have discussed the treatment of tension and some interesting phenomena concerned with it, we will see that the logbook is not necessary for protracted periods.

The Quantification of Tension and Anxiety. Tension and anxiety are general concepts that include a series of responses that do not lend themselves to simple quantification as do other behaviors, such as smoking or eating. There are certainly differences in levels of tension and anxiety, i.e., you may be tense for the same length of time on two different days, yet be more severely affected on one day than another. Certainly you could be "tense" for two hours on Monday without suffering as severely as you might after fifteen minutes of tension on Tuesday. These kinds of problems in quantification can be resolved if we have a lot of exotic equipment available and could hook you up to the machinery twenty hours a day, but this is highly impracticable. Since we cannot reasonably deal with the severity or quality of tension or anxiety, we will restrict ourselves to quantifying tension and anxiety in terms of length of occurrence or quantity. This can be done with either of the two techniques we have set forth for identifying tension. The first technique, that of logging the appearance of any responses that are indigenous to tension or anxiety at regular times through the day, allows us to graphically portray tension or anxiety by the total time it occurs or in percentages of the waking hours in which it occurred (see figure 10-1)

THE TREATMENT

Now that we have discussed how tension and anxiety are defined (or how they may be defined for you), how to identify tension and anxiety, and how to quantify them, it seems that the time has come to direct ourselves to the treatment of tension and generalized anxiety. However, before we discuss specific treatments, let us examine the effects of obtaining a baseline rate of tension or anxiety behaviors.

The reader will no doubt remember that all of our previous problem behaviors shared in the phenomenon of a decrement in their appearance after the client began to keep accurate records of the appearance of the various behaviors. Oddly enough, in our experience this phenomenon is strongest in dealing with tension or anxiety. Why is this so and what is the result?

Tension and anxiety, as we have alluded to above, are covert sets of responses, sets of responses that are not easily perceived. It is a great deal more difficult to notice the onset of tension or anxiety behavior than it is to notice the onset of eating behavior, for instance. Furthermore, it is much more difficult to analyze the behavior (tension and anxiety) than to determine what consequences of the behavior support them. However, it is possible to inhibit the respondents without altering the consequences of behavior, that is, to deal directly with the respondent without altering the environment. Very often if people become sensitive to the onset of tension or anxiety, their levels of tension or anxiety drop off precipitously. The major part of controlling tension or anxiety, evidently, is to become aware of the emotive state in the first place. Many individuals, when realizing that they are tense or anxious, can force themselves to relax and to inhibit the respondents consciously.

RELAXATION

The method that we prefer in working with tension or anxiety is that of enforced self-relaxation whenever tension or anxiety is identified. There are several ways that this can be accomplished, but we generally have the person (in our presence) relax in an arm chair as much as is possible consciously. We attempt to have the person become a wet noodle figuratively and purposely relax every muscle in the body. The person is then instructed to follow this procedure whenever tension or anxiety occurs. We have found this to be a reasonably successful treatment but it does have its drawbacks. Complete relaxation is often not practical, e.g., while driving a car or in the middle of a business conference. Strangely, however, many people, once they have practiced inhibiting tension or anxiety, are able to "step down" their levels of tension or anxiety and literally stop those responses associated with these emotions. Most have told us that this could be done just by making an effort to relax. Often we have suggested getting up from work and taking a walk or stopping for coffee as a means of helping the relaxation process.

Regardless of the efficacy of this technique for some, the best method of attenuating levels of tension is to locate the tension or anxiety producing stimuli and either remove them or extinguish the responses that they bring forth. This is only practical when the conditioned stimuli can be pinpointed. If they can be pinpointed, then they can either be avoided or paired with a reinforcing activity until they lose their potency. Desensitization, paradoxical intention and the operant control of fear responses, can also be adapted to control tension and certainly, anxiety.

An outline for the control of tension and anxiety is provided below:

1. Define the behavior so that identification of the behavior can readily be made.

2. Keep a baseline of the behavior for a period of a week or so.

3. Start forcing yourself to relax when tension first appears by consciously relaxing your muscles, leaving your work and unwinding somewhat, or just changing your task to a less rigorous one.

4. Avoid "sure-fire" tension or anxiety-producing situations un-

Figure 10-1

A Typical Daily Log for Quantifying Anxiety and Tension Behaviors

Time	Conditions	clenched jaw	clenched teeth	"nervous mannerisms"	who with
8:00					
9:00					
10:00					
10:30					
11:00					
11:30					
12:00					

Note: The chart above is an example of a chart that may be used to determine the onset of tension or anxiety by way of the responses that usually accompany it. Elapsed time of tension and anxiety behaviors can be inferred from such a graph as well as the conditions surrounding the emotional behavior.

til you feel confident that you can manage your behavior. If you are wondering how to do this, we have a few suggestions:

First, unclench your teeth, or any other muscular tightness you may feel. (If this seems odd, flex the muscle in your forearm right now. Make a fist and pull your fist back toward the inside of your arm as though you were pulling a rope. Hold your arm in this flexed condition for a moment and then relax your arm thoroughly. This is the same relaxation process you want to follow with other parts of your body during stress. It also helps to feel these tightened muscles with your hands to determine whether they are completely relaxed or not. You should feel these muscles when you are very relaxed first so that you will know how they should feel when you are trying purposely to relax.

Second, if possible, change activities until your body relaxes. If you are at your desk working on something that has elicited tension or anxiety, leave it and work on something more relaxing, or just take a break for a few moments. Third, ask yourself why you are tense or anxious. Look at the situation and see if it really warrants your emotional state. Sometimes a logical examination of the situation is enough to "defuse" the tension.

5. Inhibit tension responses to stimuli that have in the past elicited it. Refer to figure 10-1, and notice a column for describing the situation that was thought to elicit the tension response. Since our assumption is that this situation became a conditioned stimulus for tension or anxiety (or is similar in form to another stimulus that was conditioned, i.e., stimulus generalization) and since you are aware that no real physical threat is present, restructure this stimulus in your thoughts so that it does not elicit tension or anxiety. This can be done by pairing a positive experience with this eliciting stimulus until you stop responding to it as though your life were being threatened. This is similar to "getting used to things," such as driving, high places, etc.

6. Set up reinforcing contingencies for falling below an allowable level of tension (anxiety) every day. In other words, provide yourself with a reward that is potent enough for you to want it for eliminating tension or anxiety. (Note: Noxious consequences are seldom applied to anxiety or tension states because these techniques often generate their own tension. It would seem to be a self-defeating process to use either the Premack principle or contingent noxious consequences to attempt to modify anxiety or tension behaviors.)

7. If situations cannot be avoided that elicit tension or anxiety responses, an evaluation of these situations is in order. Divide a piece of paper into two columns. On the right, list all the bad, horrible, nasty things that could happen to you in this situation. On the left, list all the good things that can happen to you. Now go back and place an estimate of the probability that the bad things actually will happen in a new third column. Now stop and think about it. How bad is this

situation? Still not convinced? All right, now produce a fourth column to the extreme right. In this column count each of the bad things that could happen along with how your state of tension or anxiety helps you to cope with these bad things or helps you to avoid them. The chances are, if you get this far, that you should be convinced of the futility of tension or anxiety as a means of stopping these bad things from happening. An example of this chart appears in figure 10-2.

FIGURE 10-2

AN EXAMPLE EMOTIONAL EVALUATION CHART

problem	good things	bad things	probability	How the emotion helps

Note: The chart above may be used when considering how to reduce the levels of tension or anxiety.

8. If the tension or anxiety you experience cannot be easily treated by self-administration and you find the tension or anxiety to be irritating, see a medical doctor to determine the state of your health. If the problem is not physical, you should consider seeing a private psychologist or psychiatrist. There are as many reasons for inappropriately high levels of tension and anxiety as there are people

who experience them. We are aware that some people experience tension or anxiety or experience eliciting stimuli that provoke the emotional states from sources that are not readily apparent. As we have mentioned, the best method of treating tension or anxiety is to extinguish the respondents to those stimuli that elicit the anxiety or tension respondents. This may only be possible under the guidance of a clinician who, after all, has a considerable edge on most lay people in terms of training and experience in dealing with inappropriately learned responses. Our method, related in this discussion, is only for those who can literally "counter-condition" themselves, i.e., people who can recognize the symptoms of tension or anxiety and consciously inhibit these responses. It is highly successful for many, but many others need the direct support and help of a clinician.

EXAMPLE 1

A young, female graduate student who also worked full time came by our office complaining of tension and the headaches that accompanied the tension. She related to us that although she felt that she had the ability to perform well in school and at work, her feeling of tension often kept her from performing her duties well, primarily when she suffered "tension headaches." Our first reaction, of course, was to send the lady to a medical doctor for a complete checkup. On her return the following day she indicated to us that she had a clean bill of health but the doctor had suggested that she spend more time relaxing. Since this is what we hoped to accomplish , it seemed cogent to go on with a modification of her behavior.

We explained the physiological aspects of tension to her and talked over the signs (responses) she had when she knew that she had been in a stress situation for some time. We then agreed that she would keep a logbook, making entries on an hourly basis for one week before we went further. Figure 10-3 represents the graduate student's levels of tension.

We did not see her again for two weeks. During this period, her

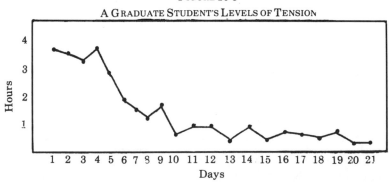

FIGURE 10-3

A GRADUATE STUDENT'S LEVELS OF TENSION

Note: The above graph is drawn from a series of daily logs that this student kept on her tension responses.

sensitivity to the detection of tension had evidently heightened and she had taken control of the situation (see figure 10-3). Since her levels of tension had dropped to almost zero (she reported that she could now feel the onset of tension and force herself to relax), we felt that nothing else needed to be done. Evidently, for this young woman, the identification of tension alone led to a heightened sensitivity of tension responses which allowed her to gain control and remove tension and the effects of tension, headaches and so forth. She told us that it had been remarkably easy, once she had known what to look for and made it a part of her daily activities.

Example 2

Not everyone, however, is as lucky as to be able to "grab the bull by the horns" and totally inhibit an undesirable set of responses. Mr. Karnes, a middle-aged businessman, had just completed a physical examination and was told in no uncertain terms that he must start relaxing and avoiding tension or anxiety-producing situations. Assuming that we knew something about this business, he dropped by our office to talk over the tension reduction plans he had been formulating. He was already planning to restrict his working day to a maximum level of six hours a day for five days a week, but felt that there might be some points he was missing. We found that he was already well versed in the physiology of stress emotions and that he felt sure that he could not avoid tension merely by being aware he was tense.

We discussed his personal signs of tension, clenching fists, clenching teeth, blinking his eyes very forcibly and other less apparent behaviors, and agreed that he would take a baseline of his tension-oriented behaviors via a logbook for a period of one week. Figure 10-4 represents Mr. Karnes' levels of tension.

On his return a week later, we were dismayed to see that his levels of tension had not been attenuated at all by merely keeping a daily log. In examining his logbook, it seemed that his highest levels of tension/anxiety occurred during times when he was in meetings of various kinds. We suggested that he try to start pairing meetings with some positive experiences and to further try to relax his body as he had done experimentally in our office. We then spent the next forty minutes having Mr. Karnes try to relax as much as he could by conscious control of his body. We had him flex and unflex his neck muscles and to touch these areas in both conditions so that he would be very familiar with how his body felt under both conditions. We suggested before falling asleep that evening he should note how his body felt while it was relaxed. He should then try to duplicate this feeling of relaxation whenever he noticed the onset of tension while at work. He agreed to start trying to shift meetings to situations which he found pleasant, and further agreed to try to become totally relaxed at least three times a day, besides trying to force himself to relax at the onset of tension. The result of his new approach is pictured in the "treatment 1" part of figure 10-4.

As the reader can see, the levels of his tension were attenuated, but were still not at optimal levels. Thoughts of "making decisions" still corresponded with tension responses. At this point we decided to try a novel approach and had Mr. Karnes draw up a "statement of importance" for each decision he had to make. In this statement he listed the possible outcomes of his decision, other people that had input into the decision, and how sure (in a percentage estimate) he was that his decision was correct, and whether or not tension could help solve the problems. He was to continue as before and check with us in another week. The results of this third week are pictured in the "treatment 2" section of figure 10-4.

The levels of his tension dropped still further, but did not reach what he felt were acceptable levels. By thinking about the outcomes of his decisions, he had been able to further lower his tension levels, but not to extinguish them. At this time we felt that Mr. Karnes would do better with a clinician and referred him to a local analyst on his agreement with this recommendation. Mr. Karnes' treatment was not a failure; it did successfully reduce his levels of tension. However, we could not totally eradicate the responses. Mr. Karnes eventually left his job and took one considerably less demanding. As we pointed out earlier, the best way to prevent tension or anxiety is to remove the stimuli that elicit them.

Nervous Habits

In a general chapter on tension and anxiety reduction, it seems appropriate to direct ourselves to "nervous habits" which, in truth, may or may not have anything to do with tension, anxiety, or "nervousness." "Nervous habits" can be defined as conditioned responses (habits) that we perform for no directly discernable reason, except, perhaps, because we are "nervous." We believe that most of those responses we identify as nervous habits (e.g., pulling at an earlobe, pulling at a beard, pulling at a moustache, snorting, drumming fingers, etc.) are superstitious behaviors. That is, they are responses that have been accidentally or vicariously reinforced in the presence of certain stimuli (discriminative stimuli) until they are fixed into our pattern of behavior. After such superstitious behaviors have been reinforced, they are highly likely to appear in the presence of those discriminative stimuli (or stimuli that are similar to the original discriminative stimuli) in the future. Sometimes they will be reinforced and sometimes not. At any rate, if they do appear frequently, it can be assumed that there is enough reinforcement to maintain them.

We've introduced some jargon and to make clearer what we're getting at, let us examine one of our favorite examples. Snorting (blowing through the nose) is an irritating habit that is difficult to extinguish. How does a person first develop this habit? If snorting is

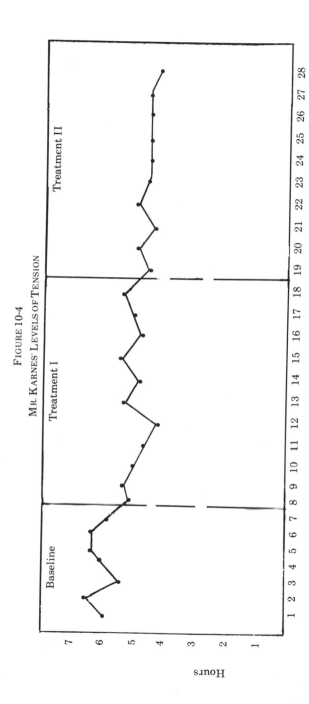

FIGURE 10-4

MR. KARNES' LEVELS OF TENSION

Note: The above graph represents Mr. Karnes' tension responses expressed by the amount of time they lasted on each day. Note the gradual decrease across the treatments, but the intractableness of the response.

not a habit, when are you likely to snort? People most frequently snort in response to blocked nostrils, discomfort in the nostrils, nasal passage or sinuses, or a feeling that there is some substance in the nasal passages that must be removed. Some of this behavior is reflexive. If a bug flies up your nose, you will probably snort reflexively without "thinking" about it. Reflexive behavior, though, seems to be just a small part of the total pattern of snorting behavior. Most of the snorting behavior is operant. Some stimulus (a noxious stimulus) causes an irritation of one sort or another in your nasal passages and to remove it you snort.

noxious stimulus   response (snort)   relief (a negative reinforcer)

This is the negative reinforcement paradigm we described in Chapter 2. Because the response (snort) removed or relieved the noxious stimulus, the person is more likely to snort given a similar noxious stimulus in the future. Snorting is then fixed into a pattern in which it follows discomfort of a certain form, as opposed to picking the nose (another irritating habit), blowing the nose, using a nasal spray, and so forth. We have explained why snorting is likely to occur, but we have not yet determined why it appears at times when it is inappropriate.

Once snorting does occur during the presence of a noxious stimulus, snorting is likely to occur in many situations that have little or nothing to do with the noxious stimulus that evokes the snorting. Your nostrils may feel uncomfortable while driving to work. Hence, you snort. Then, you may snort while in an argument, while winning a bet, or while you're struggling to wade through a difficult passage in a book. In fact, snorting may occur at the same time a lot of other things are going on.

Let us suppose that while you are putting the finishing touches on a difficult paper that has aroused considerable tension, your nasal passages become somewhat blocked, and because it has been reinforced in the past by alleviating this sort of bad feeling, you now start snorting. Further, let us assume that you are still snorting while your boss or teacher or editor looks over your paper and tells you it is a good piece of work and you are to be congratulated. All of a sudden, the tension (anxiety) drains from your body and a feeling of relief (a reinforcer) infuses you, along with the reinforcement from the evaluator of your paper. What has this accidental pairing of a few behaviors likely resulted in?

snort
+
feeling of anxiety   consequences   (reduction in
+   anxiety other
turn in paper   }   reinforcers)

Paired   together

What is highly likely is that snorting and whatever other responses were going on, such as writing in a certain way, using a particular format and so forth, are all reinforced by the reduction in anxiety and other reinforcers. What this causes is a heightened probability that given similar circumstances you will bring forth the same response(s). In other words, if you are highly anxious in the future, you will be more likely to snort than you were before. Obviously, more than a feeling of anxiety is present in such a situation. Snorting could just as well become paired with the discriminative stimulus of working on a paper, sitting in the office and other stimuli.

One reinforcement, though, is hardly likely to fix a response into your behavioral repertoire permanently. However, if snorting is paired a few more times with anxiety reduction, it soon will become an "automatic" response to the feeling of anxiety (a noxious, but nevertheless discriminative stimulus). As you can infer from our basic discussion of operant conditioning in chapter two, once such a response has been fixed, it can continue to be emitted on a schedule of reinforcement that provides very little reinforcement at highly irregular and infrequent intervals.

Well, snorting is just one example, and is one that can be traced to a reasonable operant (or respondent) behavior. How about some of the more obscure behaviors that appear as nervous habits? Can they be traced the same way? Yes, but with somewhat more difficulty. Let us examine the habit of running a thumb over the tip of the other fingers.

Running your thumb over the tips of your fingers is not likely a respondent (reflexive behavior). It is also a highly unlikely operant to occur unless you've got glue or some other substance on your fingertips. In other words, moving your thumbs over the tips of your fingers is not a behavior that seems to serve much purpose and it is a highly unlikely behavior. How does such a behavior, or other equally unlikely behaviors, become nervous habits?

SHAPING

If you will recall our discussion of shaping from chapter two, you will remember that shaping is the reinforcement of gradual successive approximations of some goal behavior until the goal behavior is reached and is fixed into the organism's repertoire of behaviors. Shaping is the process used, although accidentally, to develop some superstitious behaviors, like running the thumb over the tips of fingers. During some situation in which other responses were reinforced (finishing a paper, successfully making an oral argument, etc.) the first, rough approximation of the thumb-running behavior occurred. Perhaps this was only an accidental touching of the end of the index finger with the thumb. As you know, such a vicarious reinforcement of a response will increase the likelihood of its appearance in the future. So, the next time the person is in a similar situation to the one which accidentally reinforced the thumb/index finger contact, it will likely happen again.

Consider, however, what happens if the reinforcement occurs somewhat later than before, for example, when the thumb is touching the index finger and the next finger. Now, with similar conditions in the future, the response will be slightly different, the thumb will touch both fingers. If this accidental shaping goes on over a period of time, eventually we obtain the response of running the thumb over all the fingers, back and forth. This does seem a little far-fetched, but many far more complex superstitious behaviors can be developed totally by accident.

Setting Conditions

From the previous examples, the reader can infer that not all behaviors become paired with the discriminative stimuli of anxiety, tension, or "nervousness." Some such behaviors, in fact, can be paired with almost any discriminative stimuli that can be named. One note is of interest here. Feelings (e.g., anxiety, fear, anger, happiness, etc.) form discriminative stimuli of their own. The state of your organism in every form of feeling is different. The state of the organism is a series of literally hundreds of internal cues that tell you how to act. It is no wonder that certain responses are present during periods of one kind of feeling but not present during other kinds of feelings. It is unlikely, for example, that you would clench your teeth and growl while extremely happy. Not only do external stimuli function as discriminative stimuli, internal stimuli do, too.

Now that we have some idea as to how habits are formed, we ought to be able to find some operant techniques for extinguishing them. In the following sections, we will discuss the extinction of "nervous" habits. The same procedures can be followed to extinguish any habit; they need not be necessarily considered to be "nervous" in nature.

Extinguishing Nervous Habits

Since we have determined that "nervous" habits are operant forms of behavior, we ought to be able to apply a whole series of operant techniques to eliminate them. This is exactly the case and we will describe different forms of treatment that will allow the reader to self-administer the extinction of "nervous" habits.

Over-Kill

One method that we have found to be highly successful is based on the general nature of extinction. If a response occurs often enough without reinforcement, it will cease to occur altogether. To facilitate this we use a technique we call over-kill. In this technique, the inappropriate response is first defined and an attempt is made to determine what reinforcers are supporting the response. Then we have the person emit this response over and over (sometimes hundreds of times) while preventing reinforcement from occurring. Eventually, the response will cease to occur. The reader will note that no baseline is taken in this technique. This is a "quicky" that either works immediately or it does not work at all. If the technique works, then the response will be terminated and no need for records exists. If the technique does not succeed, we move to another treatment, one with the normally rigorous levels of measurement.

This method has the advantages of being a relatively simple technique that can be performed without guidance or help. It also generally provides quick results. The drawbacks include the possibility that the reinforcers may never be fully identified and that spontaneous recovery (see chapter 2) can occur. Let us list the steps for this procedure and then provide an example of how it has been used.

1. Define the inappropriate response.
2. Locate possible reinforcers.
3. Perform the inappropriate response as many times consecutively as possible.
4. Continue to withhold the reinforcement.

Incidentally, this technique could be used with a baseline and a follow-up record of the response to determine whether or not it is successful. If one or two trials of overkill do not work, however, we suggest that the reader try one of our other techniques.

EXAMPLE 3

One young man had the habit of snorting, the one we discussed above. His snorting seemed to have started over the Christmas vacation and had become progressively worse to the point of irritating his wife, children and co-workers. He wanted to remove this one response as soon as possible and gain some relief. While he was discussing the snorting, it became worse despite his active efforts to control it. He told us that it seemed to be worse during times when he was angry or upset, especially if someone pointed out that he was snorting.

The behavior was easy to define, the occurrence of any audible noise generated through the nose. This included actions like blowing the nose, too, but as we will see, that was not a problem in this instance.

The reinforcers for the behavior could not be observed, but we inferred that the snorting had been paired with various reinforcers that had appeared during feelings of anxiety or tension, much as in our earlier discussion.

It occurred to us that one method that could ease this habit rather rapidly would be to force it to occur over and over without reinforcement. Besides, if that didn't work, we could always try something else.

We explained to our client the idea of extinguishing his snorting behavior by literally having him snort until exhaustion. He was ready to try it, although he thought it somewhat strange. To make a long story short, he sat there and snorted continually for thirty minutes, until he could not bring himself to do it again. We instructed him to do this every time he caught himself snorting for the next few days and to check back with us.

Well, we must admit that he was rather dubious about the procedure, but we felt that if such a short procedure would work, there would be little reason to go through a longer procedure. At any rate, he returned two weeks later and announced that after two marathon sessions of snorting his habit seemed to have disappeared. He was happy and we were happy. He decided that if the snorting returned, he would try the same thing again.

This example is not a well-documented, shining example of behavior modification. It is, however, one technique that we have found to be successful on many occasions and we continue to recommend it on the basis of a high success rate as compared to the time it takes to go through it.

Contingency Management and "Nervous Habits."

Our old standby, the management of contingencies, is one of the most effective means of treating nervous habits. As one would expect, the technique is highly similar to others we have already described.

The idea of using contingency management to control or modify nervous habits is based on the concepts of response cost and competing responses. Briefly, given two possible responses, the organism will opt for the response with the greatest amount of payoff. Similarly, when two responses could occur at the same time, they are generally referred to as competing responses. The response that gains the greatest amount of reinforcement will likely be the "winner" and be the response ultimately fixed into an organism's behavioral pattern.

What we attempt to do in the management of contingencies supporting a "nervous" habit, is to make the response cost of the "habit" as unappealing as possible while at the same time making the response that competes with the habit a highly attractive alternative. Not snorting is a response or lack of a response that competes directly with snorting. Only one of the two behaviors is possible at any given time. Eventually, whichever is the most reinforcing will be the behavior that is performed. This is done by developing contingencies that will support nonappearance of the inappropriate response (the habit) which can be considered to be a response by itself. At the same time we try to develop contingencies which will make the inappropriate behavior an undesirable behavior. We try to set up the consequences of these various behaviors so that the gain from snorting (the reinforcer) will be far outweighed by the loss of reinforcers for not snorting and the gain of noxious consequences for snorting.

This procedure is not really as complex as we have made it sound. Snorting is going to be reinforced on occasion, no matter what we do. It either makes the person feel better in some way or is paired with other kinds of reinforcers. What we try to do is make the stuff that happens to you for snorting worse than what you gain by snorting while at the same time rewarding (reinforcing) non-snorting behavior.

Perhaps an example would be worthwhile. Let us suppose that you could rob a bank and gain $5000 (reinforcement). However, if you rob the bank, we guarantee that you will also be put in prison for ten years (punishment) and we are going to stop paying you $500 a month not to rob the bank. Which alternative, robbing the bank or not robbing the bank, is the best alternative? Well, the answer for most of us would be to not rob the bank. It is a simple matter of response cost. What we attempt to do with "nervous" habits is basically this same process.

Caution: Compulsions are not the same thing as habits.

Warren (1933), defined a compulsive behavior as one that cannot be controlled, even consciously. Clinical definitions have not varied much since that time.

Compulsions should be treated by clinical specialists, not by books you pick up off the shelf. Further, the techniques we describe below can generate enough anxiety and fear to worsen habits. They are techniques that have worked well for us in the past, but severe or bizarre habits should be treated by a clinician.

As the reader glances over this technique, the techniques for weight loss and speech modification will probably be recalled. The techniques are very similar. Why, then, have we been so careful in dealing with "nervous" habits as opposed to other behaviors? Our answer is that some "nervous" habits may merely be part of the symptoms of some much deeper problem (Coleman, 1956; McNeil, 1970b; Stone & Stone, 1969) and since we suggested medical advice prior to weight loss, can we do less with equally serious problems?

Remember the "piggy-bank" technique we discussed in modifying speaking behaviors? Exactly the same approach can be used in modifying "nervous" habits with equal success. To refresh the reader's memory, the following steps should be carried out:

1. Specify thoroughly the behavior to be modified.

2. Keep a baseline record of the levels of occurrence of this behavior for a period of about one week.

3. Carry a piggy bank (or other, similar receptacle) around with you and place a penny or a nickel in the bank every time the response occurs.

4. Continue keeping track of the behavior.

5. Donate the proceeds, irretrievably to some disliked source (if necessary).

As is usual, once the process of keeping track of the behavior has started, the inappropriate behavior tends to occur less frequently.

The consequences of losing a sum of money during the intervention phase (you have intervened) is a purposive attempt to make the cost of the inappropriate response higher than the return or gain from that response. This sort of technique works well when there is no high level of anxiety surrounding the habit.

In case the piggy-bank procedure has too many problems involved, if it produces anxiety and heightens the level of the inappropriate responses—we suggest the direct application of the Premack Principle to the problem. Again, this technique is highly similar to those we mentioned earlier in applying the Premack Principle to other responses. The steps to follow in implementing the application of the Premack Principle are as follows.

1. Define the behavior.
2. Keep a baseline record of the behavior.
3. Set up daily criteria (goals) for the behavior-change process immediately after the baseline period.
4. Decide what behaviors to hold contingent upon meeting the daily criteria you have established.
5. Put your treatment into effect while continuing to keep accurate records. Your records should be posted in a conspicuous place.
6. If you have trouble meeting your criteria, try setting up noxious consequences for failing to meet the criteria in addition to your Premackian consequences.
7. Still having trouble? Try setting up a daily log similar to the one discussed in the weight loss chapter and record the conditions surrounding your behavior. Determine the times of day your responses occur, who you are with, how you felt, and other pertinent conditions that may affect the response. From this information, change your habits by performing an acceptable response (chewing gum or taking a walk for example) in the place of inappropriate responses.

Either of these two techniques in which the consequences of the behavior are adjusted so as to make them undesirable in terms of their "cost" to you, can be highly successful, but only, as we have pointed out, when the behavior is not a symptom of some more serious problem. Exhaustion, malnutrition, anxiety, frustration and fear or anger are some of the sources for "nervous" habits. You may find that knocking off work for a few days or changing your daily schedule remediates the problem. If you are unable to effect change by the methods we outline in this chapter, we suggest that you first obtain a thorough medical examination. It may be that a change of diet or some rest are the prerequisites for alleviating nervous habits. If the problem is not physical in nature, then we urge you to consult with a clinician.

SUMMARY

In this chapter we applied some of the techniques of behavior modification to tension and anxiety reduction and control. First, it is necessary to adequately define the behavior. Second, the behavior must be identified as it appears and thoroughly quantified. Third, the individual on identifying tension or anxiety must inhibit those tension responses, causing the body to relax. Fourth, if inhibition is not successful, then eliciting stimuli must either be avoided or reconditioned.

Self-treatment of tension, anxiety or nervous habits has many limitations. The techniques, if properly applied, can help the behavior-change process. In situations where stress is extreme, external help by a specialist is often the best solution. One of the best methods of dealing with tension and anxiety, though, is developing the ability to identify it, and to remain aware of what is happening. Awareness is the key.

Nervous habits can be controlled as can any other operant behaviors. The adaption of overkill, the piggy-bank method, or the Premack Principle all can lead to self-administered extinction of nervous habits. As with the control of anxiety and tension, if a person cannot reasonably administer self-control, a specialist should be consulted.

A Postscript to Part II:
The Control of Emotions

Seeking Professional Help

In the last two chapters we have emphasized the importance of seeking professional help if there is any reason to believe that the problem you are working with is anything out of the ordinary. It is pertinent to consider the concept of normality for a few moments, however, before we discuss the scope of the problem and how one may go about obtaining professional help. The idea of normality is a statistical concept that has very little value to a working psychologist. Almost any person you could point to would have at least one abnormality. If a man is taller than 5'9", weighs more than 160 pounds, has an I.Q. of over 100 and has more than 11.7 years of education, then that man is abnormal in each of these characteristics. Most of us would agree, however, that all of these characteristics would be advantageous, that is, we would most likely agree that being taller than average, brighter than average, etc. would be a good thing.

Normal in its strictest interpretation refers only to the arithmetical average. Obviously, most people are not going to be average or normal; it is a statistical impossibility. For our purposes, normality is used only to exclude people suffering from psychotic reactions or severe neurotic reactions. It is most assuredly *not abnormal* to seek help for your emotional or behavioral problems. Though data is not available to prove it, we believe that at least 90 percent of us discuss our problems with other people, and if we do not receive professional help, at least we go to someone to unburden ourselves.

We have not really delved into the areas of mental health or mental hygiene, but it is necessary to note that Carroll (1969) estimates that 10 percent of the (American) population will suffer from some form of serious mental disturbance. He further estimates that the number of people with at least temporary neuroses will be much higher than 10 percent.

To give the reader an idea of how many people at times need special help, in 1972 there were sixty-four thousand psychologists and at that, many mental health facilities were understaffed (Compton, 1972). As long ago as 1962, 1.5 million people were seeing psychiatrists in one year (U.S. Department of Health, Education and Welfare, 1966). Estimates differ from author to author concerning the number who will need help and at what level they will need help. Our purpose here, however, is not to show the reader statistics concerning how many people see clinical specialists in a given year, but rather to try to convince the reader that it is a common occurrence and one that should not be a source of embarrassment or shame.

There are many sources of help available and we will briefly list and describe these from our point of view. Incidentally, if you happen to be one of those listed and do not like where we listed you, we are, at least, allowed to have an opinion about it, whether or not it is absolutely correct.

COUNSELORS

The term counselor is a highly ambiguous term that includes, from time to time, car sales personnel, finance counselors, employment agency counselors, guidance counselors at all levels, and, counseling psychologists. Generally speaking, trained counselors (those with at least a master's degree in guidance and counseling or counseling psychology) are professional helping-people who work with 'normal' people with 'normal' problems. (Read normal problems as problems that are not psychotic in nature, problems that are not extremely severe). Doctoral-level counseling psychologists usually have a clientele with far more serious problems than the master's level counselor. In any event, trained counselors are a good place to start if you have determined that you need help in dealing with your problems. Professional counselors are bound by a highly rigorous code of professional ethics (The American Personnel and Guidance Association or the American Psychological Association) which will either help them determine that they can help you, or if necessary, refer you to someone who may be of more assistance.

Counselors are available at all institutions of higher education and most secondary schools. If you are in such a setting, the counselor is a good person to see.

ASSORTED BEHAVIOR-CHANGE PSYCHOLOGISTS

There are all kinds of psychologists who may dabble in behavior change as a part of their professional work. These include behavior modifiers, educational psychologists, social psychologists, school psychologists, and community psychologists among others. If you know of such a person, determine whether he is licensed before approaching for consultation. Chances are that if not licensed, the psychologist will not take you on as a client, but still can be of great help and may be able to refer you to someone who more directly meets your needs.

Licensing is generally carried out by the various state boards of healing arts in conjunction with the American Psychological Association guidelines. The reader can be assured that if the person is licensed with the state board of healing arts as a psychologist (clinical psychologist in some states) that he probably has a doctorate and has had the necessary experiences to conduct a practice. The reader should find very often, though, that the great majority of psychologists will not treat problems that are out of their area of special training. For example, it is extremely doubtful that the reader could locate a licensed psychologist who is an expert in behavior modification who would be willing to perform any kind of hypnotherapy.

CLINICAL PSYCHOLOGISTS

Clinical psychologists are doctoral level non-medical clinicians with expertise, training and an internship in working with all forms of mental and emotional problems. They generally have had extensive training both in theory and in direct application under the supervision of practicing clinicians. Clinical psychologists are equipped to work with any form of emotional, personal or behavioral disorder. The reader should carefully determine what the guidelines for licensing are in the particular state. Some states have a Clinical Psychologist II level of licensing which generally indicates a person not holding a doctorate degree.

PSYCHIATRISTS

Psychiatrists are medical doctors in addition to having training similar to that of clinical psychologists. Whenever organic problems are in any way associated with emotional, personal or behavioral disorders, we recommend psychiatric help. Only psychiatrists of all the workers in mental health areas are able to prescribe medicines and conduct physical examinations.

Who should you go see? When should you go see someone and how will you know who to choose?

If you are currently at an educational, military or business organization, we believe that your first step should be to see the people at the organization counseling center. You and the counselor should be able to determine rather quickly whether his services will meet your needs or not. If the answer is not, they will have a list of other professionals to whom you can be referred.

If it seems that the counseling services are what you need, you still have the right to shop around and find the counselor with whom you feel most comfortable. Whether we like to admit it or not, human nature is such that you may not hit it off with some counselors and vice versa. If you are going to counseling, the prime concern should be that you feel that the counselor has your best interests at heart, is really interested in you, tuned in to what you say, and that you feel at ease in his or her presence. Don't expect miracles or some amazing rapport that cannot be established with strangers. Counselors are human and so are you. Any professional counselor will try to have your best interest in mind. This may not be communicated to you, though, if he doesn't feel that you need the sympathy you think you do.

If you are not within a locality that provides psychological services, you have fewer options. Basically, you can choose private services from a psychologist or a psychiatrist, or you can choose public services from mental health centers. If you choose mental health centers, you will receive adequate services, but you probably will not have the choice of practitioners. If you choose to see a private practitioner, of course, you may shop around and see whom you wish, assuming that your choice can work you into the schedule. The advantage of public services is the cost. Most public mental health facilities adjust their costs to fit what their clients can afford. The disadvantage is that you are a part of the public being served rather than a regular client. (Note: We are not going to put our feet in our mouths and go any further; the reader will have to personally judge the merits of public and private mental health agencies.) The disadvantages of private service is the cost which can be exorbitant.

If you choose to go the route of finding a private clinician, either a psychologist or a psychiatrist, you can probably be referred to one by your physician. If this doesn't work, they are listed in the yellow pages or you can contact your local board of healing arts. In any event, choosing a mental health specialist is much like choosing a physician and there is no way to guarantee that the person you first see is the person you will work with best.

FINAL COMMENTS

There are many other forms of behavior modification techniques that have been used to reduce levels of inappropriate behaviors. Due to the nature of anxiety, tension and stress situations,we have not described these techniques. Our feeling is that if simple techniques do not work well for developing self-control, the more dramatic or complex treatments should be administered by specialists rather than self-administered. Further, the reduction of some forms of treatment do not lend themselves to self-application and can only be properly administered by trained clinicians.

Our purpose in writing this part of the book was threefold: First, to introduce the reader to some readily available techniques for managing emotional behavior; second, to introduce the reader to the concepts underlying the learning and development of emotional behaviors and third, to point out the necessity of obtaining professional help when problems cannot be managed in the home.

PART III
Therapy, Counseling, and Self-Control

Introduction

One of the major concerns of psychologists is the number of books, articles and pamphlets that are being produced on the psychology of self-control. Self-control, because it deals with human behavior, is a popular topic, and consequently, is sold in bulk to the buyer of "popular" psychology. The reason that there is such a mounting concern about self-control as a psychological technique is that writers assume a good deal of sophistication on the part of their readers and the result is that self-control, or the use of operant procedures to govern one's own behavior, has often not been put in the proper perspective with psychiatric, clinical, counseling and other psychological helping procedures. The reader sometimes reaches the conclusion that self-applied operant processes provide the answers to virtually all human emotional and behavioral problems. This is a gross misconception. When writing for professional journals, it is proper for the research psychologist to assume some interpretive expertise of his readership. But when writing for the general public and the beginning student, the psychologist has the ethical and professional responsibility to place operant treatment procedures in the proper perspective along with other methods that are necessary and effective in the proper instances. This does not deny the power of operant conditioning and self-control methods. It is simply a statement that is intended to set the stage for clarification of the various behavioral disorders, their types and degrees of intensity, and the various methods that seem most appropriate to their treatment.

THE ANALYSIS OF HUMAN BEHAVIOR

It is pertinent to set forth the three major components one must consider when attempting to explain, describe, predict and control the behavior of any organism, including Homo sapiens. The three major components are: the state of the organism, its history of reinforcement, and the current conditions that are operating in the environment of the organism under consideration.

STATE OF THE ORGANISM

The state of the organism is an expansive consideration and covers a very wide spectrum of facts, figures, conditions and concepts. In general, "state of the organism" includes genetic considerations or inheritance, the comparative integrity of the operation of the organism's central nervous system, any chronic or acute physical condition that deviates substantially from the norm of what is considered to be "healthy." It includes the functioning of the sympathetic and parasympathetic nervous systems and the system of glandular processes—the endocrine system. A comprehensive list of possible disorders that should be considered under the schema "state of the organism" would be too long and ponderous and would not be appropriate to the purpose of this section. It might be useful to provide a general list, however, just to demonstrate the scope of the concept.

Heart diseases
Respiratory diseases
Bone, joint or muscle disorders
Gastrointestinal disorders
Organic central nervous system disorders
Endocrine system disorders
Major impairments of sensory receptors
Major variations of weight and height
Premature or delayed appearance of secondary sex
    characteristics.
Urinary disorders
All addictive conditions

The state of the organism obviously has an effect on both the qualitative and quantitative aspects of human responses. In general, if the state of the organism is to be manipulated, the medical profession is the one to do it, or at least supervise its being done. It is for this reason that it is necessary to rule out possible organic causes of behavior before one attempts to modify behavior, whether it is one's own behavior or that of a client. It is important for the lay reader to realize that most of the non-medical helping professionals have been trained to discriminate between problems of behavior that have an organic etiology and those that do not. Among these professionals are the psychologist, the counselor, and the psychiatric social worker. It is also important to note that these professionals, when licensed by their various states to engage in private practice, are required to establish an on-going professional relationship with one or more physicians to whom they refer clients and from whom they receive referrals. This arrangement is not for the pecuniary benefit of these professional groups, it is in the interest of patients and their needs.

State of the organism, therefore, is an important consideration critical to the understanding and changing of behavior. Proof of this rests in the requirements for interprofessional practices cited above. Much of the self-control literature overlooks or implicitly denies the importance of the state of the organism. It is the hope of the authors that none of the material of this text is construed to negate the important relationship between certain organic functions and human behavior and thereby cause some individual to deny himself or a loved one the proper care.

History of Reinforcement

History of reinforcement is a concept of behavioral psychology and has already been discussed at length in earlier sections of this text. In brief, history of reinforcement is the life experiences an individual has had since birth, the effect these experiences (the consequences the individual's behavior has obtained for him), and how those experiences and consequences affect his present behavior, both internal and external. We can observe an individual's behavior and listen to his report of how he feels and reacts to given conditions and be able to get a general idea of what kind of history of reinforcement he has experienced. However, a moment's consideration will tell the most naive reader that it is impossible to identify with the degree of precision we would like the exact experiences an individual has had, and the exact degree to which those experiences are influencing what he is presently doing and feeling.

Psychologists refer to this imprecision as "error term," or unexplained variation. It is expressed in the research findings of psychological experiments in which groups of persons are evaluated on one or more dimensions or variables, and is usually found in the tables that explain what research design was used, what statistical technique was employed, and the results of the research. The error term is expressed numerically, is usually very large, and its largeness is evidence of the lack of precision of nomothetic research procedures. It is also evidence that history of reinforcement is an important consideration to make when trying to come to more accurate assessments of why a person is doing what he is doing.

Current Conditions Operating

The above is also an operant psychology term or concept, and it involves a thorough analysis of specific target behaviors currently being exhibited, the stimulus events immediately surrounding the behavior being observed. The latter includes not only the specific stimulus, but the general setting conditions, such as the room, location, time of day, and so on, and all the elements of the environment under which the behavior occurs. It also includes what the consequences the specific behavior under consideration obtains for the individual. This is terribly important, as previous sections of the text have indicated. At this point it is necessary only to mention in brief form that the current conditions operating, that is, the events that precede the target behaviors (the discriminators) and the events that follow the target behavior (the reinforcer, punisher, or neutral effects) are tremendously useful in determining how to describe, explain, predict and control how the organism will behave in the future.

It is also important to realize that with few exceptions, the most accurate and useful information is obtained through the examination of the current conditions operating. The next, in rank order, are history or reinforcement and state of the organism. The exceptions to this general rule are to be found under the state of the organism category. Medical science and psychological diagnostic procedures have vastly improved the availability and accuracy of certain facts to be evaluated under the state of the organism category.

CLASSES OF BEHAVIORAL DISORDERS

Four general classes of behavioral disorders will be described: the neuroses, the psychoses, the character disorders and brain syndromes. There are several other ways in which behavioral disorders could be delineated and classified, but the method chosen seems to be the most appropriate with which to present a process whereby the lay reader and the beginning psychology student can begin to make discriminations and judgments about the relative value of self- control to other treatment methods, and to help put self-control as a regulatory procedure in its proper perspective.

Examples of specific disorders will be used to demonstrate problems that are manifest under the four major categories, and will show when it is appropriate to approach a professional person for help with troublesome behaviors or feelings. The examples and descriptions will help the reader to discriminate as to which professional discipline one should turn and how to raise questions as to whether one should attempt self-control or to seek truly professional help. The lines will not ever become completely clear, of course, as to when one should see a clinical psychologist or a psychiatrist, whether one should turn to a school or community counselor or a clinical psychologist, or whether one should simply pay a visit to any one of these individuals for perhaps nothing more than a "check" on one's perceptions before beginning the institution of self-control procedures. The section to follow will not clear up all the questions that could possibly arise, however, it will shorten the path and lessen the "hassle" for anyone, regardless of whether the use of self-control is ultimately the best treatment choice.

This section will discuss problems in terms of whether they are "clinical," "sub-clinical," or simply "troublesome." These tags for classes of behaviors will become useful to the average person, not only in knowing more about himself, but will help him better understand his family and friends. They are not intended for use by the lay reader or beginning psychology student to make themselves diagnosticians; they are merely guidelines that will help discriminate in a general way the type and seriousness of the problem being considered, and to help make the choice of whether to use self-control procedures or to seek out professional help. It is also hoped that it will clarify self-control as a therapeutic tool with a valuable but narrow usefulness rather than something that will "cure" anything.

An essential part of the format of this section involves the presentation of "case histories." These case histories have not actually taken place; instead, they are composites that have been drawn from the medical and psychological literature, the authors' experiences in teaching, counseling, and clinical practice, and are organized and presented because they are believed to be the best way to illustrate the critical points this section of the text has to make. It should be clearly understood that the names used are fictitious, the symptoms and setting conditions are contrived, but *are* a fair representation of reality that has and will continue to take place in some degree.

The use of fictitious case histories is considered best to illustrate the points *not* because they are more dramatic, have greater literary appeal or that the authors believe they in some way know "what's best." Instead, there is an ethical consideration having to do with the preservation of individuals' rights to privileged communication with the helping professions. In the recent past, even the individual's prerogative to sign away his privacy to a writer or researcher has come under careful scrutiny. When dealing with the self-disclosure of emotionally or genetically-based human behavior, one must not only consider that an individual may later change his mind about disclosing such data, but that an individual may later assert or be adjudged to be incapable of rationally deciding to release his own personal information. There is a permanence and finality associated with recording human behavior in print, film, etc. that is often not perceived by the grantor until it is too late. For these ethical reasons it is important to avoid presenting actual case histories in their entirety in a way that would allow persons to be identified.

THE NEUROSES

The neuroses are all characterized by what is called anxiety. It is useful to immediately distinguish between fear and anxiety. Many people, including some professionals, use the two terms interchangeably. Fear is a withdrawal or the avoidance response to a known danger. Fear is a natural and desirable response, mainly because it has what biologists would call survival value. Without the response of fear it is likely that Homo sapiens, or any other species for that matter, would not survive. The positive value of fear as a response extends beyond that which is related to the interpersonal behavior of fellow creatures; it has to do with the relationship of the organism to the *total* environment.

Anxiety, although it is characterized by the same accompanying feelings and physiological components as fear, is different in that the source of the fear is not known to the respondent, or that the anxiety has been linked to the incorrect source(s), or that it is "free-floating." Free-floating anxiety is the emotional and behavioral response of fear which is not attributed to anything in particular; the individual experiences the feelings and exhibits the accompanying behaviors of fear without consciously linking the feelings and behavior to anything specific.

Primarily, neuroses are clinical in nature, however, neuroses may be treated by methods ranging from psychiatric-chemotherapeutic techniques to techniques of self-control. The techniques employed and the individuals' using them are determined by the type and severity of the neurosis symptoms, and, of course, the professional area of the helping person being consulted. The neuroses can be incapacitating or can range all the way down in severity to being simply troublesome or annoying. As such, neuroses may be treated at all levels of difficulty: clinical, sub-clinical, or troublesome.

Although persons who are diagnosed by a qualified professional as neurotic may be severely handicapped by their difficulties, they are not considered to be in as much "trouble" as certain other categories of dysfunction. First of all, with one possible exception, neurotic individuals are in contact with reality, and know that there is something wrong with their mental and emotional functioning. Secondly, although the neuroses can range widely in severity of functional impairment, it is the general category of problems, when expressed only to the troublesome degree, that lends itself to the use of self-control most readily.

In general, the clinical categories of neuroses are the following:
1. Hysterical
   A. conversion type
   B. dissociative type
2. Phobic
3. Obsessive compulsive
4. Depressive
5. Depersonalization
6. Hypochondriacal
7. Unspecified (this is for mixed diagnosis).

Examples will be presented from the above list and each will be shown to decrease to the sub-clinical level through various treatment techniques. At that point, a list of behaviors will be given that are similar to each of those in the clinical category chosen, but which are manifested only at the troublesome level. This does not mean that the use of self-control techniques are only appropriate to behaviors in the troublesome category, but rather, that this is the most appropriate level at which one may apply self-control procedures with great confidence. Examples will be given, in some instances, at the clinical level where self-control may be applied by the individual, but usually only after professional consultation and/or supervision.

THE PSYCHOSES

There are two general categories of psychoses: the functional and the organically based. Functional psychoses, in a very loose sense, are situationally or environmentally determined, such as by trauma, stress, and so forth. However, a functional disorder may also be complicated by a medical condition, either acute or chronic, which may exacerbate the problem. Organically-based psychoses are traceable to brain syndromes of various types—genetic, pre-peri and post-natal insult, intoxication by various agents, injury at any time during growth, development, or adulthood.

There is growing evidence and opinion that some of the organic psychoses are biochemical in origin.

In general, persons are described as psychotic when their mental functioning is sufficiently impaired so as to interfere significantly with daily living activities. Such an individual may not be able to distinguish reality from nonreality, may suffer from hallucinations and delusions, and mood changes may be so rapid and profound that he is unable to respond appropriately to the simplest and most commonplace stimuli. In most instances, the person is unaware of his illness.

There are several sub-categories of psychoses, but for purposes of illustrating the main point of this section of the text, we shall confine our discussions and examples primarily to the non-organic psychoses, i.e., those of the major affective types.

CHARACTER DISORDERS

Character disorders or personality disorders, as they are sometimes referred to, are manifested by deeply ingrained maladaptive behaviors that are distinctly different from the previously discussed categories. These behavior patterns are usually established early in life and are extremely difficult to change. There are several diagnostic types subsumed under character disorders. The primary focus here will be upon two: the obsessive-compulsive personality and the passive-aggressive personality.

ORGANIC BRAIN SYNDROMES

There are two general categories of organic brain syndrome: psychotic and non-psychotic. In both instances the disorder is caused by or associated with impairment of brain tissue functioning. In addition, the conditions may be specified to be either chronic or acute, depending upon whether the condition is permanent or temporary, respectively.

The symptoms of organic brain syndrome include the loss of

memory (or impairment of memory), loss of time or space orientation, impairment of judgment, emotional liability and shallow affect, and problems in normal intellectual functioning.

Diagnosis is usually made by a combination of behavioral observations, gathering and evaluation of medical history, and psychological evaluation with certain diagnostic tests, such as the Wechsler scales, the Graham Kendall Memory for Designs Test and the Bender Gestalt. Combination is a critical word in the above as will be seen in the fictional case study to be presented in a subsequent chapter.

Organic brain syndrome was chosen to be included in the text for two main reasons: (1) the high incidence of the diagnosis of "hyperactivity" among school-age children in recent years, and (2) the large number of individuals damaged each year by physical trauma, such as by auto accidents. Both of these general categories of organic brain syndrome are diagnosed and treatment attempted by a wide range of professionals and nonprofessionals. The disagreements between various professional groups and individuals as to the relative efficacy of medical as opposed to behavioral management of these disorders will be presented. It is hoped that the reader will have a better understanding of prognosis and proper treatment procedures after consideration of the data presented in this chapter.

The chapters to follow will present several fictitious cases, describe clinical treatments which moved the patient to a sub-clinical level of functioning, and finally to the troublesome stage of behavior. Again, the purposes for presenting such material are to show how the psychological-helping professions are in both a continuous and cooperative relationship at various times, and that the full spectrum of helping professions need to maintain close contact. Perhaps a stronger purpose is to help the sub-clinical professionals such as the counselor, the school nurse, the school psychologist, the social worker, the pastoral counselor, and so on, to better understand the various roles and functions involved in helping others. A final purpose is to assist the beginning student and readers in the general population to understand and place in proper perspective the utility of self-control as a method and to help the student and lay reader discriminate as to when and how self-control procedures are to be properly used.

Chapter 11

Neuroses

A forty-year-old female brought her forty-seven-year-old husband, whom we shall call Jack, to a private clinic for psychological diagnosis and treatment. Jack had no significant medical history of unusual psychological or physical trauma, and had never before presented himself for psychological help. During the intake interview he described himself as "always being shy, backward, nonaggressive, and somewhat fearful of social situations." He further described himself as "not being competent at anything" and referred to an early memory of being afraid to go to school, and being retained for the second year in the first grade. He was an only child, with one parent deceased ten years prior to Jack's presentation of himself for help, and the other parent, his mother, still living. Examination revealed no particular trauma surrounding the death of the parent.

Until six months before his presentation for treatment, Jack had spent his adult working life with the same organization in one job classification. At that time he was transferred out of his position as a display artist and painter to a nearby out-of-state position with the same agency as an outside painter (a laborer's job). It was at the point of the transfer that Jack's anxious behavior became extremely troublesome to him and his family, and when he first began to attribute his problems to his "incompetence." He maintained that "the company just put me there hoping I would quit; they didn't want to just fire me because I had so many years service." Jack was extremely unhappy with his new job, but he apparently lacked the assertiveness to petition for a different assignment, and refused to consider other sources of employment. One reason he gave for his inaction was the retirement pay he had accumulated over the years. If he were to terminate, most of the retirement equity would be sacrificed, especially that portion that had been contributed by the company. The other stated reason, of course, was his perceived incompetence. He appeared convinced that there was no other organization that would even consider hiring him due to his "incompetence."

Jack and his wife had four children: two older boys aged 16 and

18 who were still living at home, and two girls, one of whom was in the second grade and the other was a preschooler. During the interview the couple passed over the children very quickly and there appeared to be nothing significant in the interactions of the children with the parents that had any relationship to Jack's problem.

Jack's wife exhibited a low profile during the initial interview. She contributed very little to the content of the discussion, although she did corroborate Jack's impressions of his problems whenever he asked her to do so. It was obvious, however, that she had been the person responsible for persuading Jack to seek professional help. She did not appear to be overtly aggressive or controlling; she did, though, appear to be somewhat over-solicitous and motherly in her responses to Jack. In view of Jack's extreme anxiety complaints, the interviewer deemed her attention to Jack to be within normal limits and consequently did not focus on the husband-wife interactions at that time.

When Jack was asked to describe his problems in detail, he produced a saga of virtual constant anxiety over the previous six-month period. Upon awakening, which was usually several hours before time to prepare for work, Jack would experience an extreme anxiety attack. His ideation ranged from indecision about what to wear, what to prepare for breakfast, what to take with him for lunch, to feared circumstances on the way to work and anticipated catastrophic events while at work. At night he would endlessly review the hopelessness of his job plight, his "stupid" mistakes and his perceived inappropriate social interactions during the day, and fears about being "crazy" due to his inability to control the intrusion of the unwanted thoughts.

Jack had done some reading on the classic fears of heights (he had to paint five-hundred-foot towers in his new job), closed spaces (he had become extremely fearful of getting in his car), and several other well known phobic reactions, and had come to the conclusion that he was severely neurotic. He was correct.

When asked what he thought should be done for him, Jack said that he felt he should be admitted to a hospital. Yet he was not quite able to request admission. When pressed for a reason, Jack admitted that he was afraid that if he were hospitalized, he would never get out after "they" discovered how "crazy" he was. He mentioned the possible use of medication to help him feel better. The therapist agreed that it would certainly be worth a try. Pursuant to that, Jack agreed to a psychiatric interview. It was believed that the psychiatrist would recommend some medication to lower his anxieties and possibly shorten the treatment process. Jack reluctantly agreed to undergo a physical examination, a blood sugar count, and a psychiatric interview.

He was normal physically; his blood sugar was within normal limits (which ruled out a hypoglycemic reaction), and medication was recommended. Jack never filled the prescription; he was too afraid of "becoming addicted." During the session following his psychiatric interview and his subsequent refusal to take the recommended medication, Jack sighed that, "I guess I'm so afraid of everything that there's no way I'll ever get any better. I really don't know what's going to happen to me."

In the three or four interviews immediately subsequent to the one in which Jack and his wife reported on the results of the psychiatric evaluation, various methods were used to elicit as much about Jack and his problems as was possible to obtain. Day-to-day problems of a current nature were discussed in depth: Jack's relationships at work, with his children, with his wife, and lengthy and detailed descriptions of how Jack spent his time at home. While these discussions were going on, the therapist described various approaches to the problems which might be attempted, but more importantly, *how Jack was interacting in the interview situation* was carefully noted by the therapist.

At work Jack
1. was very sensitive to typical injustices that are common in work situations;
2. was intellectually superior to the people with whom he worked, including his supervisors;
3. was not interested in any of the things and ideas that concerned his fellow workers;
4. was keenly aware of peer pressures to "force him" to carry out work assignments that he thought were dangerous or that were fear-arousing in him;
5. felt alone in his behavior, ideas, beliefs and values;
6. believed himself to be incompetent at all the activities necessary to "good" job performance and acceptable social interaction.

At home Jack
1. was not consulted by his daughter in the second grade for study help; he remembers that the older boys did not consult him either;
2. reported that he could not do the annual income tax report, could not balance the check-stubs, could not make good decisions about shopping, etc.;
3. would usually wait until the children had actually engaged in behavior that he deemed inappropriate and then attempt to invoke punishment;
4. would occasionally stipulate that certain behaviors were inappropriate but would never say what the consequences of undesirable behavior would be;
5. said that "nobody" respected him at home and that the children thought he was "weird" or "crazy."

With his wife, Jack
   *1. always consulted her on decisions;
    2. recalled that during the course of their marriage when he had to be out-of-town, he called her frequently at night and was usually very upset about "being alone";
    3. was afraid he was "driving her away by being so incompetent";
    4. was afraid that he was "being dictatorial when he asserted himself";
    5. disagreed on disciplinary matters.

In general, Jack
   *1. believed that there was something organically wrong with him that caused him to feel "peculiar" and "afraid";
   *2. believed that these feelings *caused* his behavior.

In the lists, above, three of the propositions are asterisked to denote their critical relationship to Jack's problems. Jack's statements and descriptions leading to the conclusion that he "always consulted his wife" is especially important. During one of the interviews, the therapist unobtrusively recorded a tally on the number of times Jack asked his wife to confirm his feelings, beliefs, or behaviors. In a fifty-minute session he asked (and received) either verification or denial thirty-seven times! The fact that he asked for verification so many times is highly significant; the nature of the responses Jack received and how he reacted to them is even more important.

Successful therapy for Jack involved two steps: (1) a procedure social psychologists call cognitive restructuring, and (2) radically changing the nature of the environment.

One of the purposes of chemotherapy as an adjunct to other types of therapy is to bring the client's feelings to within a normal range. This permits the individual to respond from a more intellectual and less emotional standpoint. Jack had dismissed chemotherapy as a method of alleviating his undesirable feelings. Since he perceived that his bad feelings (which he incorrectly thought stemmed from an organic condition) caused his inappropriate behavior, it was necessary to somehow change his feelings.

Cognitive restructuring was chosen as the technique. One of the procedures in cognitive restructuring involves the therapist refusing to talk of feelings as being determined by internal processes that have gone askew. Another procedure is to demonstrate that behavior is not the result of feelings, but rather, is tied to elements of the environment. The critical elements of Jack's environment were the responses of his wife and the way in which Jack structured the responses of people around him.

Step one of Jack's therapy involved telling him rather dogmatically that his behavior was not caused by his feelings. Further, a ground rule was established in which Jack agreed to allow the therapist to point out and censor any statement or inference that Jack made concerning the so-called organic cause of his feelings and the believed causal relationship between feelings and behavior.

Step two involved pointing out to Jack each instance in which he asked his wife to verify his feelings, beliefs, attitudes, etc. Especially pertinent was that no matter what the nature of his wife's response, Jack would interpret her remark so that it confirmed his illness and worthlessness, and the hopelessness of his situation. For example, the following is typical dialogue between Jack and his wife.

JACK: I really am nervous almost all of the time; isn't that right, honey?

RESPONSE

WIFE: Well, yes, I guess so.

JACK: See, I really am in bad shape, I feel so bad all the time. That's why I act this way.

ALTERNATIVE RESPONSE

WIFE: Well, no, not *most* of the time. Maybe sometimes you are.

JACK: You see how she tries to protect me. She's just saying that to make me feel better.

With this kind of feedback system operating, the verbal contingencies support a stable cognitive position of illness for Jack. Structuring Jack's wife to turn away and not answer to any request for verification of his behavior tended to decrease his asking for the confirmation. A no-response from his wife also served as a discriminator in that it made Jack keenly aware of how often he engaged in this kind of behavior. Initially, Jack became very anxious when his wife refused to answer him. Later, he became angry with her. In a third and final stage, he began to accept that he was engaging in dependent and self-defeating behavior, and began to talk about other aspects of his life in which he behaved in much or the same way. For example, he cited several instances when he had been out of town overnight and felt compelled to call his wife to report his anxiety. Although Jack had insight into his behavior and would speak freely about his out-of-town anxiety being related to his wife not being present to confirm his helpless condition, Jack was still unable to behave appropriately in a consistent fashion. His wife was required to maintain the therapeutic verbal contingencies for some time.

A third step in Jack's therapy involved the first level of self-management. With his cognitions restructed such that he no longer saw his behavior as the *result* of his feelings, and with the demonstration that his anxiety diminished when he was no longer allowed to self-confirm his illness, he was ready to try self-management.

Jack had experienced a good deal of difficulty with his older children. They never seemed to act responsibly, and openly refused to "mind" him most of the time. After examining his transactions

with the children, it was pointed out that often Jack did not stipulate which child's behaviors were appropriate and inappropriate, and
almost never established a contingency for inappropriate behaviors.
Jack was asked to prepare two lists of behaviors for his children,
with one list made up of "good" behaviors and one of "bad" behaviors. He was also asked to list a contingency for each. After doing
so, Jack was asked to read the proclamation to his children and to
post it in a conspicuous place at home. He also agreed to follow
through and apply the contingencies.

For most parents, such an undertaking would be relatively
simple. But for Jack it was extremely difficult. His first week with
the program was largely unsuccessful. He found himself not following through with the contingencies or, in the case of "bad" behaviors, trying to apply contingencies more stringent than those listed
on the proclamations. A review of his failures served as discriminators in two ways: (1) He was able to see that his poor relationships with the children were largely the result of his own violations
of the contract and, (2) that his anxiety went up when he violated
the contract and "lost control." In subsequent weeks he managed
to implement the program successfully, with drastically improved
relations with his children and lowered anxiety.

While the above ensued, it was noted that Jack had stopped
talking about his anxieties surrounding going to work, work activities, his peer relationships at work. When asked how he was getting
along on the job, he sheepishly replied that he had it "all figured
out." "It seems natural," he said, "to assume that if you feel out of
control and lack the respect of those in your own home where it is
supposed to be safe and comfortable, that you would feel even more
so away." "When I started feeling better at home, without realizing
when it happened, I began to feel okay at work." When Jack's therapy was terminated, he was actively applying self-control procedures
to control his sleep, social relationships, eating, smoking, and im-
pulse buying.

It was especially pleasing to see a person in as much anguish as
Jack improve dramatically without medication. Although we do not
maintain that insight brings behavior change, it did seem to be a
critical element for Jack. At termination he expressed pleasure that
he had not taken medication, and mentioned that the medication
might have made him feel better sooner, but it would certainly have
heightened his belief that there was something organically "wrong"
with him. His statement should not want to make us abandon the
use of medication, but it certainly should serve as a reminder that
medication is to be used judiciously.

Anxiety Neurosis: Jill

The increased incidence of parents who continue regular
pediatric service for their children through the early school years,
and the increased public use of mental health centers and the services

of private psychologists in child practice has led to the discovery of parental neuroses that otherwise might have gone unattended.

Clinical hyperactivity has a definite cluster of symptoms that are both behavioral and psychometric in nature. At this writing, hyperactivity is the most overdiagnosed and perhaps most misunderstood childhood malady. Parents, teachers and lay-readers of popular psychology constantly misapply the term. Almost any child who exhibits an uncomfortable amount of curiosity or stimulus-seeking behavior is called "hyperactive." Hyperactivity is technically a clinical diagnosis. It is listed under the organic brain syndromes, and the diagnosis should be made jointly, in most cases, by the pediatrician and the psychologist or child psychiatrist. With the most pronounced evidence of brain syndrome, it is not necessary to obtain supporting psychometric data. However, the psychologist should provide the parent-teacher adjunct therapy, and should direct the management of supportive contingencies for the child.

Clinical hyperactivity requires chemotherapy. There has for some time been a controversy over "drugging" children. Settling the controversy centers on proper professional diagnosis at the outset, and a follow-up with well-managed chemo and behavioral therapy by a medical-psychological team. The use of chemotherapy should not proceed immediately at the insistence of a parent or a teacher and without a thorough diagnosis and evaluation preceding such action. Children without the clinical cluster of hyperactivity should not receive chemotherapy; behavior modification leading to self-management is the appropriate treatment. But more about hyperactivity under the chapter on organic brain syndromes.

Upon presentation of a child for evaluation and possible treatment, the mother (Jill) told a story familiar by now to most pediatricians, elementary teachers and psychologists. The child was said to exhibit a very short attention span, "could not sit still" at school or at home, argued with mother frequently and refused to respond to repeated requests to perform minor household duties, school work and many basic self-management tasks that are commonly mastered by first graders. The mother reported the child was taking dexedrine and ritalin, and that there was little (if any) discernable effect on her behavior. The teacher reported over-aggressiveness on the playground and hyperactive "rebelliousness" in the classroom. Average to below average classroom academic performance was reported by the teacher, who acknowledged that her "grading was influenced by the behavior of children;" she practiced the lowering of academic grades if undesirable social behavior was exhibited.

Prior to testing, the child was interviewed by a psychologist. It was noted there was no hyperactivity, but some "tic and nail-biting behavior" characteristics of anxiety reaction. The child spontaneously expressed open hostility for the mother during the interview and asked for an explanation of the visit.

The child was administered the WISC, an individual test of

intelligence, which consists of ten sub-tests and two alternate sub-tests. The five performance and five verbal sub-tests (without alternates) were administered. The full-scale IQ of the child was in excess of 130, with the performance component slightly higher than the verbal IQ, but not significantly so. The within-verbal and within-performance test profiles were high and flat, a condition that does *not* suggest organic brain syndrome. The Bender Gestalt test, a design-drawing test that will indicate brain syndrome, yielded the developmental score of a normal adult. Again, certainly not indicative of OBS.

The tests were administered in two sessions, thus the psychologist had observed the child on three occasions for approximately one hour each time. The child's behavior was stable and normal for a child her age and intelligence across the three situations. The mother was given the findings along with the suggestion that the child was normal, and was perhaps responding to a stressful familial or school situation. At this, the mother began to weep hysterically and asked if she could obtain psychiatric help. She was subsequently diagnosed as having a chronic and rather severe anxiety neurosis, and required medication. Her condition had placed her marriage and family relationship in jeopardy via her anxiety outbursts and hyper-critical behavior toward others, the inability to obtain sexual pleasure, and poor relationships with both peer and authority groups at work. One of the anxiety behaviors was overeating; the woman was approximately ninety pounds overweight.

As the mother's medication, Diazepam (valium) 15.20 mgs., lowered her anxiety reactions, her child, who was originally brought for evaluation, was gradually removed from medication. The mother continued in psychotherapy with the initial purpose of analyzing the social interactions in her home, and in particular, her relationship with her child. The advanced goals of therapy involved the application of behavioral techniques to teach her child appropriate behaviors. This was necessary due to the long-standing nature of the mother's neurosis; her behavior across time had established a behavioral repertoire that was maladaptive in the child. It was also necessary for the mother to "see" in a direct way how her behavior influenced the child. Finally, self-control techniques were introduced to help the mother withdraw the valium and to regulate her sexual and eating behaviors. Satisfactory levels of performance were achieved in all the goals and formal therapy was terminated after twenty-seven sessions.

Although removing the "hyperactive" tag and medication from the child no doubt prevented much future psychological damage to the child, the most satisfying (to Jill) achievements were the lowering of anxiety, the achievement of sexual satisfaction, and eventually (after about eight months) the loss of excess weight by the mother, all produced primarily by self-control methods. It is believed that the use of valium was important in the treatment only to the extent that results were produced more rapidly. This seems especially appropriate to mention because valium has since been placed on the Schedule IV (highly regulated) list of medications.

The most effective rewards for the child were found to be (1) a specified amount of time each day to spend with mother "doing what I want," (2) afternoon playtime with specified friends, and (3) certain early evening TV programs, in that order. The reward listed first above was initially the most aversive to the mother, but was one of the most productive and growth-producing behaviors for the mother. Through this daily activity, the mother desensitized herself to contact with the child, gave the child some social control over the parents, and eventually learned to play normally with her. The rewards were furnished the child on an earnings and "response cost" schedule; i.e., all rewards were earned by producing specified levels of certain behaviors, and could be lost if the child exhibited pre-specified behaviors. The contingency system became very elaborate, and the child eventually came to participate in various revisions of the system.

The mother's overeating and consequent overweight were apparently linked directly to anxiety reactions over the poor family interactions, rather than to the sexual problem specifically. She responded to lowered anxiety by immediately lowering the amount and frequency with which she ate. Her weight loss was regular and uniform. The sexual problem was highly resistant to change, and the first reported changes occurred long after other positive results were obtained. Later, it was discovered that the husband was ejaculating prematurely; the wife believed the sexual problem to be hers entirely. After successful Masters and Johnson-type training for premature ejaculation, the sexual problem was rather easily resolved by artificial stimulation of the clitoris alternated with entry by the husband while his partner was stimulated.

As is often the case with child problems, especially hyperactivity, what began as a simple evaluation of a child for hyperkinesis became a highly involved family treatment process involving medication, supportive psychotherapy, behavior modification, sex therapy, and self-control measures.

Chapter 12

The Psychoses

Some of the most acute, bizarre, and disruptive human behavior problems are classified as functional psychoses. Although people who have such problems are severely incapacitated, they are sometimes helped dramatically with self-control procedures, but only when applied at the proper stage of recovery. An example is furnished which illustrates several points about diagnosis and treatment. First, with this example one can readily see how persons can be misdiagnosed, or certainly, clinicians can disagree about the nature of the problem. Second, it can be seen that treatment procedures can vary widely among clinicians. Finally, it will be shown how persons who are recovering from certain psychoses under medical treatment typically respond, and how self-control procedures can be a significant part of the total treatment procedure.

Ann: Manic-Depressive Illness, Circular Type or Schizophrenia, Schizo-affective Type

Ann was a twenty-eight-year-old female in her second marriage on the occasion of her hospitalization for severe emotional disturbance. She was of middle-class origin, the last of five children, and was a college graduate. Her first marriage, which terminated in divorce, was to a physician several years her senior. Her second marriage was also to a professional man, doctoral level, who was several years older than she.

Her childhood was unremarkable except for family interactions that typically center on the "baby" or last child, an adolescent head injury in which she was comatose for several days, and a fundamentalist religious orientation in which Ann's mother was dominant and exhibited guilt-producing behavior control over all the children. There appeared to be no residual from the head injury, but elements of the early religious training showed up in the content of Ann's psychotic break which hospitalized her. There was no evidence of emotional disturbance in any of the siblings or in either parent, although one would suspect that Ann's mother was heavily defended, perhaps to the neurotic level, against the recognition of her own "sinful" impulses. Ann was a high achiever academically, related a normal history of adolescent and early adulthood heterosexual behavior, and entered her first marriage a virgin. Her college scholastic and extracurricular activities were characterized by high achievement, which Ann enjoyed immensely.

Ann's first marriage lasted only a year, and she described it as sheer drudgery. Her husband expected her to contribute all her income to a common "pool," and to cook, clean, and do general housekeeping maintenance chores. In addition, she described her husband as cold, unaffectionate, and rather domineering. Early in the marriage, he refused to kiss her or tell her he loved her. She said her husband accused her of being childish, irresponsible, and dependent, and chose to spend all his free time golfing or fishing. She grew despondent, and at her husband's coaxing, got a divorce. However, just prior to the divorce she sought psychiatric help which she described as completely ineffective. No medication was prescribed; the therapy was traditional psychoanalytic.

After the divorce, Ann moved to a neighboring state and completed a graduate degree. During that time she had several "affairs" of varying duration. All the involvements were sexual in nature, and Ann claimed a complete inability to achieve orgasm with any of the men. At the outset of each affair, she believed she was in love, only to grow disenchanted as she successively failed with each man to achieve sexual satisfaction. Just prior to receiving her graduate degree, she entered into an affair with her second husband-to-be, and this culminated in marriage in about six months. During this time Ann had no other affairs. She was able to reach orgasm frequently, and she was certain she was in love.

During the first two years of their marriage, Ann's behavior was characterized by mood shifts that were calendar-cyclic in nature. From April through July, her husband described her behavior and mood as normal. August brought on an irritable, hypercritical behavior phase accompanied by criticism of her husband's sexual prowess. Beginning in September and continuing through December, her behavior was described as manic. From January through early March, Ann's behavior was markedly depressive, and as was discovered later, was characterized by sexual promiscuity.

In the second year of her marriage, the manic stage involved sexual liaisons with almost fifty partners. During the second revolution of her manic behavior, Ann became pregnant and was not certain of the identity of the unborn child's father. It was certain that her husband did not father the child, for he had undergone a vasectomy prior to their marriage. Ann carried the child through an uneventful pregnancy, and the child was born mongoloid in June. In late summer her behavior, which had been "normal" since April, began to cycle again, and in October she was forcibly hospitalized with full-blown psychotic symptoms.

After Ann's behavior stabilized, she maintained that she had recall of her beliefs, feelings and behavior up to the point of hospitalization and medication. Her descriptions coincide with admission data. They involved delusions of grandeur: she and her lover at that time were planning (and reporting to all who would listen) that they were going to make the "movie of the century." Ann was extremely manic: she slept only every other night, and then for only a few hours; her eating was erratic; she went several days without bathing or washing her hair. During her manic stages, menses always ceased for the duration of the episode.

When Ann was apprehended and admitted for treatment, she remembers talking with a minister, and watching in amazement as the minister's face would "fade out" and reorganize successively into the faces of each of her lovers. She remembers "talking" with each face as it appeared, and hearing the voices of the lovers (rather than the minister's) respond. While being admitted Ann recalled screaming repeatedly, "I am a perfect schizophrenic" and earnestly requesting "come on God—fuck me now."

When her behavior was stable, and she was questioned about the latter statement, she said she believed herself to be the mother of all mankind, and that her request was not a religious mockery, but stemmed from the sincere belief that she was "mother earth." Ann described the feeling accompanying the request as one of "giving, loving, expansiveness—somewhat like a peak religious experience." When asked if she would like to experience it again, she admitted that she would, and that it "was the most euphoric feeling I've ever had." Ann hastened to add that she did not, however, wish to be psychotic to have the feeling. Contrary to popular belief about psychoses, Ann insists that she knew all along that she was "sick, but just didn't care."

In summary, Ann experienced abnormal euphoria, delusions of grandeur, visual and auditory hallucinations, exhibited bizarre verbal behavior, and extreme manic behavior. There was disagreement about the admitting diagnosis: one clinical opinion was schizophrenic, schizo-affective type, with a strong circular component; another was manic-depressive illness, circular type.

Ann was hospitalized for five months. Her treatment consisted of phenothiazine in heavy doses, which very quickly diminished her manic behavior and accompanying symptoms. She plunged into a deep depression, however, and remained depressed through her dismissal, which came only at her husband's insistence. Ann had received some gestalt-type therapy while hospitalized, but it seemed largely ineffectual. Ann was brought to a private clinic for help during the first week after her dismissal. She was given a mild (child-level) dosage of Tofranil along with lithium. Her mood stabilized within two weeks, and the Tofranil (for mood elevation) was removed. Ann and her husband entered joint therapy with the purpose of trying to bring permanent stability to her behavior, and to help work out the feelings brought about by Ann's behavior. Although both Ann and her husband understood and accepted her behavior on an intellectual level, there was a strong emotional residual of the events for both of them.

During the early stages of therapy (in which Ann was still on maintenance levels of lithium), she reported an interesting phenomenon. Prior to her manic cycles, she reported playing what she called "memory games." The memory games were obsessive-compulsive (and largely private) activities in which she tried to recall insignificant minutia, such as, "When I last used the garden hose, how long did I cook the beans, how long has the water been boiling, how many times have I worn this article of clothing this year," etc.

One function of the memory games, obviously, was allowing Ann to bridle her impulsive thoughts by converting them to non-emotional content. Another was to prohibit the emergence of anxiety when thinking of the future; the memory games focused on the past. An analysis of the content revealed no projective trends, and contained no material about which inferences could be drawn about childhood trauma. She was distressed over playing them, professed a desire to stop, but yet felt a good deal of stress to continue. Ann spoke with her husband about the games, and even persuaded him to play them with her on occasion.

When Ann introduced the idea of memory games to the therapist, they spent several portions of sessions discussing whether to eliminate the games and how to do so. After making several tentative explanations of the games and how they might be eliminated and observing Ann's reactions, the therapist suggested that Ann choose the interpretation she thought most plausible to decide what (if anything) to do about them, and to pick a method from those offered (or to construct her own). Ann would choose a technique. The therapist would begin the process with her, and she would refuse to cooperate. This happened with several techniques. After dropping each successive proposed treatment, Ann would be critical of herself and of the therapist, and then move on to the next treatment method. The therapist pointed out the consistencies of her behavior and suggested that the memory games were also probably a defense mechanism to avoid working with more potent material, but readily agreed to continue "playing her game." Subsequent to this maneuver, Ann reported decreased memory games and spent increasingly less time talking about them until talking about them was finally extinguished.

One of the characteristics of people with psychoses in remission, particularly the major affective disorders, is that they tend to feel so much better that they refuse any kind of continuing counseling. Ann was apprised of these characteristics, and she was requested to use self-control procedures to help herself remain stabilized. She learned to monitor her affect and behavior and to adjust her medication intake accordingly. For instance, when she began to play memory games and/or began to feel anxiety, she would take a single dose of mellaril (which was not a part of her maintenance program). She plotted the amount and time she took lithium, which had to be taken carefully as prescribed. This allowed her husband to double check to make certain she kept her lithium at the therapeutic level. With the onset of depression, she would take Tofranil until her mood lifted. Thus, she used self-control to keep her illness within manageable boundaries.

Ann was taught to use self-management techniques to reestablish the social acquaintances she had lost during her illness. One of the aspects of her illness involved the inability to form and maintain proper social relationships. She carefully plotted the number of calls she made, to whom they were made, the general nature of the conversation, etc. She began the process by overcoming the fear of answering the phone by using systematic desensitization. Then she began to place phone calls. These records were used in the therapy process. The therapist provided reinforcement for increases in "other" contact, for appropriate explanations of her behavior to inquisitive callers, and for forming and carrying out normal, day-to-day social contacts, such as going shopping with Mary, attending a lecture with Ellen, etc. Ann also kept information on material of an intimate nature that she self-disclosed, and eventually learned how to disclose appropriate levels, to discriminate as to whom she should disclose, and how to manage the disclosures of others.

The use of self-control in medication and the use of social self-management has played an important role in keeping Ann functional. It is believed that without them, she would have been hospitalized again. To date, she has remained functional for almost a year.

Too often, persons who are psychotic are thought always to be incapable of decision-making and responsible behavior, not to be trusted, and sometimes unjustly believed to be somehow intellectually deficient. These assumptions preclude the use of self-management techniques as an important part of the total therapy program. Consequently, many psychotic individuals never reach the functional level that it is possible for them to attain, and many are returned to the hospital because their therapy program is missing this very important property.

Chapter 13

Organic Brain Syndrome

Organic brain syndromes, as stated in the introduction to this section, may be chronic or acute; they may be psychotic or non-psychotic in nature. What is very troublesome is that it is often extremely difficult to determine in organic brain syndrome diagnosis which behavioral manifestations are psychotic and which are not, especially when physical brain trauma by an external agent is involved. For example, there may be memory loss, distortion or impairment; there may be pronounced personality changes which would be attributable to the psychodynamics of either guilt or brain injury, and ideation involving notions of reference and religiosity in the post-trauma condition. In observing individuals with severe adult brain injury, it is often believed that self-control could not ever be a part of the treatment program. However, there are instances in which self-control may be used. The case of Ed is such an example.

Ed is a thirty-four-year-old city civil servant who was seriously injured in the line of duty. His injury was such that he was comatose for approximately a two-week period, and his brain injuries were so serious that he was irrational and had to be restrained and fed intravenously for about sixty days after he had recovered from his physical injuries. He was hospitalized for a continuous period of just over three months immediately subsequent to his accident.

Ed was released in the care of his wife and neurologist. The neurologist tried several combinations of medication to help Ed manage his behavior and was unsuccessful. Ed was referred to a private clinic for psychological and psychiatric evaluation. The neurological report accompanying the referral listed a series of troublesome behavioral symptoms and included the opinion that there were widespread (but unspecified) "closed head" injuries contributing to the patient's behavior. The psychological evaluation was needed to determine the sites of brain injury and their relationship to the patient's current behavior, and to determine a tentative prognosis. The psychological information was also needed for the psychiatrist to place the patient on the proper medication regimen. The following is an abbreviated list of symptoms and conditions observed in the patient.

1. Rapidly alternating mood swings from deep depression to elation.

2. Outbreaks of rage at the slightest stimuli.

3. Short-term memory loss, especially surrounding accident circumstances.

4. Apparent loss of memory for certain familiar objects.

5. Gross personality change from that of a person who drank alcohol, was known to be a bit promiscuous, and used profanity freely, to one who attended church and exhibited much verbal religiosity and no longer engaged in the pre-accident behaviors listed above.

6. Frequently expressed remorse over his past life and spoke of being punished by God for his behavior.

7. Frequently spoke of committing suicide.

8. Could not write, could only print name and few other basic items.

9. Would frequently give a bizarre response to a question or make a statement obviously absurd, and would express as much surprise as the listener at what he had said.

10. Impairment of many sensory-motor functions.

The patient was administered the Wechsler Adult Intelligence Scale, the Bender Gestalt Test of Visual Motor Abilities, and the Graham-Kendall Memory for Designs Test. These data and the information gained from the clinical interviews with Ed and his wife yielded a primary diagnosis of non-psychotic organic brain syndrome, and a secondary diagnosis of severe depressive neurosis.

The very complicated and profound personality changes observed were apparently due primarily to damage to the frontal lobe and to probable damage to the "connecting" functions of tissue between the old and new brain. The latter explained much of the rage behavior and extreme sensitivity to very slight stimuli. It was impossible to rule out some personality change due to identity and role changes necessitated by the accident results, that is, psychogenic causes, but the correspondences found between areas of the brain damage and the functions tended to point to organic rather than psychogenic etiology.

There was also tissue damage to the brain areas governing smell and taste, and to an area controlling tactile sensations, medial anterior left forearm.

Dilantin was prescribed for the rage attacks. Elavil was used at night to enable the patient to sleep; depression had been so severe there was not only the classic symptom of awakening early, but a pronounced inability to fall asleep at night. Up to 20 mg. of valium was prescribed on an "as needed" daily basis for lowering anxieties. The medication was reasonably effective in stabilizing Ed's behavior; however, he had experienced a profound weight loss (from 190 to about 150 lbs.), was not eating regularly and would never eat more than one meal a day, was still dysphasic, dysgraphic, confused about the moral and religious aspects of his new identity, and very concerned about his loss of motor abilities and whether he would be able to return to work.

Psychotherapy involved the use of Rational Emotive techniques of Ellis to assuage guilt associated with the accident and to reconcile his new "moral and religious" self. Dysphasic and dysgraphic exercises much like those employed by special educators with brain-damaged children were used to help tissue take over as many of the damaged functions as was possible. Recovery in these areas was rapid.

Self-control procedures were used in the areas of environmental management and in acquiring a more normal eating regimen. Ed learned to structure his children and social situations so as to remove the noxious stimuli that triggered his rage and anxiety. Ed had been a part-time carpenter prior to his accident, mainly because it was his hobby. He lost very few of his carpentry skills, and he discharged much of the "hyperactivity" associated with his brain injury by doing carpentry work. In addition to the emotional therapy this provided, it also allowed him a "natural" way of rebuilding motor and "thinking/judgment" skills. Since carpentry activities were rewarding to Ed, he learned to make engaging in them contingent upon performing some other activity, such as establishing a better eating pattern.

Eating was a special problem. Because of the injury, Ed had lost much of his taste sensation, and that which was left was mildly unpleasant. The same was true for smell. In addition, smell and taste were in some instances mixed; that is, he would experience a familiar taste as a smell, and vice versa. Therefore, the natural reinforcement of pleasant taste and smells could not be relied upon to help recondition eating. A behavioral technique was required. Eating behavior, and to some extent, sexual behavior, were highly resistant to retraining. This is believed to be due to the damage incurred to the mediational functions of the new brain (frontal lobe), their "connections," resulting perhaps in a malfunctioning of a part of the hypothalamus. However, the behavioral approach did eventually bring about normal behavior with respect to eating and sexual behavior, but perhaps with a moderate permanent loss of the pleasures previously experienced.

Ed's case is a dramatic demonstration that it is necessary for a full range of helping professionals to be involved in some behavior problems. It also demonstrates the efficency of behavioral techniques without taking any of the therapeutic thunder from medicine or "traditional" psychotherapy.

HYPERKINETIC REACTION OF CHILDHOOD OR ORGANIC BRAIN SYNDROMES, MILD: BOB, CAROL, TED AND ALICE

Bob, Carol, Ted, and Alice are the fictitious names of four children in a fourth grade class who were referred for evaluation and treatment for suspected hyperactivity. All four children had a history of disturbance in the classroom; all had taken either Ritalin, Dexedrine, or both. And none of the medical treatments had been effective in improving classroom demeanor. Prior to initiation of the treatment described herein, all the children were administered the WISC and the Bender Gestalt. All children scored within the normal range of intelligence, and all made borderline scores on the Bender Gestalt Test, indicating possible emotionality and possible minimal brain injury. Following an analysis of the results and the case histories of the children, it was decided that a self-control approach to academic and social control would be in order before exploring the effects of different medications.

Two high-school-age students were enlisted and trained as behavioral observers. The observers were then stationed unobtrusively in the fourth grade class and their presence in the classroom was desensitized to the children. When the students recovered from the novelty of the presence of the observers, behavior recording began, with the purpose of obtaining baseline measures of disruptive behaviors common to the four target children. It was decided that the academic-dependent measure would be the number of math and reading series problems solved correctly. Baseline measures on both of the factors were obtained on each of the children. Baseline period was arbitrarily established as fifteen minutes.

Following the establishment of baselines, the four students were informed that the school day (while in classroom) was to be divided into fifteen-minute units. They were told that during some of the units they would be "checked" on their academic and social behavior progress. They were given general verbal descriptions of behaviors to be checked. Also, they were told that in some instances a point system of reward would be used, and that points would be exchanged for pennies, which could be saved or could be spent for edibles (cookies, etc.). Four randomly selected fifteen-minute units were chosen at the beginning of each day; these four units were designated as the point system reinforcement periods. Four other periods were randomly chosen as secondary reinforcement periods. When the latter contingencies were in effect, points were not rewarded, but lavish praise from the teacher was administered for progress. Progress was defined as any improvement from the previous fifteen-minute period. The rest of the fifteen-minute time segments during the day were "control" periods; that is, students were evaluated but were not informed on how well they did and no reinforcement was provided. Contingencies as described above were in effect for one week.

During the second week, each of the four children received a chart of five disruptive behaviors. The behavior chart was fastened to the desk of each child, and was covered with a clear sheet of plastic. Each child was given a transparency marker for recording behaviors on the plastic cover over the chart. This allowed the plastic to be erased and the charts to be used over and over. The contingencies during the second week were as follows: each child was asked to record the frequencies of his or her own disruptive behaviors during each fifteen-minute segment. Points or praise were provided for those students who *matched* the observer's recorded frequency (within $+ - 1$). Increases or decreases from previous trial were *not* a factor. All children were checked, but only *one* behavior was checked, which was chosen by the observers and students were not informed before the check as to the target behavior. Academic progress (as previously defined) was checked by the teacher and both points and praise were awarded on each trial.

During the third week, the four were divided into two teams. The same contingencies were in effect. Reinforcement was applied only when matching occurred and progress was shown. Only one team was chosen by a random procedure during each time for checking.

During the fourth week, the same contingencies as above were in effect, except that only one person was randomly chosen for checking. Praise continued and token reinforcement was discontinued.

During the fifth week, one student was randomly chosen for checking at four random times during the day, with a continuation of no tangible reinforcement and continued teacher praise. At the beginning of the sixth week, the disruptive behaviors were all extinguished, the on-task behavior was high and steady, and "problem solved" was slightly above the average for the entire class. Observation and self-checkings were discontinued, and the target students were placed on a schedule of intermittent reinforcement schedule of "praise and A's."

The first week of the contingencies was designed to establish the primary and secondary reinforcers, and to help establish the teacher as a source of reinforcement. This was accomplished by the pairing or association between appropriate target behavior and the various kinds and sources of reinforcement.

The second week of contingencies involved discrimination learning in which students were made "aware" of the kind and frequency of their behaviors. All behaviors were not checked, but the students had to continue to monitor all their target behaviors, since they did not know which would be chosen for checking and possible reward. This is the first real element of purposive self-control.

The balance of the treatment procedure involved gradually shaping the students to monitor and control more and more of their behavior, and the eventual transference from primary to secondary reinforcement.

The account of the treatment procedure in this chapter illustrates the kind of professional discrimination that is required when diagnosing and treating "hyperactivity." Hyperactivity may be diagnosed in one of two general ways: as a transient childhood reaction or as an organic brain syndrome. Children who are properly diagnosed as organic brain syndrome should exhibit the clinical symptoms of brain syndrome. It should be reflected in some aspect of their intellectual behavior, such as measured by the WISC and Bender, and furthermore, this manifestation should be rather pronounced. In this eventuality, medical treatment is a necessity, and sometimes behavior therapy as an adjunct is helpful. In the absence of a pronounced clinical cluster, the "hyperactivity" observed in the child is probably a primary function of history of reinforcement rather than "state of the organism" factors. Therefore, a behavioral approach which utilizes medication only as a last resort is probably the most appropriate treatment procedure.

Chapter 14

Character Disorders

The personality disorders represent the largest category of un-diagnosed mental problems, and of those that are diagnosed, are the most resistant to change. Among them are: paranoid personality, cyclothymic personality, schizoid personality, explosive personality, obsessive-compulsive personality, hysterical personality, asthemic personality, anti-social personality, passive-aggressive personality (and its variations) inadequate personality, sexual deviations and orientation disturbances, alcoholism and drug dependence.

Persons with some types of character disorders never adjust to social norms and spend much of their lives in prisons. Others make a kind of marginal adjustment or manage to avoid imprisonment, but make themselves and those around them very unhappy. Still others use their character disorders in a positive way and become very suc-cessful by certain standards, but remain basically maladjusted and unhappy. Intelligence seems to be the major factor determining whether a person is successful (i.e. earns a lot of money, status, etc.). Intelligence, however, is the very factor that prohibits such an in-dividual from obtaining benefits from therapy. Those with character disorders rarely present themselves for therapy; when they do ap-proach a therapist it is usually the result of some kind of external pressure or desperation situation. The therapy process usually ter-minates when the patient, either successfully or unsuccessfully, manipulates the therapist, or leaves because the therapist prevents the manipulation. The example to follow is such an example.

Eva: Passive-Aggressive Personality

Eva was a twenty-eight-year-old psychiatric social worker whose husband, also twenty-eight, was in a professional position. Eva presented herself for therapy after her husband threatened to leave her and their two children if she did not seek help. She came to the first interview, along with husband, relatively calm and surprisingly open about their problems. She admitted they had sought profes-sional help on two previous occasions, and that the therapy was inef-fective in both instances. Eva had terminated the sessions after two or three interviews in both instances. In prior attempts, Eva had steadfastly maintained that it was her husband who had the problem, and that she was in joint therapy only "to help him." Neither the therapists nor her husband really accepted Eva's premise, but the husband said that he "went along with her" to see if they could "get some relief." When the therapy began to focus on Eva, she became angry, attacked the therapists' competence, and removed herself from therapy, taking her husband with her.

On this third occasion with a new therapist, and under the threat of a broken marriage, Eva came for help, finally admitting that she "had a problem" and committed herself to a program of change. The scheduled fifty-minute initial interview lasted two hours. Both Eva and her husband were asked to state their perceptions of "the problem" and to express what they expected therapy to do for them.

Eva's husband described his early life as uneventful except for a series of minor illnesses beginning at the onset of adolescence. He expressed satisfaction with his academic achievement in high school, college, and graduate school. He saw himself as successful in his work, although a bit disorganized, and as a person who was easily stressed. Some aspects of his job were anxiety-producing for him, and he believed his anxieties were heightened by his wife's general dissatisfaction with him and with their life. He had been hospitalized for a "stomach operation" after their first child was born. He said that he visited his physician "about twice a month" and when questioned about medication, reluctantly admitted that he was taking about 40 mg of valium daily. The therapist expressed concern over this level of valium intake (which had persisted over a year), suggesting that gradually withdrawing the valium might be one of the first things he should do. The man was resistant and then defiant. He said that it made him feel better, and that he would find another physician who would get it for him if this one were to stop prescribing it. He agreed to any other therapeutic tactic suggested except the removal of medication. The valium appeared to be the method he had hit upon to control the aggression he felt toward his wife. When asked what he thought would happen if he could not get the valium, he said that he would have to leave his wife or kill her —that is, if she persisted in her "nagging."

Eva described a childhood characterized by extreme competition for both her mother's and father's affection. Her two older brothers were, in her words, "brilliant" in school, and she had to struggle constantly to "keep making the A's—all the way through college." She learned early in life to feign anger and hurt feelings to help her control mom, dad, and her two brothers. As are many sociopathic individuals, Eva was extremely bright verbally, and had developed a caustic verbal repertoire with which to devastate her opposition. When things did not go in her favor, she could always turn her verbal skills on her "enemies" and make them feel responsible for all of her misfortunes. Her husband was no exception; she made him feel totally responsible for all her unhappiness, and appeared to feel no remorse in doing so. On the occasion of her current presentation for therapy, she had driven her husband to the point of leaving the marriage, and had seduced him into believing that she was "serious" this time about changing. It seemed rather clear to the therapist that it was a calculated maneuver. Eva spent a good deal of time talking about how ineffective the other therapists were and in structuring the therapist in the current situation. She closed her presentation of the problem by demanding that the therapist provide an immediate program, and left the impression that if it were not successful from the very beginning that she would certainly not be responsible. After all, she had come for help and had been "completely honest"; it was now up to the therapist to get everything straightened out—and in rather short order.

The therapist countered with a statement that he would "do the best he could," but did not offer a lot of hope for change on her part. He pointed out her interaction characteristics that were giving her problems, both in her marriage and in her work. He further suggested that her motivation for therapy was inappropriate, that it appeared to stem more from the threat of her husband (therapy by blackmail) than from discomfort with herself. Toward the end of the session the therapist asked if they both would be willing to take the Minnesota Multiphasic Personality Inventory, MMPI, so that he could check his perceptions of them against a somewhat more objective measure. The husband agreed readily; Eva was somewhat reluctant.

The following week, Eva came in with her husband to take the MMPI. She asked for the therapist when a psychological examiner was preparing them to take the MMPI. When told he was not available and that it was not necessary for him to be there to administer the self-report instrument, Eva flew into a rage, refusing to take the exam and refused to allow her husband to take it. She cancelled all future appointments. Thus, she used a minor incident to avoid entering therapy seriously, illustrating her tendency to place responsibility for not going into therapy on someone else.

The example of Eva is an extreme one, but if not in intensity, certainly in character, it illustrates the nature of sociopathy and its resistance to change. Behavioral techniques could have been used to circumvent the incident and kept the couple coming to therapy sessions. However, such procedures fall into the "seduction traps" typically set by such patients. In responding to manipulation with manipulation, the therapist is playing the game according to the patient's rules, and in such cases, the therapist always loses. It is much better to confront the patient at the outset, agree to try to help, but make it clear that deception is inappropriate for both patient and therapist. This forces the patient to decide whether help is really wanted—to accept the fact that the therapist refuses to be a tool in the patient's continued expression of pathology under the guise of "treatment."

As one might guess, behavioral therapy is the only kind of therapy approaching effectiveness for character disorders of the type just described. However, a minority of those affected ever seek help, and of that group, probably fewer than five percent actually enter "real" therapy. Such clinical levels of character disorders are probably second in commonality (neuroses being the most prevalent) in the general public for which self-control measures can help.

Most readers who are honest with themselves can see traces of the behavior of character disordered persons in their own behavioral repertoire. Self-control measures can be applied to reduce these behaviors, as long as they are at the "troublesome" level. Whenever an individual's social interactions reach a level that produces chronic stress in those around them, then professional assistance is in order. Unfortunately, the person so affected is usually the very last to admit that help is needed.

Chapter 15

Normality

Am I normal? Are the things that I do normal? Are my desires and dreams normal? These three questions are the result of a great deal of concern and worry by many people. From time to time most of us are faced with one or more of these questions or others similar to them. To help the reader deal with those questions, several things must, of necessity, be settled first. These are:

1. What is normal?
2. Who is normal?
3. Is normal good?
4. If I am "negatively" abnormal, what do I do?
5. How can I recognize signs of "negative" abnormality?
6. How abnormal is abnormal?

NORMAL

The term normality is one of the most ambiguous and most misused terms in the English language. A healthy nine-pound baby girl is born and the doctor pronounces that a normal baby has been delivered. What does the doctor mean and what is actually the case? A nine-pound baby is abnormal because the baby is larger than normal. The doctor, of course, recognizes this, but his pronouncement of normality is more properly synonomous with the concept of "no defects" or saying that there is nothing wrong with the baby.

A young man with an intelligence quotient of 130, with high academic achievement, and who also happens to be a first-string halfback on the high school football team, is labeled a "normal," "all-American" boy. What is meant by this pronouncement and what is actually the case? What is meant is that this young man is superior both intellectually and physically. The case actually can be interpreted as a boy with abnormally high mental and physical abilities.

Consider the average, or "normal," man-on-the-street. If he earns $15,000 a year, is six feet tall, weighs 190 pounds, has three children, and drives a motorcycle, he is abnormal in each of the five

categories mentioned. He earns more than normal, he is taller than
normal, heavier than normal, has more children than normal, and
does not travel normally. Would we, however, refer to this person as
abnormal?

The term normality has come to be synonomous not with the actual meaning of the word normal, but rather with "better than
average," or "having no defects."

In each of the three instances above, we were concerned with
human characteristics that do not often enter into the conception
of normality-abnormality. When we are confronted with the statement, "She is abnormal," most of us are likely to infer that the
speaker means that some facet of the person's *behavior* is abnormal.
Before we discuss the kinds of behavior that are or are not normal,
it is important that we define normality.

Normality in its strictest sense refers to the arithmetical average of some characteristic that a group of organisms have in common. Normality is a useful and workable reference point when some
characteristics are considered, but not for others. Let us examine
something called the normal curve and explain what we mean.

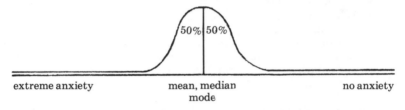

| extreme anxiety | mean, median
mode | no anxiety |

A normal curve is an hypothetical construction that may or
may not really fit most human characteristics, but the similarity between the real data and the hypothetical curve is so great as to allow
its use. In any normal curve the mean (arithmetical average), the
mode (the most frequently observed score), and the median (that
point at which fifty percent of the people fall above and fifty percent
fall below) are all at the same point. This is at the center of the
curve denoted by the verticle line bisecting the curve. What this
means is that half of the people are above average and half the
people are below average. In our example, one-half of the people are
more anxious than normal while the other half are less anxious than
normal. Those folks that have very little anxiety are just as abnormal as the folks that have extremely high levels of anxiety.
Where does abnormality start, though? If a person is fairly close
to the mean, he or she is obviously not too abnormal.

First things first. Abnormality is not necessarily bad. Positive
abnormality, in fact, is something for which most of us strive. We
would all like to be abnormally free from anxiety, to be abnormally

happy, to be abnormally successful and so on. Hence, we need not concern ourselves with positive abnormality.

We would all agree, however, that there are a whole series of things that we would not want to be. We would not want to be abnormally anxious, abnormally unhappy, abnormally unsuccessful and on and on. What is actually meant by abnormality, then, is the concept of being worse off than other people, i.e., negatively abnormal. When, though, does normality stop and negative abnormality start?

(negatively abnormal)   (optimal)
extremely maladjusted   extremely well adjusted

There is no standard or easy answer to such a question. Some writers (Carroll, 1969; Baughman and Welsh, 1965) point out that abnormality and pathological behavior are taken synonymously by many people. Our answer, then, about when negative abnormality begins, is structured around the concepts of dealing with life and the severity of the various problems. Negatively abnormal conditions exist when the person possessing these conditions can no longer function at an adequate level, when no answers are seen for the problems, when the problems come to dominate life, when the problems are severe enough to merit remediation.

In our example of anxiety, most of us have some anxieties and we deal with these or suffer them, but the anxieties do not come between us and an adequate performance of life, i.e., the anxieties do not disrupt our marital harmony, do not keep us from job advancement or keep us from relaxing and having a good time.

Our definition of "normality" is one of exclusion. Everyone that is not negatively abnormal is "normal." People who are negatively abnormal are ones who have various problems that interfere with their harmonious life functioning.

Some human characteristics lend themselves well to "normal" descriptions. Height, age, number of children and economic status are all variables that can be cogently placed into statistical terms for evaluation. Cars are built for people of average physical dimensions. The concept of normality fits well here to allow automobile companies to manufacture cars that will fit well for the majority of people. Clothing manufacturers make their clothing for persons of different sizes but they make most for average people of average dimensions.

Human behavior, however, does not lend itself well to the little optimal, negatively abnormal continuum that we pictured earlier. Statistical infrequency itself is not a good index of negatively abnormal behaviors. Very few people, statistically, gather in crowds of fifty thousand, drink beer and shout themselves hoarse. This is, however, exactly what a good crowd at the World Series might do. Certainly these fans cannot be considered negatively abnormal based on their behavior of going to a ball game. If one of these individuals chose to perform the same behaviors at noon time at his place of work, we would no doubt, then, think the behavior negatively abnormal.

HUMAN CHARACTERISTICS AND NEGATIVE ABNORMALITY

We have not specified exactly what we mean when we consider negative abnormality. Every human characteristic can be placed into a continuum from extremely bad to extremely good (given that someone, somewhere makes a value judgement). The "normal" person will not be in an extreme in whatever area we are concerned with. We could discuss normality with respect to age, eye color, length of fingers, number of heads, education and on and on. For our purposes, we will restrict the discussion of negative abnormality henceforth to that of behavior.

This restriction to behavior, however, still allows for an amazingly complex topic. Consider the following areas of behavior: sexual behavior, interpersonal relations, anxiety, frustration, habits, eating behavior, etc. A person may be "normal" in all or any of these behaviors. Persons may also be "normal" in all but one area of behavior.

At this point let us restate our first question with respect to behavior. What is normal behavior? To answer this question, we must consider the following points.

1. Societal impositions
2. Sub-cultural guidelines
3. Peer group standards
4. Family standards
5. Frame of reference

Our society prescribes some behaviors and censures others. While a thorough analysis of our society's acceptable and unacceptable behaviors is a topic deserving its own book, we can briefly mention that behaviors differ from society to society. The hard-charging businesswoman, teeth clenched, while she demands, wheedles and commands those around her, is a fact of life in the American culture. Some of us might still think of her as unusual, but no one would consider her behavior as negatively abnormal. If a woman were to behave the same way (if indeed, it were possible for her to attain a position to allow the behavior) in Polynesia, she would be seen as emitting negatively abnormal behavior. Not all the examples we could draw are as striking as this one but there are many differences between the American society and others.

In the American culture, certain sexual behaviors are labeled as abnormal: fetishism, masochism, sadism, homosexuality, exhibitionism, etc. Certain behaviors that may be lumped together and called manners are frowned upon: flatulence, belching, eating with the mouth open, not bathing, etc. Aggressive behaviors are labeled as abnormal on occasion: mugging, murdering, raping, maiming, etc.

The list of all society-condemned behaviors would fill several hundred pages so we will leave the remainder to the reader's imagination.

SUB-CULTURAL GUIDELINES

Various sub-cultures within the larger framework of American society have far different standards for normal and abnormal behaviors. For example, the majority of us might consider contests between young males where the distance one can expell urine is the important factor, to be abnormal behaviors. In one particular sub-culture, however, this was a normal and accepted game. Violence, speech mannerisms, sexual behaviors, manners, every facet of human behavior can have different standards within different groupings. In fact, various sub-cultures have been viewed as abnormal components of society.

PEER GROUP GUIDELINES

Smaller units than sub-cultures also provide standards of reference with respect to the normality or abnormality of behavior. Consider the sight of twenty adult males spending all day on Saturday consuming beer until they have all drunk themselves into a stupor, replete with vomiting and passing into unconsciousness. Abnormal behavior if you've ever heard of abnormal behavior, right? Maybe. If all these young men are members of a fraternity on a college campus, it may not be abnormal to them. In fact, it may be the only acceptable way of behaving on that day. Pressure to conform to peer groups is enormous at all levels, from middle childhood through old age. Perhaps the reader has heard of the American neighborhood that literally fenced itself in from the surrounding areas of the town. This may seem like a bizarre behavior to some of us, but it certainly was not to the residents of that neighborhood.

FAMILY

Even smaller reference groups for normal and abnormal behaviors are families. Behavior patterns are developed and fixed uniquely for each family unit in the United States. What is an absolutely normal behavior might be seen as strange or bizarre by other family units. The most obvious examples are the references to parents by first names from the children in some families while in others the parents are always called Mother and Father. Another example we often see is the way affection is expressed in different families. In some families affection is open and expressed in a very physical manner, complete with lots of hugging, kissing and touching. Other families, with the same degree of love, are much more restrained, showing little, if any, of the physical aspects of affection.

FRAME OF REFERENCE

The brief descriptions we gave above for the various frames of reference for behaviors were only exiguous, non-inclusive ones. Bizarre, negatively abnormal behavior in one area may be quite acceptable in other situations. The purpose of our descriptions was to lead the reader to the following point: behaviors can only be interpreted from the frame of reference from which they are emitted. Hence, the whole idea of what is normal is tied to the *frame of reference for the behavior*. We can only interpret other people's behaviors when we are familiar with why they appear and whether or not their behaviors are appropriate to their reference group. Let us examine our first three questions again with reference to our discussion.

1. What is normal (behavior)?
2. Who is normal?
3. Is normal good?

The answers are that we cannot establish what is normal for everyone. It is an impossibility. What is normal behavior in one setting is likely to be viewed as negatively abnormal behavior in other settings. The only valid statement that can be made about normal behavior is that it is common, acceptable or optimal behaviors from the frame of reference from which it is produced. Negatively abnormal behavior is behavior that is personally harmful either to the person emitting the behaviors or to others. This definition includes neurotic and psychotic behavior as well as many other habits that we discuss throughout this book.

Who is normal? None of us and all of us. At one time or another almost every person will emit negatively abnormal behaviors. The old saw that we are all neurotic, it's just that some of us are more neurotic than others, is very true. The normal person, though, is one who is able to cope with negatively abnormal behaviors from time to time. The normal person may be severely depressed for a time and then work out of it. The same can be said for fears, frustrations and anxieties. The normal person *adjusts* and returns to a level of productive functioning. The person who we would identify as negatively abnormal is the one who does not adjust, who cannot overcome negatively abnormal behaviors and is impeded by those behaviors from living a productive and fulfilling life.

Is normal good? In the sense that normal is the ability to adjust and to deal with life, yes, normal is good. In the strict statistical sense, the term normal loses its value altogether, for obviously we would prefer to behave more optimally than normal.

AM I NORMAL?

In determining whether the reader identifies himself as normal, let us set the following conditions. First, everything that is actually normal (statistically speaking) and more optimal than normal shall be defined as normal. Second, we must assume that the reader is capable of relatively objective self-judgement and lastly, we are not the final authorities on what is abnormal and what is normal, and neither is anyone else. From these three guidelines, let us list a series of conditions that can be employed as guides for the reader's self-discrimination of abnormal behavior.

1. Depression. Depression in an ambiguous term referring loosely to a feeling of personal loss, hurt, or pain. Depression that occurs in any of the following forms is a sign of an adjustment problem: if depression is severe and of lengthy duration, if a person swings from extreme depression to extreme elation in a cyclical manner, if depression is frequent and prolonged, if depression occurs frequently "without cause" and if depression is an inhibiting factor in life, i.e., damaging the self or relations with others.

The reader will note that we have been ambiguous in our description of depression and less so in our listing of depression conditions that indicate adjustment problems. We have done this purposely for what we feel to be extremely good reasons. First, if the reader is having serious concerns about his mental health, we urge the reader to contact a professional clinician for advice. Normal depressions can be as full of anguish and pain as any abnormal depression can be. Objective judgements concerning personal mental health are difficult, at best, during periods of depression, and are made much more effectively with the guidance of a professional clinician. Second, if the reader is able to identify one or more of the depression conditions we cited above, we also urge consultation with a clinician. It may be that the reader has merely blown the problem out of proportion or it may be that a real adjustment problem exists. At any rate, consult a clinician in order to facilitate a proper judgement.

Third, we have noticed a tendency for people to adopt symptoms that they read about as their own, whether or not there is any basis for this. This can be due to other problems or just a source of worry. Inevitably, the identification of abnormal behavior is difficult and must be made by the individual or those close to him. In the remainder of the possible problem areas we discuss, the reader should infer that these same statements stand.

2. Anxiety
   a. Has it led to physical illness?
   b. Does it inhibit the normal pursuits of life?
   c. Is it frequent and/or severe?
   d. Has it resulted in interpersonal friction?
   e. Is anxiety "free-floating," i.e., not directed at any specific stimulus?
3. Tension
   a. Has it lead to physical illness?
   b. Does it inhibit normal pursuits of life?
   c. Has it resulted in interpersonal friction?
   d. Are there frequent headaches or upset stomachs without medical cause?
   e. Is tension frequent or severe?

Only the individual and his or her immediate friends and family can decide or help to decide whether or not help should be sought. The answer to our last question posed at the beginning of this chapter is, seek help if you feel it is warranted.

Obviously there are a tremendous series of behaviors that can be considered in determining what is normal and what is not. We have counseled people who were worried about their normality with respect to sexual behavior, interpersonal relations, vocational goals, dreams and daydreams, habits, feelings about self, feelings about others, feelings about parents, guilty feelings about manifold topics, and on and on.

Probably the most important criterion in assessing your normality is how you feel about yourself. If you are questioning yourself, or do question yourself occasionally, you probably are like thousands of others. We all question ourselves from time to time. If the problems you face seem insurmountable and if questions of normality are constant, we suggest you seek the aid of a clinician.

WHERE DOES NORMAL END?

The line between normality and negatively abnormal is vague at its very best. When do individuals stop being normal and start being abnormal? There are statistical answers for this question when we consider such quantifiable human variables as height, weight or intelligence. Consider the hypothetical normal curve below that represents the distribution of intelligence quotient scores in a population of students for some standardized test.

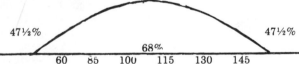

In this set of scores, as with any human variable that fits a "normal" distribution, exactly fifty percent of the people score above the mean and fifty percent below. A score of 100 is exactly average. Let's suppose that we have a valid measure of intelligence and that we have a good reason for setting up a criteria for students who are abnormally unintelligent. Perhaps we want to give them some special training. Where will we set this criterion? To help in making this decision, there are some standard points along any normal curve that may be identified.

Standard deviations are statistical devices best left to a statistics text for explanation that denote equal spaces along the horizontal axis of the normal curve. While the scores may be different from normal curve to normal curve (for example, instead of 100 at the mean as in our example, the mean may be 69 inches if our curve was to represent height in inches of male adults), the distance of the standard deviations will always be the same. Notice how the scores in the printed curve are clustered around the mean as represented by the height of the curve. As we go further from the mean in either direction, the frequency of scores decreases until, as we get to a score of 130 or so, there are very, very few scores at that point. This relationship is described by the standard deviations. Between a plus one standard deviation and a minus one standard deviation, we find 68 percent of all the scores. To put it another way, on the intelligence test example, 68 percent of all the scores on that test will be between 85 and 115. In other words, in any normal distribution we could consider, height, weight, intelligence, reaction time, levels of anxiety, etc., 68 percent of the people will fall within one standard deviation above the mean and one standard deviation below the mean. That means that 16 percent of the scores will be above one standard deviation above the mean while 16 percent of the scores will be below one standard deviation below the mean. To take it a little further, 13.5 percent of the scores fall between the first and second standard deviations above and below the mean. This means that 13.5 percent of the people in our example fall between a score of 60 and a score of 85 as well as 13.5 percent of the people scoring between 115 and 130. If we consider the people that fall between two standard deviations above the mean and two standard deviations below the mean, we now encompass 95 percent of all the people.

Well, as the reader can infer from this discussion, we can set our criterion at any of these points. Even though standard deviations allow us to pick scores on different variables that correspond with any percentage, we must still decide what percentage is abnormal. That is, shall we choose the lowest five percent of the students and treat them as abnormal or should we choose the lowest 15 percent? Those kinds of decisions are invariably arbitrary decisions. After all, who can say that a child with an intelligence quotient of 71 does not need just as much special attention as a child with an intelligence quotient of 70? Gross differences can easily be made, say between intelligence quotients of 90 and 70, but the finer discriminations are arbitrary.

This example was necessary to point up the fact that the difference between normality and abnormality is an arbitrary decision. Further confounding such decisions are the different frames of reference from which behaviors are generated, which are discussed elsewhere. There are persons who are obviously abnormal, severe psychotics whose bizarre behaviors are beyond the bounds of reality. Most people's behaviors, though, cannot be so easily distinguished. The definition of abnormality is one that must be employed for each individual in turn with little possible generalization.

bizarre,   normal?
severely disturbed   optimal behavior

In the little continuum pictured above, we could all recognize *severe* behavior disorders and there would be no question as to whether or not people with such disorders are abnormal. However, as we move along the continuum to optimal behaviors, we soon reach the point where there are maladaptive behaviors present, but we are unable to say "this person is normal." There can be no definite dividing line with respect to normal or abnormal behaviors just as there can be nothing but arbitrary divisions between below-normal intelligence and normal intelligence.

<u>   </u>

optimal

<u>   </u>

normal

<u>   </u>

abnormal

Perhaps a series of three continuums such as the one pictured above is more appropriate when we consider abnormal, normal, and optimal forms of behavior. The ambiguity is still there, but at least this form of pictorial conception does not allow us to forget the "overlap between normal and abnormal." The answer to our third question, then: "how abnormal is abnormal?" cannot be found except in an individual sense.

FINAL COMMENTS

In this section we have discussed the problem of normality from the statistical point of view and from an applied vantage point. We have pointed out the extreme difficulty of determining what is normal behavior and who is normal. These kinds of questions can only be answered when the frame of reference of each individual is considered. Normal is not synonymous with good in its strictest sense, but when defined as non-negatively abnormal behavior, it can be considered to be "good." Negative abnormality is debilitative abnormality, abnormal behavior or other human characteristics that are in some way detrimental to the person's functioning.

It is impossible to determine how abnormal abnormal is. Beyond a doubt there are severe negatively abnormal behaviors and there are optimal and normal behaviors but we cannot make fine discriminations between the beginning and end of normality. The question is very much like asking "how high is up?" or "if a vest has no sleeves, why are oranges round?"

The "signs of abnormality" are quite individual. Intelligent or realistic determinations of normality/abnormality can only be made by the individual and those close to him except in obvious, severe cases. If a determination has been made that a person is exhibiting negatively abnormal behavior, or if strong doubts persist as to whether or not a person is normal, then a clinician should be consulted. The process of locating and identifying a clinician is discussed elsewhere.

We feel no compunctions in stating unequivocally that everyone, at one time or another, questions his or her normality. Asking yourself whether or not you are normal, whether your dreams and desires are normal, is—"normal"! What is abnormal is the debilitation of life's functions by behaviors that are irrational. That is, we would expect that severe grief following the death of a spouse or loved one would disrupt life until an adjustment was made. Grief, anxiety, tension, fear, any behavior, etc., that disrupts life without a real or rational source of the behavior, is abnormal.

It is interesting to note that there are several synonyms for abnormal behavior. Among them are maladjusted behavior, maladaptive behavior, irrational behavior, disturbed behavior, mentally ill behavior, and so forth. Of all of them, we prefer "maladaptive" because it comes closest to describing what we feel negatively abnormal behavior is—behavior that is the result of the organism's inability to adjust to situations, events or people either through history of reinforcement, organic disorders, or a traumatic event. The purpose of this book has been to help the reader deal with the process of making these adjustments for a happier, more satisfying life. We hope that we have contributed to this in some small way.

Bibliography

Ax, A. F. The physiological differentiation between fear and anger in humans. *Psychosomatic Medicine*, 1953, *15*, 443-442.

Bandura, A. Influence of model's reinforcement contingencies on the acquisition of imitative responses. *Journal of Personality and Social Psychology*, 1965, *1*, 589-595.

Bandura, A. *Principles of behavior modification*. New York: Holt, Rinehart and Winston, 1969.

Bandura, A. *Psychological modeling*. New York: Aldine/Atherton, 1971.

Bandura, A., Ross, D. and Ross, S. A comparative test of the status envy, social power, and secondary reinforcement theories of identification learning. *Journal of Abnormal and Social Psychology*, 1963, *67*, 527-534 (a).

Bandura, A., Ross, D. and Ross, S. Imitation of film mediated aggressive models, *Journal of Abnormal and Social Psychology*, 1963, *67*, 601-607 (b).

Bandura, A. and Walters, R. H. *Social learning and personality development*. New York: Holt, Rinehart and Winston, 1963.

Baughman, E. E. and Welsh, G. S. *Personality: a behavioral science*. Englewood Cliffs, New Jersey: Prentice Hall, 1965.

Bem, D. J. Attitudes as self descriptions: another look at the attitude-behavior link. In A. G. Greenwald, T. C. Brock, T. M. Ostrom (Eds.), *Psychological foundations of attitudes*. New York: Academic Press, 1968.

Beneke, W. M. and Harris, M. B. Teaching self-control of study behavior. *Behavior Research and Therapy*, 1972, *10*, 35-41.

Bernstein, D. A. Modification of smoking behavior: An evaluative review. *Psychological Bulletin*, 1969, *71*, 418-440.

Bridges, K.M.B. Emotional development in early infancy. *Child Development*, 1932, *3*, 324-341.

Briggs, R. D., Tosi, D. J. and Morley, R. M. Study habit modification and its effect on academic performance: A behavioral approach. *Journal of Educational Research*, 1971, *64*, 347-350.

Carroll, H. A. *Mental hygiene*. Englewood Cliffs, New Jersey: Prentice-Hall, 1969.

Castenada, A. and Lipsitt, L. P. Relation of stress and differential position habits to performance in motor learning. *Journal of Experimental Psychology*, 1959, *57*, 25-30.

Champion, D. J. *Basic statistics for social research*. Scranton, Pennsylvania: Chamber Publishing Company, 1970.

Coleman, J. *Abnormal psychological and modern life*. Glenview, Illinois: Scott, Foresman and Company, 1956.

Compton, B. E. Psychology's manpower: The education and utilization of psychologists. *American Psychologist,* 1972, *27,* 335-518.

Frankl, V. *The doctor and the soul,* New York: Alfred A. Knopf, 1957.

Frankl, V. *Man's search for meaning.* Boston: Beacon Press, 1969.

Frankl, V. Logotherapy and Vicktor Frankl. *Saturday Review,* September 13, 1958, 20-21.

Franks, C. M., Fried, R. and Ashem, B. An improved apparatus for the aversive conditioning of cigarette smokers. *Behavior Research and Therapy,* 1966, *4,* 301-308.

Freeburne,C. M. and Fleischer, M. S. The effect of music distraction upon reading rate and comprehension. *Journal of Educational Psychology,* 1952, *43,* 101-109.

Funkenstein, D. H. The physiology of fear and anger. *Scientific American,* 1955, *192,* 74.

Gary, A. L. and Glover, J. A. *Sex, eye color, and children's behavior.* Chicago: Nelson Hall Company, 1975.

Gendreau, P. and Dodwell, P. An aversion treatment for addicted cigarette smokers: Preliminary report. *Canadian Psychologist,* 1968, *9,* 28-34.

Gerz, H. O. Experience with the logotherapeutic technique of paradoxical intention in the treatment of phobic and obsessive-compulsive patients. *American Journal of Psychiatry,* 1966, *17,* 123.

Glover, J. A. and Gary, A. L. *Behavior modification: Enhancing creativity and other good behaviors.* Pacific Grove, California: Boxwood Press, 1975.

Grimaldi, K. A. and Lichenstein, E. Hot, smoky air as an aversive stimulus in the treatment of smoking. *Behavior Research and Therapy,* 1969, *7,* 275-282.

Guess, D., Sailor, W., Rutherford, G. and Baer, D. M. An experimental analysis of linguistic development: The productive use of the plural morpheme. *Journal of Applied Behavior Analysis,* 1968, *1,* 297-306.

Heine, R. W. *Psychotherapy.* Englewood Cliffs, New Jersey: Prentice Hall, 1971.

Hilgard, E. R., Jones, L. V. and Kaplan, S. J. Conditioned discrimination as related to anxiety. *Journal of Experimental Psychology,* 1951, *42,* 94-99.

Holland, J. G. and Skinner, B. F. *The analysis of behavior: A program for self-instruction.* New York: McGraw-Hill, 1961.

Homme, L. E. Perspectives in psychology: XXIV, control of coverants, the operants of the mind. *Psychological Record,* 1965, *15,* 501-511.

Horn, D. and Waingrow, S. Some dimensions of a model for smoking behavior change. *American Journal of Public Health,* 1966, *56* (12), 21-26.

Isaacson, R. L., Douglas, R. J., Lubar, J. F. and Schmaltz, L. W. *A primer of physiological psychology.* New York: Harper and Row, 1971.

Jones, H. E. and Jones, M. C. Fear. *Childhood Education.* 1928, *5,* 136-143.

Jones, L.C.T. Frustration and stereotyped behavior in human subjects. *Quarterly Journal of Experimental Psychology,* 1954, 12-20.

Johnston, J. M. Punishment of human behavior. *American Psychologist,* 1972, *81,* 1033-1053.

Keutzer, C. S. Behavior modification of smoking: The experimental investigation of diverse techniques. *Behavior Research and Therapy*, 1968, *6*, 137-157.

Kirkpatrick, F. H. Music in industry. *Journal of Applied Psychology*, 1943, *27*, 268-274.

Korchin, S. J. and Levine, S. Anxiety and verbal learning. *Journal of Abnormal Social Psychology*, 1957, *54*, 234-240.

Lazarus, R. S. and Erickson, C. W. Effects of failure stress upon skilled performance. *Journal of Experimental Psychology*, 1952, *43*, 100-105.

Lublin, I. Principles governing the choice of unconditioned stimuli in aversive conditioning. In R. D. Rubin and C. M. Franks (Eds.), *Advances in Behavior Therapy, 1968*. New York: Academic Press, 1969.

Malott, R. *Behavior Modification*. Kalamazoo, Michigan: Behaviordellia, 1972.

McCandless, B. R. and Castenda, A. Anxiety in children's school achievement and intelligence. *Child Development*, 1956, *27*, 379-382.

McNeil, E. B. *The quiet furies: Man and disorder*. Englewood Cliffs, New Jersey: Prentice Hall, 1967.

McNeil, E. B. *Neuroses and personality disorders*. Englewood Cliffs, New Jersey: Prentice Hall, 1970 (a).

McNeil, E. B. *The psychoses*. Englewood Cliffs, New Jersey: Prentice Hall, 1970 (b).

Meldman, M. and Hatch, B. *In vivo* desensitization of an airplane phobia with penthranization. *Behavior Research and Therapy*, 1969, *7*, 213-214.

Mikulas, W. L. *Behavior modification: An overview*. New York: Holt, Rinehart and Winston, 1970.

Morgan, C. T. *Physiological psychology*. New York: McGraw-Hill, 1965.

Mussen, P. H., Conger, J. J. and Kagan, J. *Child development and personality*. New York: Harper and Row, 1974.

Ober, P. Modification of smoking behavior. *Journal of Consulting and Clinical Psychology*, 1968, *32*, 543-549.

Oliveau, D. C. Systematic desensitization in an experimental setting: A follow-up study. *Behavior Research and Therapy*, 1969, *7*, 377-380.

O'Neil, D. G. and Howell, R. J. Three modes of hierarchy presentation in systematic desensitization therapy. *Behavior Research and Therapy*, 1960, *7*, 289-294.

Palermo, D. S. Proactive interference and facilitation as a function of amount of training and stress. *Journal of Experimental Psychology*, 1957, *53*, 153-167.

Perkins, H. V. *Human development and learning*. Belmont, California: Wadsworth Publishing Company, 1974.

Powell, J. and Azrin, N. The effects of shock as a punisher for cigarette smoking. *Journal of Applied Behavior Analysis*, 1968, *1*, 63-71.

Rachman, S. Studies in desensitization: I. The separate effects of relaxation and desensitization. *Behavior Research and Therapy*, 1965, *3*, 245-251.

Rachman, S. Studies in desensitization: II. Flooding. *Behavior Research and Therapy*, 1966, *4*, 1-6(a).

Rachman, S. Studies in desensitization: III. Speed of generalization. *Behavior Research and Therapy*, 1966, *4*, 7-15 (b).

Rachman, S. and Hodgson, R. J. Studies in desensitization: IV. Optimum degree of anxiety reduction. *Behavior Research and Therapy*, 1967, *4*, 205-207.

Reynolds, G. S. *A primer of operant conditioning*. Glenview, Illinois: Scott, Foresman and Company, 1969.

Reynolds, G. S. *A primer of operant conditioning*, revised edition. Glenview, Illinois: Scott, Foresman and Company, 1975.

Saltz, E. *The cognitive bases of human learning*. Homewood, Illinois: Dorsey Press, 1971.

Sarason, I. G. and Sarason, B. Effects of motivating instructions and reports of failure on verbal learning. *American Journal of Psychology*, 1957, *70*, 92-96.

Schachter, S. The interaction of cognitive and physiological determinants of emotional states. In O. Klineberg and R. Christie (Eds.), *Emotion*. New York: Columbia University Press, 1963.

Schachter, S. Cognitive effects on bodily functioning: studies of obesity and eating. In D. C. Glass (Ed.) *Neurophysiology and emotion*. New York: Rockefeller University Press and Russell Sage Foundation, 1967.

Schachter, S. The assumption of identity and peripheralist-centralist controversies in motivation and emotion. In M. B. Arnold (Ed.), *Feelings and emotions*. New York: Academic Press, 1970.

Schachter, S. and Singer, J. E. Cognitive, social and physiological determinants of emotional state. *Psychological Review*, 1962, *69*, 370-399.

Schlingting, H. E., Jr., and Brown, R. V. The effect of background music on student performance. *American Biology Teacher*, 1970, *32*, 427-429.

Sloane, H. N. and MacAulay, B. D. Teaching and the environmental control of verbal behavior. In H. N. Sloan, Jr., and B. D. MacAulay (Eds.), *Operant procedures in remedial speech and language training*. Boston: Houghton Mifflin, 1968.

Stone, A. A. and Stone, S. S. *The abnormal personality through literature*. Englewood Cliffs, New Jersey: Prentice Hall, 1966.

Stone, J. L. and Church, J. *Childhood and adolescence*. New York: Random House, 1973.

Sutton-Smith, B. *Child Psychology*. New York: Appleton-Century-Crofts, 1973.

Tweedie, D. F. *Logotherapy and the Christian faith*. Grand Rapids, Michigan: Baker Book House, 1961.

Ullmann, L. P. and Krasner, L. *A psychological approach to abnormal behavior*. Englewood Cliffs, New Jersey: Prentice Hall, 1969.

United States Department of Health, Education and Welfare. *Occupational and personal characteristics of psychiatrists in the United States*. Washington: United States Department of Health, Education and, Welfare, 1966, February, 1-2.

Warren, A. B. *Dictionary of psychology*. New York: Houghton Mifflin Company, 1933.

Werner, H. and Kaplan, B. *Symbol formation.* New York: John Wiley and Sons, 1967.

Williams, R. L. and Anadam, K. *Cooperative classroom management.* Columbus, Ohio: Charles E. Merrill, 1973.

Winer, B. L. *Statistical principles in experimental design.* New York: McGraw Hill, 1971.

Worthy, M. W. Eye darkness, race, and self-paced athletic performance. Paper read at Southeastern Psychological Association Convention, Miami, Florida, 1971.

Worthy, M. W. *Eye color, race and sex.* Anderson, South Carolina: Droke House/Hallus, Inc. 1974.

Young, K. *Personality and problems of adjustment.* New York: Appleton-Century-Crofts, 1952.

Index